W9-AOD-792

THE

CHANGE

AGENTS

THE
CHANGE
AGENTS

Decoding the

New Workforce and

the New Workplace

LIZ NICKLES

ST. MARTIN'S PRESS ✖ NEW YORK

www.stmartins.com

Book design by Jessica Shatan

Library of Congress Cataloging-in-Publication Data

Nickles, Liz.
    The change agents : decoding the new workforce and the new workplace / Liz Nickles.—1st ed.
        p. cm.
    Includes index.
    ISBN 0-312-27535-8
    1. Organizational change. 2. Industrial sociology. I. Title.

HD58.8 .N499 2001
650.1—dc21   2001041719

First Edition: October 2001

10 9 8 7 6 5 4 3 2 1

This book is for my son Drew,

knowing that someday he too will change the

future, in his own way.

CONTENTS

ACKNOWLEDGMENTS

Thank you to all the people who generously offered time and expertise in the writing of this book. Those who wished to be identified have been cited; some, however, preferred to remain anonymous. Particular thanks to Greenfield Online, Nick Ellison, Elizabeth Beier, Sascha Brodsky for research assistance, and to Laurie Ashcraft, whose insights have documented a changing world for two decades.

INTRODUCTION

When Daedalus the craftsman had finished making [the wings], he balanced his body between the twin wings and by moving them hung suspended in the air. He also gave instructions to his son, saying, "Icarus, I advise you to take a middle course. If you fly too low, the sea will soak the wings; if you fly too high, the sun's heat will burn them. . . ."

. . . the boy began to exult in his flight and, drawn by a desire to reach the heavens, took his course too high. The burning heat of the nearby sun softened the scented wax that fastened the wings. The wax melted; Icarus moved his arms, now uncovered, and without wings to drive him on, vainly beat the air. . . . The sea received him.

—Ovid, *Metamorphoses*

A legend that is thousands of years old has never been more current. Every generation has its Icarus. For our great-grandparents, it was Charles Lindbergh. When he became the first person to fly solo across the Atlantic Ocean, bets were placed on whether he too had been overly ambitious and would be hurtled into the waves by his hubris. But he made it, and his flight evoked the beginning of a new world for his entire generation, linked from that point forward in ways never before imagined possible.

The pattern continues today, with the technology revolution, the launch of the Internet and its mass adaptation and embrace, and with the evolution of the new economy and a generation that lives and works within that sector. Today the descendants of Icarus are a group we will call the Change Agents, an advance force born to the technology revolution, empowered by electronics at an early age, and catapulted to independence and power that have allowed them to soar closer to the sun than even the mythmakers could have imagined. We have all watched as their flight took them higher and higher, until, sure enough, their wings became singed.

The media rushed to capture the drama. First, they lionized: all hailed the virtual Lindbergh, the business press poster boy and the Madonna of the NASDAQ, rolled into one. And as with all stars, there were those who have eagerly awaited the inevitable fall from grace.

What's next for E-carus? Will he indeed plunge to his destruction? White-knucklers brace themselves: *Will he take us down with him?* Old economy naysayers rub their hands, awaiting not a mere "correction" but a just comeuppance and a return to the status quo, where a person could navigate a well-trodden, earthbound path without interference. The fan club eagerly await the next release, consigning rumors of the early demise of E-carus to the Baby Boomer category of "Paul is dead."

But to understand the fate of any contemporary celebrity, you have to know the person, up close and personal as they say. Who is he, where does he live, and why should we care what happens to him?

We have to know, and we need to care, because, whatever happens to E-carus, to the Change Agents, will happen to us.

That's the nature of Change Agents. They leap while we are still afraid to look. If they make it, the rest of us do eventually follow. By keeping our eye on the Change Agents, we are really observing ourselves in a crystal ball.

This book is a story of change, an attempt at explanation of things we see happening around us that, so often, seem inexplicable. The past, which once provided a comfortable fall-back for explanations and patterns, is less relevant in a world that is increasingly defined by technology that did not previously exist. The technology revolution and, particularly, computers and the Internet have indelibly changed the face of society and those who inhabit it. Children who grew up in this world are coming of age in adult society and the workplace and, as a result, bringing a distinct set of psychographics to an arena that must understand them if conflict and miscommunication are to be avoided, not to mention if the total pool of talents and capabilities is to be maximized. The vanguard of this group, the Change Agents, began to filter into our lives a decade ago. Now they are a truly integrated force.

Are you ready?

You could not step twice into the same rivers; for other waters are ever flowing onto you.

—Heraclitus

THE
CHANGE
AGENTS

1 PASSING THE SWORD

BlackBerries. We've got to get them their BlackBerries. Have the BlackBerries been ordered?" The mood in the New York conference room of one of the world's largest financial institutions was tense. Over the speakerphone in the middle of the table, one of the senior officers, let's call him Mr. Euro, sounded uncharacteristically anxious as he called in from France. Even in his absence, those around the table could imagine him at the moment: iconically dressed in suit, crisply impeccable button-down shirt, tie, and gold cuff links—in spite of the recent global edict for five-day-a-week "business casual." Mr. Euro was one of the more conservative bastions of the old school. But, as was becoming clear in the meeting, even his stolid foundations were crumbling.

The six people around the conference table leaned closer to the speakerphone, styluses poised at the screens of their Palm

Pilots, ready to carry out Mr. Euro's wishes. He wished for BlackBerries. Now.

Mr. Euro was not talking about a field trip to the blackberry patch or a foray to the gourmet produce stand. The BlackBerry was, at the moment of this conversation in the spring of 2000, the newest, hippest, and most in-demand technology toy—a handheld, wireless device that allows access to and sending of e-mail from anywhere. Forget the archaic pager or the paleolithic cell phone. The BlackBerry had become the must-have business accessory, the Prada electronic of the backpack/briefcase set. As such, the younger associates had recently put in a demand for BlackBerries—among other things. However, this particular firm, being on the leading edge—or so they had thought—had actually anticipated this and had proactively initiated the process of harvesting BlackBerries for its employees even before this latest request had hit.

One of the midlevel executives shifted uncomfortably in his chair as he addressed the speakerphone. "Um, we've got good news and bad news on that." The good news was that the Tech department had gone on a quest to get the BlackBerries at a lower price, which it had achieved; the bad news was that this cost-consciousness had delayed the process a good month.

Over the speakerphone, Mr. Euro's voice tightened, although he did not raise it. He was a very polite man, more given to understatement. "Well, that is not good. We need to accelerate this process." Styluses flew across tiny electronic tablets an ocean away. "Now they're going to think we got the BlackBerries because they demanded them. We won't get credit."

They being the young associates. *We* being the senior management of the firm.

What's not wrong but *different* about this picture?

The executives sitting in the meeting exchanged glances. Everyone sitting there knew the answer: This was a pivotal moment, one of those instances when everything is about to change, when the bottom card is being pulled from the carefully constructed house.

Even a year before, the young associates on Wall Street — or new, first-year hires at almost any traditional company, for as far back as anybody could remember — were the voiceless slave labor of the organization. They were invisible. They were learning, contributing, gaining necessary expertise and momentum, but they were also doing something that was, once upon a time, quaintly referred to as "paying their dues."

Remember the trainee? I can assure you the Baby Boomers do, because they spent the first quarter of their careers being one. They got the coffee. They answered the phones. They typed their fingerprints off. They canceled their vacations. They practically licked their bosses' feet — and were lucky, if not always happy, to do it. Because they knew this was the way in, the first step in the long arc that would lead, say, forty years hence, to the gold watch, as it had for their fathers (and, in rare but heroic instances, mothers) before.

I remember my first job at an advertising agency. I was a junior junior copywriter. After my first client lunch, I was soundly berated by my boss. I stared at him, bewildered: I had spoken intelligently about the account, been polite and knowledgeable — so why the scolding? As I was quickly to learn, it had to do with the food. The client had ordered dessert. Nobody else had ordered dessert, including me. *Especially* me. "It's called 'Eat the dessert!'" my boss said, exasperated — actually, he was yelling — the implication being that I should have known my place in the pecking order, which was the rock bottom. "If the client orders dessert, the junior member of the team — that being you — orders dessert too. And eats it!" Every Baby Boomer I have ever worked with has stories like this.

Fast forward to the conference room in New York, where this

firm, along with other firms on the Street, was trying to make sense of a paradigm shift that seemed to them to have dropped from the sky. The culture was traditionally one of the most selective, and most demanding, that a new graduate could join. Just one year before the BlackBerry meeting, the territory was familiar, expected, and reeked of the status quo. It was the world of three-piece suits and ties for men; dark-colored skirt suits, blouses, and heels for women. Today it was five-day-a-week business casual (to assist in the re-wardrobing, Banana Republic opened an in-office shop on one investment bank's New York premises; the firm sent out the notice over the intranet). And, lurking around the corner, concierge service.

For decades, the elite young financial recruits, the cream of the Harvards, Whartons, and Stanfords of the world, could look forward to hundred-hour workweeks crunching numbers, dredging research, and assembling pitch books and reports from behind the scenes. Their status within the firms, according to a junior analyst quoted in a front-page article in the *New York Times*, was a "general perception of inferior creatures." This was, simply, the way it was. It was the price paid for a career path in financial services, for a shot at the megabonuses somewhere down the line. It was unimaginable that a junior staffer would confront, say, a Bruce Wasserstein or Henry Kravis with anything more bold than "Good morning, sir."

But in an instant, things were different. New hirees, strong in self-confidence if short on experience, were making demands. Yesterday's self-termed slave labor force had wrested control of the tiller, and the captains of the ship were charting a new course.

George Anders, senior editor and Silicon Valley bureau chief of *Fast Company* magazine, observed "more of a sense of 'I'm here, I'm ready for responsibility. Let me go do it.' I think, by and large, this is good. We don't need a version of the old

German apprentice system where at age thirty-six you were finally declared a master craftsman and you could begin doing whatever it was you wanted to do."

Upheaval at Salomon Smith Barney was also cited in the same piece in the *New York Times*. "The youngest workers are having their dues paid for them," trumpeted the article, headlined "At a Wall Street Firm, Junior Voices Roar." A twenty-three-year-old analyst had submitted a list of demands that detailed thirty-six ways the firm could retain their junior members (in addition to their $70,000-a-year salaries). The list included—in part—concierge service, videotape return service, free toothbrushes for business trips, stock perks, free gym memberships, better car service, and beds where the burned-out could relax at work. And BlackBerries.

The sword had been passed. The question remained: Just who was in training for what?

Instant entitlement has swept upon us like a tidal wave, in the turbulent wake of the Tech Babies, just one of a flurry of trends that is spawning a fundamental paradigm shift in how we work, live, love, and, even, exist in a world that is changing underfoot as we attempt to negotiate the shifting sands. In a speech to the Women of Silicon Valley Summit in April 2000, Hillary Clinton called the wiring of the country and its impact "as significant as electrifying the country in the 1930s." Certainly few circumstances in history can compare with the impact of the Internet, and even those that can cannot claim the swiftness with which the Internet has been embraced. According to Jupiter Media Metrix, in 1996, 14 percent of Americans were online; in 2000, the number had surged to 44 percent. In 1998, the average person spent nine hours a month online. Two years later, the number was nineteen. The Strategis Group in Washington released statistics including the facts that in 2000, more than half of all U.S. adults were online; that daily home use of the Internet skyrocketed 50 percent from the previous year; and 57 million adults, or 28 percent of the American population, used the Internet from home every day. In the same year, the percentage of adults who shopped online more than doubled their spending, from $1.72 billion to $3.6 billion. And they're getting plenty of early exposure. According to a *Newsweek*/Kaplan poll of parents with children in kindergarten through eighth grade in the fall of 2000, 75 percent of them had computers at home and 62 percent were connected to the Net. More than half of the children in grades K to 4 used computers at least a few times a week.

OK, they use computers. Doesn't almost everybody, certainly everybody in the business community? How does this entitle anybody to cut to the head of the line? The answer is, for this group it's irrelevant, because there is no line. True, a lot of people are standing there, queued up like the line exists. But there is a whole group of people who are line phobic. You're thinking a volatile stock market, job market, or economy is going to shake them to their senses? Think again. For the most part, it's beyond the point to them, because they were born outside the line, they grew up outside the line, and that's where they're operating, even if they are starting at ground zero of the career trajectory.

In every sea change, of every generation, there is an advance force of early adopters who set the tone for the mass movement that will follow. This time a new breed of early adopters—a mutation in the DNA—has tossed out a virtual stone, and the surrounding ripples are creating a new culture that is infusing every aspect of our lives until, one day, we will look up and recognize it, indelibly changed, as our own.

It's tempting to slap a ubiquitous "dot com" label on the swirl we see happening around us. Clearly, technology is chipping at the mortar of the once-unshakable pillars of our economic superstructures, and evolving new economies are increasingly renegotiating culture as we know it. But economy and culture are only part of the equation. In fact, the evidence behind this shift points to something more personal, a convergence of technology and attitude that is unique to this time and place.

One of the greatest impacts of the Internet has been a new capacity to allow—and, in some cases, force—people to interact with each other in different ways. In any human interaction, attitude is the critical link; however, it is also the forgotten element. We live with the impact, but we ignore the human engine. The motivations behind behavior are the driving force of action, which in turn lead to reaction. Why are people acting and responding differently from how they used to? Or are they? And what does this mean? What it means to the economy is critical—but what does it mean to me? What can I expect, and how can I prepare myself to handle it?

I was having lunch not long ago with Carl, a very intelligent and accomplished man I've known for two decades. He has led innumerable businesses to profitability, won many awards in his field, been president or CEO of several major companies, and currently holds a distinguished position at the top of a highly respected professional association, where he is responsible for the strategic overlay of an entire industry. But before the waiter could recite the specials, Carl began telling me about the new–versus–old economy culture clashes he was experiencing at his firm and his inability to get a grip on what he saw happening around him and where he fit in. We joked about a commercial that was running on TV, where a woman in her young twenties announces that after ten weeks on the job she's ready for her seat on the board, and Carl rolled his eyes in confusion. "I just don't get it," he said.

Carl is not alone.

Even the most recent historical equivalent to the socioeconomic upheavals we are seeing today, the movement of women into the workforce, failed to produce the kind of instant impact, not to mention resonance, of the New Economy Change Agents. The comparison helps shed some light on the current scenario.

For the past twenty years, researcher Laurie Ashcraft and I have tracked lifestyle trends and changes. Almost two decades ago, Nickles & Ashcraft, via the mail panel of Market Facts, fielded the first nationally projectable, in-depth survey to track women's changing attitudes, motivations, and behaviors, called Update: Women.™ The implications have ranged from the explosion of the divorce rate to single parenthood to the advent of the Supermom to the "Martha Stewartization" phenomenon.

The movement of women out of the home and into the workplace is one of the most significant socioeconomic shifts of the past century, but there are major differences between what happened in the women's sector and what we are seeing evolve from the new economy, and these differences help underscore the uniqueness and impact of the issues we are experiencing today. For instance, it has taken women nearly twenty years to gain their current position in the workplace, which is still significantly below that of men, while the population of the new economy and an empowered young segment of men and women established an entrenched culture that managed to slice into the establishment in a matter of only a few years. Why is this the case?

Although technology and other factors played a role in providing tools that enabled women to work more effectively outside the home, women's migration into the workforce was an attitudinal revolution, spurred by empowering changes within women themselves. Entering the economic mainstream gave them a new socioeconomic status, but real financial motivation actually played a lesser role. In 1981 the Nickles & Ashcraft Update: Women™ Survey showed that while 46 percent of all women age twenty to fifty worked primarily for income, the rest were motivated by having an interesting job and seeking self-respect. And the power women acquired by entering the economic mainstream was neither fast enough nor great enough to impact the overall economy to the point where all Americans could see their power reflected in their personal stock portfolios. Although strides were made toward economic equality between the sexes, there was no great engine for the amassing of wealth when women hung up their aprons and got jobs in the late 1970s and 1980s; in fact, the job sectors populated by women tended to be traditionally underpaid arenas labeled "pink-collar ghettos," which were a very long way from Silicon Valley. Partly as a result, women have still not completely broken through the glass ceiling. They have integrated, but not populated, the elite sectors of the economy. Women's advances have been based on performance within a status quo, not its reinvention.

In-depth questionnaires and interviewing of more than 5,000 women in our Update: Women™ surveys from 1979 to 1989 revealed little to no impact on their attitudes that could be traced to technology or any other outside force. In fact, in spite of the fact that it could be argued that technology produced the dishwashers, washing machines, telephones, cars, and countless other inventions that made daily life and, indeed, having a career, more feasible, none of these was an overnight innovation, and most had been in place since the birth of these women's mothers if not grandmothers. There was no external force to help launch women into a more elevated career trajectory.

Further, unlike those in the technology sector today, women had virtually no career-relevant role models to emulate or follow. In the 1980 Update: Women™ survey of 2,400 women, which allowed women to write in their selections, not a single respondent named a prominent executive or entrepreneur as her role model; almost universally, women's role models were family members such as their mothers, with the exception of a few who named fantasy figures such as glamorous movie stars.

The end of the twentieth century saw another kind of attitudinal shift that had not previously been seen. In 1999 Ashcraft and I partnered with Greenfield Online for the Gen Y2K study,™ a groundbreaking online survey of 2,000 young men and women age sixteen to twenty-four. This study revealed attitudes, motivations, and behaviors of an emerging empowered mind-set among younger people that has been playing out from the family room to the boardroom. Behind the data lay a complexity that was not apparent from surface observations.

Instant entitlement can be traced to a powerful cocktail of factors:

- The impact of socioeconomic speedup

- The enablement of a wired world

- The in-your-face sensibility of a new, empowered attitude

- The amassing of wealth in the sector

- The lionization of the culture

The Gen Y2K Study™ revealed that younger men and women are vastly more ambitious than their older counterparts. Roughly 64 percent of the sixteen- to nineteen-year-olds in the survey revealed that their goals in life are "quite ambitious" — compared to one-third of Baby Boomers. A third of the male teens believe they could run a company tomorrow. Fifty-three percent of the male teens age sixteen to nineteen and 65 percent of female teens set long-term goals for themselves.

This is not just attributable to the generalization that younger people, no matter what their generation, have a more go-get-

'em attitude. In fact, Baby Boomer women, as they age, appear to have less ambition than their generational counterparts of the two most recent decades. For instance, in the last twenty years, Ashcraft and I have seen the percentage of twenty- to twenty-four-year-old women who say they have ambitious plans move up 11 percent, while the number of women age thirty-five to fifty who claim to have high goals has declined 16 percent.

Unlike the empowerment mind-set shift that occurred among women in the 1980s, which was largely attributable to the snowball effect of acquiring new earning power in the economic mainstream, sixteen- to nineteen-year-olds are not being emboldened primarily by the fact of earning their own income. They have an ingrained attitude that has become a part of their DNA. They walk into the workplace with that attitude, because they had it *before* they walked in.

Donny Deutsch, chairman of Deutsch, Inc. and iDeutsch, advertising and communications companies, has experienced the impact firsthand. Not so very long ago, Deutsch, now in his early forties, was one of the so-called young Turks of the advertising world, and he has had the professional temerity and expertise to advise everyone from the president of the United States to Puff Daddy. "The entitlement thing is fascinating," says Deutsch, shaking his head. "And I have seen it. I can sum it up in an anecdote.

"We have one area of the office which is a kind of pit or open area where there are maybe twenty young people sitting— they all happen to do a job where they are all in their early twenties. A couple of times a year, I will go into this area, so I walk in not long ago, and I say, 'Hey, how's everybody doing?' and, you know, out of the twenty people, maybe fifteen kind of quickly hang up the phone and turn to the big boss, or whatnot. And I happen to see that there is one young woman still on the phone. I come up to her, face her, and I say—kidding around,

'Hey, that must be a really important call—who are you on the phone with?' It was a kind of 'Why don't you hang up—after all, the big boss is here?' Finally she hangs up the phone, and I say, 'That must have been an important client.' And she says, 'Well, no, actually, it was a friend of mine.' "

Deutsch shrugs. "Now, if you think back twenty years ago, and you are a junior person and the head of the company walks in, you would stand up, you'd salute. I am not somebody who is ceremonious"—there are scooters and the occasional dog in the polished concrete halls at Deutsch—"but the fact is that she not only didn't do that, but she was so comfortable saying 'Oh, this is a friend on the phone.' I don't want to say this is a lack of regard for authority. It's not. It's this entitlement thing. This is 'I have a great job here, but I can get another one tomorrow, and I can probably get more money.'

"And, you know, everybody believes that at a very young age they should be making millions and they are the future. They've all read about the millionaire that just did their IPO. I think in the next couple of years, this is going to change a bit, for obvious reasons. But certainly these last few years, there is this sense of not only entitlement but lack of the feeling that you have to work your way up, or of the things that have fundamentally been driving young people in this business and country for two hundred years. It has just completely changed."

That opinion is ubiquitous, because the attitude is. Across the country from Deutsch, Valerie Frederickson, president of Valerie Frederickson & Company, a human resource, career management, and executive search firm in Menlo Park whose clients include Intuit, Philips, and Silicon Valley Bank, tells a similar story. One of Frederickson's staff members, a few years her junior, got a call on her cell phone during an important marketing meeting at 5:30 P.M. The woman took the call and left, explaining that she had to go, because friends were waiting for her at a bar. "I was actually more upset with her for taking a cell phone call in the middle of the meeting than for leaving to go to the bar," says Frederickson, a Gen Xer who is sometimes taken aback by those even a few years younger than she, although, she says, she understands where they are coming from because she is on the cusp and sees both sides. "I myself didn't come into work today until 10 A.M. because I was upset about something and didn't want to come in to work, so I called my office manager and said I wasn't coming in till ten."

In explaining the issue of instant entitlement, Frederickson adds, "We were the first generation to be raised by parents who were off busy, doing other things. They didn't spend so much time with us, they were off doing other stuff. They were also able to buy us more stuff because moms were working, too — there was more disposable income. And there was just more stuff to buy. We grew up in the era of inexpensive Japanese electronics, and so from the time when we were little kids, we were used to using technology and were the first generation to have it as kids. We're not intimidated by it, and we have this sort of *droit de seigneur* attitude toward it, where we have the right to have it all."

Companies are addressing this by stepping up to the plate like never before. The kinds of perks that were being offered to the in-demand members of the Internet space — many of them first- or second-time job holders — certainly paled alongside the traditional "packages" of health insurance and two weeks' paid vacation. Companies have found that retirement packages do not make a big impression with this crowd, because they can't imagine themselves sticking around until retirement age. Here are a few of the perks and quirks that were glittering on the dot com landscape — even in a downturned technology market: a $700 Aeron chair, the type formerly reserved for the executive suite, for every new hiree; a two-day, all expenses–paid corporate

"Winterfest" at Lake Placid for employees and their families; on-site yoga classes; "theme" parties and nights, such as a regular, weekly barbecue, Mexican, or Italian night—or a corporate scavenger hunt with ten teams of six, each team scavengering Manhattan in its own limo, winner announced at a chic restaurant with the tab, of course, picked up by the company. "We have a morale budget," explained one executive.

"I know people who are under the age of twenty-seven who are commanding salaries of $100,000 and more," said Frederickson, "and I know thirty-one-year-olds who are now getting a quarter of a million dollars in just straight salary. For perks, you see cars, you see four-year interest-free home loans—and, you know, out here in Menlo Park, a small home can be a million or two—you see large amounts of vacation, companies paying for vacations, nice offices." Frederickson provides her own employees with perks that include paid vacations, makeup lessons, and the services of a personal shopper. "When an employee starts with us, they expect automatically that they're going to get absolutely top dollar, they're going to have the latest technology, a beautiful office, their opinions are going to count just as much as my opinion, and they don't take no for an answer," says Frederickson. "They just expect that there will be a full kitchen; paid-for breakfast, lunch, and dinner; and, if necessary, the plant person from the office will go to their home and water their plants. They know that they can get another job immediately, and they're just not worried about it."

But when faced with a downtrending market that has the savviest economists on alert?

"They're *still* not worried about it. They know that they can walk into just about anywhere and present a good-value proposition for them to be working there, and they'll be hired immediately."

The attitude is pervasive and has moved beyond the Internet space. For instance, in the legal area, Web sites such as Greedyassociates.com, a site for law associates, have sprung up so that entry-level lawyers can make sure they are up to the minute with the salary and benefits status quo; for the more analog, bonus figures can be checked out in industry publications, including the *New York Law Journal*. Bonuses, which swelled during the period of the raging market, remain higher than ever, even in the face of economic volatility, because the market for talent remains fiercely competitive; in New York at the close of the year 2000, the "package" for first-year lawyers averaged an all-time high of $165,000.

As Donny Deutsch sees it, the media plays a major role in the advent of creating and sustaining instant entitlement. "These are kids who grew up of the media age, and it is what they saw all around them, on TV and in the news. It is what gets written about because it is sexy and it is exciting. Unfortunately, the media has created this illusion that, yes, it can happen to you at age twenty-five, and it does happen all the time, because this is what you read about every day — the twenty-one-year-olds and twenty-four-year-olds making on paper $20 million, or even $100 million, so this kind of attitude goes, of 'Why not me?' and 'It is only going to take me a few years to get there — I just need to have the right idea, or know the right VC guy, and it is really easy to do. I mean, why not? I look at this guy from college and, you know, they liked basketball so they came up with this idea to watch it; it turns into Broadcast.com and they made a billion dollars and they went out and bought a basketball team.' And that is entitlement — or a false sense of it."

On the other hand, Deutsch notes, the attitude can be empowering, which in itself can become the edge that breaks the barriers. "Sometimes people sweat and bleed and don't have that sense of entitlement," he says. "And I find that is always a difference between supersuccessful people and people who don't quite get there, whatever their definition of success is."

Ray Gaulke, president of the Public Relations Society of America, feels that the loss of the mentoring system is one reason for this wave of instant entitlement. Gaulke has seen the entitlement story evolve from inside a system that he feels used to sponsor interdependence but now fosters the opposite scenario. "There's a big difference," Gaulke says. "Twenty-five years ago, there was a mentoring system. When you did something at work, there was always somebody who knew more than you who was available to look at what you did, review it, take the time to help you perfect it. There was a pursuit of excellence and a track to get there. Now everybody is self-mentored."

The Internet is a world that promotes the no-mentors mentality precisely because the culture is too green to have produced the necessary depth of seniority. It is also a world in which the junior people actually have more expertise than the seniors. In spite of the enormous advances of the past ten years, almost everyone in the field is learning as they go, and with every advance or fluctuation in technology, the paradigm shifts again. The knowledge base and the culture carriers are constantly being revised, if not reinvented. As the head of marketing for one dot com noted, "So much is changing so quickly. Everyone's using different tactics, techniques, and philosophies. There are no standards. The chic business model changes every quarter."

Carley Roney, cofounder of TheKnot.com, is proof of the point. "When we started, the Internet was just so new, there were no companies to look at for examples or models. And that was exciting, this whole thing of having to make it up as you went along. There were not any rules that you were going to break, there were only rules that you were making. And we had to create it from scratch. And that was interesting.

"Who were my mentors? Well, there were no mentors for this because there were no people who knew how to do it, so we were sort of all on our own. We did have people we got advice from now and then, financial people and advertising people, things like that. But in terms of what we were actually doing, I think we were people who liked the idea that we were doing it on our own and liked the idea that we would have to be relied on for our own — for lack of a better word — genius. Not that we are geniuses, but you would have to be relied on to come up with the answers to the questions. It was just you."

"Now you have got the sort of electronic media where there are no filters," Ray Gaulke says. "Nothing to slow you down or make you think twice. People are self-managing themselves and self-filtering. I think the thing about speed is that it has become more important than content. Education has played a role in this, technology played a role, self-empowerment played a role — it all contributes to what is this generation."

And what *is* this generation? Statistics prove Gaulke is on the right track when he says they're not being mentored. Most likely, not only do they not miss it — they wouldn't sit still for it. Unlike their predecessors, today's sixteen-to-thirty-four-year-olds feel ready and able to run a business *now*. According to the Gen Y2K Study, one-fourth of sixteen-to-twenty-four-year-olds, for instance, believe they could run a company tomorrow. This group is, in fact, almost twice as ambitious as thirty-five-to-fifty-year-olds. This is not simply a natural function of that life stage. Nickles and Ashcraft's comparable research among the younger age segment of women even ten years ago, for example, did not show this keen ambition level. Add to that the fact that young people's motivations are now, more than ever, validated by reality: In the dot com community, twenty-somethings saw their counterparts become millionaires overnight. They want their piece of the pie, and it starts young: Almost two-thirds of online teens say they play to win in a competitive situation.

Need convincing that these kids could leave tire tracks on a Baby Boomer's forehead on their way to the foosball table? Forty-three percent of the sixteen-to-nineteen-year-olds said they are under so much pressure that they feel they could explode. Sixty-one percent of boys and 41 percent of girls said they would use a gun if they "had to"—leaving one to wonder exactly what those compelling circumstances might be.

Clearly, these figures do not indicate a group of young people who will sit at their desks, hands folded in their laps, awaiting their turn.

The other shoe is bound to drop. "The reality is," says Donny Deutsch, "that all these young people who have made their millions and millions are still such an infinitesimal fraction. There is this false sense of entitlement that has been created for people to strive and reach for. These people you read about, they are the rock stars of the new millennium. And just like there are only a handful of rock and roll wannabes that make it, there are many, many people who are playing music in their garage and waiting tables. The difference being that young people aspiring to be a rock-and-roll star always knew it was a one-in-a-million shot, so there was never that sense of entitlement in a twenty-three-year-old starting a rock band, because there are only so many Rolling Stones. The irony is that there is this misperception today that it is so easily attainable. I can't tell you the number of people—not just young people, even people who actually understand the business fundamentals—who come to me with business plans that are so half baked: 'Yeah, we will raise our first $60 million here, our next $100 million there.'

And you know this is the Emperor's New Clothes. People just played the same absurd Ponzi game that everybody else is playing. And were kind of blind to it."

The fluctuations of the market serve as a built-in governing device to some extent, but even after the market correction of April 2000, the sense of entitlement did not abate. The explanation was simple: Since this empowered attitude existed before the New Economy wave crested, it should not be surprising that it did not wash away when the market valuation tide receded. This mind-set is the key factor. Instead of causing a retreat to the former status quo, a falling back into "line," a return to the days when, as one *New Yorker* cartoon caption put it, "a CEO looked like a CEO," there has simply been an evolution of the paradigm's reinvention. Market corrections, consolidations of the technology sector, untenable burn rates, crunched funding for IPOs, the winnowing of the dot com community—all are leading to the survival of the fittest, a scenario for which the no-prisoners' Millennials are particularly well suited.

Six months after we first talked, one survivor whose e-company had gone through market correction contortions and bloodbaths—but was still standing—told me, "Since I talked to you last, we've had two waves of layoffs, and we fired the general manager, the old director, and the director's staff. We now have much more a spirit of team-building."

Do you need to ask whose team?

The instantly entitled who are fast-forwarding through their careers are on a collision course. Dead ahead: the Baby Boomers, that 1960s generation that thought their reign would go on forever, for whom retirement was a dirty word, who initially saw the younger generation as a bunch of nonthreatening "slackers." Well, slackers no more. What we have is an entire generation that is gunning for the Boomers' jobs and is not willing to spend a couple dozen years waiting in the wings. A clash is on the horizon. And it would be a misconception to think that they simply want the Boomers' jobs. They don't. They want to deconstruct those jobs and put them back together on their own terms. BlackBerries and concierge service may stave off the tidal wave momentarily, but they are just a finger in the dike.

There's fallout in our future. Inevitable? Maybe. But possibly, if we have some insight into what's happening, we won't be caught by surprise, and, perhaps, we'll be able to muster some mutual understanding and constructive solutions. The Baby Boomer who insists that the economy will swing back and cause a reversion to the old status quo is wearing a blindfold. Not about the economy—but about the kind of people they are dealing with.

The e-generation. Gen N. Gen Y3K. Wireds. There's a market basket of nomenclature out there. Whatever you call them, they are the new order that is confronting and changing the world as we have known it. Collectively, they have one thing in common, and it's more about the DNA than the résumé. They are the Change Agents, and if these Change Agents are hard to harness with a "handle," there's a reason. We are used to generational nomenclature linked to demographics: Baby Boomers. Gen Xers. Yuppies. Guppies. But this group is different. Undeniably, many of them are young, in their teens, twenties, or thirties, but that span of ages alone should tell us something—this is a psychographic group, an affinity tribe, brought and bonded together by attitude and lifestyle rather than age. Their relationship with technology has been symbiotic: It's both the reason and the catalyst.

Change Agents are a lifestyle segment. This cutting-edge, trend-setting group is using the new wave of technology and the attendant economic power it has driven as a catapult to incite major socioeconomic shifts, in much the way that Boomers in the 1960s bonded around the issues of love, peace, and youth culture. This book, however, is not about technology or the economy. It is about the Change Agents and how they are not just adopting but in a symbiotic relationship with technology, and how their responses are exacting an entirely new set of rules to work and live by in uncharted terrain, where speed and uncertainty are perhaps the only common denominators.

Jack Sansolo, former executive vice president of Global Brand Direction at Eddie Bauer in Seattle, a person who has introduced a few things himself (as president of a major ad agency, he introduced the Infiniti car to America), sees the Change Agent as a more empowered version of the classic early adopter. "Certainly early adopters are Change Agents, in the fact that we look to these people to change the general trends and whatever," he says. "I believe that these particular people are different from early adopters of other kinds of things in the past. I believe that these people we are seeing today are really advocates and proselytizers for the technology. And that is different from simply adopting something, being the first on the block, and because you are the first, you are the prom queen and everybody copies you. But in this case, the prom queen is going out and proselytizing and saying 'You know what? This is a better way to live. This is a better way to get information, a better way to shop, a better way to do your job, a better way to form your community.' And in that sense, I think they really are Change Agents, more than any other early adopters. I think that has made a huge difference. The media was sucked in right from the beginning, and that worked hand in hand with all this proselytizing. And so the early adopters were absolutely in this case massive Change Agents in record time."

Every generation or period in time has its Change Agent population. Once upon a time, they were the guys who picked up rocks to start fires when others were just throwing the rocks. Today's Change Agents actually have more than a little in common with the fire-starters, because they are inextricably linked to something that cannot help but impact every other segment of the society in which they exist. Because of this, these Change Agents have taken us off guard. And before we saw them as anything but an oddity, a bunch of geeky kids out there doing God knew what, they had permeated our way of life. And changed it.

"There is all kinds of data about introductions of new technologies over the years," says Sansolo, "and the adoption curve of the Internet is a fraction of what anything else was. And I think that is because these early adopters were Change Agents."

What does it take to be a Change Agent? Look around you. You may see a fifteen-year-old in your den who qualifies, or a forty-year-old veteran of the traditional economy who finds himself on the front porch of a sheep farm with a headset and a laptop. You will see a parallel universe, sharing our space on the planet while operating under a quite different set of standards and practices.

As Caryn Marooney, thirty-two-year-old partner in OutCast Communications, a San Francisco public relations firm specializing in high-tech clients, puts it, "This whole world is unlike any other. You have to be able to walk a wire without a net, to feel your way in a fog and just keep moving forward. Everyone feels like they are in the middle of a gold rush, and we are willing to change and even give up our lives for our belief in what we are doing. Fundamental shifts are happening very quickly. The lifestyle is fast, opportunistic — and empowered."

Esther Drill, thirty and cofounder of gURL.com, the most popular interactive Web site for teen girls (800,000 unique users a month), builds on the thought: "This lifestyle is young, vibrant, and exciting. There's a sense of being connected with others like yourself, being wired. And being wired is about faster motion, faster thinking, faster moving, being quicker, more flexible. New solutions to new things. It's a constantly evolving model. It's a faster pace. You expect things to happen more quickly. When people don't keep up, you think, 'What's wrong with them?' "

Abbi Gosling, twenty-six, a founding partner and creative director of Agile Industries, a New York Internet advertising firm, notes, "The Internet is the industry that happened to have saved my generation from obscurity." She's in her company's Soho loft, dressed in casual pants, baggy sweater, and work boots. "We were 'slackers,' and suddenly the Internet came along, and we were millionaires! It gave us something to do that was *ours*, that we could get into and work really hard—I work fourteen-hour days—but it was something Boomers didn't have. It was not of our parents' generation; in fact, they didn't even *get* it. Then, for goodness sake, we made money at it."

Yes, there is a digital divide. Some of us are on one side of that line in the sand, ordering groceries over the Net, courting via instant messaging and image downloading, working 24/7 from virtual offices, turning our babies over to teachers with tongue studs. Others of us are still trying to figure out how to program our VCRs and wondering what the hell is going on. Most of us are the new unholy equation—X parts old economy over X parts new economy. Arguably all of us are struggling to put it all together, because one thing's for sure: The smooth surface we skated over for so long has been shattered forever. The Change Agents are incubating an entirely new culture where it's not just fast forward, it's fast*er* forward. And, damn the market fluctuations, they're not going back.

Whether we are consciously aware or not, we are all living in an incubator, where seeds of a lifestyle shift we can only begin to imagine are germinating in the virtual hothouse. But how can we tell what indicators are real? Is it possible to see the future, to read the map of a road not yet graded?

Actually, you don't need a crystal ball. The key is the Change Agents themselves. They are a mutation of a group of the early adopters, which are the vanguard, the first to try new things, to go not against but *ahead of* the flow, to forge new territory. Early adopters reside in every segment and geography of every society, every age and socioeconomic bracket. We all know them, we met them young. When he was six, my son had a junior early adopter in his class: Michael was the first kid to collect Pogs, and he talked the Pog gospel; soon every boy in the class collected Pogs. Michael moved on to making lanyards; soon the entire class wanted to try it. Next came yo-yos, then finger skateboards and sports card collecting. As they get older, early adopters are the first kids on the block to know about the hot new bands. They are the first triers of cutting-edge technology. Sociologists segment the early adopters by polling them on attributes that have been identified as keys to the prototype. To find out if you are an early adopter, quiz yourself with these questions, which are similar to those used by marketers to segment people psychographically:

- Do people come to you for advice on new products?

- Do you like to buy new things, even if they're not proven?

- Do you belong to more than two social groups (clubs, church, book discussion groups, sports, etc.)?

- Do you generally like new ideas?

- Are you flexible in your daily life?

- Are you comfortable giving opinions to others?

- Do you feel you have more friends than the average person?

If you answered "yes" to five or more of these questions, you qualify as an early adopter.

How do we know the impact of early adopters? There has been plenty of precedent in the research community, but Ashcraft and I have documented it firsthand. Thousands of people participating in Nickles & Ashcraft research studies have been asked these same questions over the course of the past eighteen years. Invariably, those who were classified as early adopters held opinions or exhibited behaviors and attitudes that led their peers by a range of eighteen months to two years. Where they lead, others follow. For instance, when we began a twenty-year tracking study of women's attitudes in the early 1980s, we identified an attitudinal subsegment of women early adopters that we termed the Pacesetters. These women were highly ambitious, career-motivated, and much more likely to be divorced or in a crumbling relationship. Like the Change Agents of the New Economy, these Pacesetters were highly vocal and visible proselytizers of their lifestyle; however, in this case, their segment was much smaller than the population of women in general at the time, and, as such, their potential impact tended to be discounted. In addition, the potential social consequences the Pacesetters brought along with them were so unsettling and unpopular at the time that people *wanted* to discount them. When the data came in from all 1,885 women in the study, there were statistical bellwethers that the larger population was following the pattern that had been established by the Pacesetters—albeit at that time in smaller numbers. As a result, we predicted, for instance, that based on the propensity of Pacesetters to divorce, the overall divorce rate would accelerate dramatically within the next few years. This was a highly unpopular prediction among traditionalists, and one that was actually derided at the time in the media — as we have found unpopular observations often are. The fact was that within five years, the divorce rate soared to nearly 50 percent, and many of the attendant predictions and projections hinted at by the attitudes and behaviors of the Pace-setters of the early 1980s became realities within the decade.

The Internet, with its capability of adding a supercharging, speeded-up level of overdrive and its massive economic impact, has provided a new force that has taken the early adopter paradigm and spun it into hypergear, creating another subgroup that I call the Change Agents. They have much in common with traditional early adopters, but by growing up in a wired world, they have imbued themselves with the characteristics of the medium: speed, intensity, reinvention.

The Change Agents are true mutants, a kind of ultracharged superspecies, like those power strains of sea kelp that scientists say may someday nurture the world. But they are also the water-testers, the temperature-takers for the rest of us — in hyperdrive. We watch, while they surge at warp speed over the chasm to — what? — on the other side. And, when they make it, we're right behind them. Maybe a few paces back, but there.

2 GETTING IT

"**S**hort term. Wired. Funky. Fast. Different. And an aesthetic."
Chris Whittmann, New Economy landlord, executive vice
president of TechSpace, describes the kind of real estate his clients want. In an antithesis to the mahogany-and-marble sensibility that defined prime office space for a century or more, the
Change Agents have shaken off the cobwebs and ripped out the
wall-to-wall carpeting. Not to mention the walls.

It used to be that there was a strict architectural hierarchy of
the workplace. For instance, walls and floors used to reflect stat-
ure. At one company where I worked, wall-to-wall carpet was
alternately laid and ripped up from office floors, depending on
if the occupant had the initials "VP" after his (rarely, her) name
on the door plaque. Senior VPs rated clear plastic protectors
between the carpet and the rolling desk chair, and it seemed
like there were always carpet-layers on the premises. The carpet
and the plastic served an unspoken purpose of marking every-

one's place in the hierarchy. The mere act of walking on the floor kept one in a constant state of realization that all employees were not created equal.

The stakes rose with the title. At another company where I worked, I remember coming across a fleet of workmen hauling down the hall dollies stacked with enough marble slabs to panel the Acropolis. A high-up executive was moving to a new office on the floor, and he was moving his marble with him. They had actually chiseled the stuff off the walls and floor. One reason could have been, I suppose, that the guy had become attached to the marble. More likely, the incomer to the former office was not high enough up the pecking order to rate the marble. Ergo, musical marble. Today such physical emblems of the corporate hierarchy are increasingly viewed as quaintly archaic, if not downright undesirable, and this can be credited to the influence of the Change Agents.

With the birth of the New Economy came new criteria for workspace and its integration into the lifestyle of those who worked in it. In the aftermath of market fluctuations and dot com shakeouts, one truth is left standing: The office will never again be sacrosanct in the same way. Icons of corporate identity such as the corner office, the conference room, even the coffee-maker have been literally torn down and reconstructed around new needs, and this revised landscape has leached into the old economy as well. Cappuccino and juice bars have invaded lobbies; conference rooms are being blasted away for breakout spaces with crash couches, ottomans, and music; Ping Pong and foosball tables are rampant; corners have rounded into curved walls; free juice, Starbucks, tea, bottled water, snacks, and, after hours, beer are on tap; state-of-the-art gyms are status quo; creative furnishings abound; light streams through glass walls; and executives work in open spaces alongside their staffs.

Opportunities for creativity and productivity are integrated into the furnishings at every junction. The myriad uses of the whiteboard are illustrative. In the past, whiteboards, like blackboards, once stood, stolid and silent, at the front of a conference table — because most "idea-generating sessions" or "brainstorms" took place in conference rooms and conference table surroundings. People were called into the conference room at the appointed time, then they sat down at the table and forced themselves to come up with ideas, which were then duly jotted onto the whiteboard in marker. After the session was over, everybody left the conference room and went back to regular work. The whiteboard was wheeled back into the closet. Creativity time was over. Today it is recognized that creativity is not a function of time and place. That's why so many New Economy companies have led the way in twenty-four-hour services for employees — and whiteboard reinvention. In one Internet office, whiteboards are used as sliding dividers, so if inspiration strikes, the wall can simply slide into place and scribbling can begin. At another, the doors are whiteboards. At a third, the cafeteria tabletops are whiteboards.

The philosophy seems to be: Just because you work in a pressure cooker, it doesn't have to look or feel like one. In fact, for those who practically live at the office, it makes sense to provide all the comforts of home, whether that means an on-premises kitchen to whip up an omelette, a VIP spot under your desk for your dog, a twenty-four-hour media rec room, or, on lesser budgets, a chance to paint your unfinished door-desk any color you choose. At the birth of the New Economy, talent was at a premium, and companies found themselves doing what it took in terms of space to get and hold desirable employees. If that meant converting a vice president's office to a massage room for free reflexology on Fridays . . . well, why not? The feeling was, if they feel comfortable and relaxed, they're going to work longer, more happily, and be more productive. These were business decisions as much as they were human decisions. Open spaces promote teamwork; natural light induces creativity; if Fido is in the office, you don't have to rush home to walk him. And free food is—well, free food. What was once desirable became no longer tenable.

Carrie, a mid-thirties new media CEO, whose office is in a retrofitted Soho loft, described her firm's space. "We have no walls. We were going to blow a good portion of our hard-earned money on an architect, but we got rid of him. The space he proposed was not Zen. He didn't get it—the people are the energy, not the place. We needed a quiet space. He showed us plans for a Lucite conference room, a sunken room . . ." As she talked, Carrie was sitting on a somewhat worn, round sectional velvet sofa, nine pieces fitted into an L shape. "This sofa has been there from day one," she said. "It's a member of the family." She laughed. "The architect didn't see that at all. We have a blankie and a pillow for naps—one of our people really does well if she has a nap. And we socialize on the couch, like a family coming together at a table for dinner. At six at night, whether we've been fighting or whatever, we end up on the couch. This couch has a meaning and a power."

And so does the space, open, with desks and computers and phones. "I don't want a conference room or wall," said Carrie. "We have a conference table that came with the space. We never use it. To put something between the client and me—never! I've been at conference tables all my career, and I find that if I take the head of the table, I'm viewed as an authority figure, and that can be negative as well as positive. The architect had this one piece of furniture—it was like an egg on wheels that opened up. He showed us a 3-D computer-designed space—and it wasn't who we are." She sighed. "Oh, it was competent. It would have won him design awards. But I didn't want an egg. He just didn't get it."

There is a sense of a necessary perspective, according to Carrie's cofounder and partner. "The Net was where we all started, and there is a sense of, this is a really cool thing, but no one else really gets it but people of our ilk," she says.

Getting it, understanding the sensibility.

Chris Wittmann gets it.

TechSpace is a New York–based incubator environment that caters to Internet and new media start-ups, offering them cradle-to-graduation services that start with real estate and can take you from a one-person shop with a desk made out of orange crates all the way to the IPO.

TechSpace is not your father's office. It's a self-contained hive of activity, like one of those Jules Verne–esque bubbles at the bottom of the sea, an experimental, cultivated ecoculture where species are nurtured and maintained until they are strong enough to survive on their own or are winnowed out in the survival of the fittest.

Every single one of the baby businesses within the TechSpace environment is an Internet-related start-up venture, each at a different point along the continuum of its life cycle. And everything these infants need to be born, live, and thrive is right there within the four walls — or lack thereof. Traditionally, small start-up companies were birthed in one of two ways — in a basement or in common office space that was usually efficient, but — even when high end — purposefully bland. The closest thing to an amenity was usually the Mr. Coffee. You could call these spaces functional but hardly aspirational. But now ventures like TechSpace are showing that start-up environments — even those consisting of one person, one desk, and one phone — can be sexy.

"We want to stay away from Class A buildings," Wittmann confided, disdaining what was once real estate nirvana to a fledgling company. "They don't have the sensibility that our people are looking for in a work environment. It's a different attitude, and it starts from there."

From the outside, the TechSpace offices look like any other vintage high-rise New York building, albeit one that is located in a very hip, downtown area nestled among antique shops, trendy boutiques, and gourmet take-outs. The lobby of the substantial, sedate gray limestone building is a mixture of marble and exposed pipes — old economy elegance meets new economy utility. Upstairs, however, the resemblance stops. TechSpace offers real estate and support services for Internet and new media start-up companies. Unlike traditional "office services" spaces, TechSpace offers a wraparound yet cutting-edge environment that fits its clientele. Here the drab, faceless, institutional setting we have come to expect from shared office spaces gives way to space with as much personality as the businesses it houses.

It's postpeak in the technology market, but that hasn't leveled the optimism here. Walk in, and there's an excitement, a buzz in the air, a feeling that something is happening, a sensation of hopefulness no matter how the market is performing. An open, skylit entrance faces onto a snack bar with stools, where cereal, cookies, salads, and Terra Chips can be had from 8 A.M. till 7 P.M. There's also a pantry and a kitchen. Beyond is a veritable beehive of basketweave steel hallways of interconnecting small office spaces, most no more than six by ten feet, and holding two or three people. At any given time, between fifty to one hundred companies occupy 40,000 square feet of space on two floors, and, in most cases, each office space houses a different fledgling company. Steel-grated sliding doors with sandblasted glass panels, some with portholes for windows, reveal simple, stripped-down, cagelike offices furnished with simple, natural birchwood desks and galvanized steel. Each door holds freshly printed business cards that attest to the variety of fetal business here: 2 Glow.com; i syndicate; astrology.com; Rate Yourself.com; eyeweb.com; Sundial.com. Et cetera.

The traditional office services are there, in a different form. Conference table? It's a pool table with a top. (After hours, the top comes off and the pool cues come out.) Copy machine? Behind the circular, suspended red velvet curtain. Basically, there's everything a start-up could want—including a receptionist, secretaries, technical support, project management services, recommendations of designers and printers for your cards and letterhead, corporate ID service, legal advice, and, when the time comes for you to spread your wings and fly—say, after your venture capital funding has come in—real estate brokerage to help you find a bigger space, recruiting services to help you staff up, and even caterers to plan your launch party. But, says Wittmann, TechSpace services are there for you even before you are a business at all. It starts when you're an idea, a concept. A business plan, to be precise. The idea is, before you even come in to look at the real estate, you submit an executive summary of your plan. The founders of TechSpace include investment bankers who will then review your business plan. They know what makes a successful start-up, and to get space in this incubator, you have to walk in with an idea with a better than good chance of making that venture capitalist materialize. TechSpace received 1,600 business plans last year. A percentage made the cut and scored leases for space in the New York facility, and some got more than space. TechSpace has a venture capital offshoot, Tech Space Exchange, that puts its own funds into selected start-ups. The company is expanding to San Francisco, Boston, Austin, Miami, and London.

Chris Wittmann, low key in chinos and a blue shirt with his sleeves rolled up, came from a traditional commercial real estate background that couldn't have been more different. "I had a very defined existence. I was doing tenant leasing deals in Midtown. I wore a suit every day and worked in a Class A building. Coming here, it's been such an incredible experience. It's become not a job; it's who I am. It's kind of scary."

Wittmann feels he understands the start-up mentality because he lived it himself. "It was lonely when we started this," he says. "It was a lowly experience. I found this space, then we signed a deal where the partners put down a security deposit and got six months free rent. During that period, the partners put together their own business plan. At that time, it was actually difficult to sell people on the idea. It was hard to raise money, because people didn't understand. We built the space without having the money raised, working on it while we continued pitching to raise money—till it got to the point where the contractors were looking for money. I was so freaked out, I had a skin rash going on just from all the stress. I had to put getting married on hold for a while because I couldn't handle any more pressure. To her credit, my fiancée understood. I needed some kind of sense of stability. We had conversations about it. So I understand what companies who come here are dealing with.

"A start-up can't be just a nine-to-five thing, you can't shut it off. It's nerve-wracking. You have so much personally invested, and you're working for less and for equity. Finally we got the money to pay everybody. But we knew all the time that as soon as we got the space up and running, it would take off and we'd lease it all immediately. And it did finally get to the point where our vision was confirmed. We were funded with $47 million financing."

Wittmann proudly points out a publicity mailer he designed to send prospective tenants and investors. At his former real estate company, such a piece would have taken the form of an expensively printed, glossy brochure. Here, however, the promotional mailer is not even on paper. It's a lime-green plastic

View-Master, a hip version of the funky toy from the 1950s. The photos of the TechSpace area are on the little circular disc that you slide into the View-Master. When you look through the View-Master, the photos have an open, 3-D quality. That's the idea. "It's fun to be here," Wittmann says. "This is the opposite of what it was like where I worked before. People want to be part of this community. It's industry-specific, it has a lot of synergy, people trading ideas—that whole thing. It's not a lonely existence anymore when you come here. You're part of a community right away, even if you're working alone."

One of the tenants, munching a salad at the snack bar, confirms, "There's a lot of camaraderie here. You're working around the clock, and at any hour of the day or night there is someone in the corridor, the snack bar, or one of the communal spaces for you to bounce ideas off. There's even potential for partnerships to develop. I mean, if you're going to look for partners, why not look across the hall?"

"One of the most important things is having the right space and the right image and projecting that to potential employees," says Wittmann. "We've had people come in, and all they use the space for is to hire people. They say it gives them an incredible edge. It says, 'These guys get it. The understand the whole culture.' Some people become so passionate about their work that it consumes their life and it becomes their life *and* their work."

The offices attest to the lifestyle nature of the work that goes on at TechSpace. "There's a preference for this sensibility," Wittmann says. "This is what our clients want. High ceilings, exposed mechanical systems, an open collaborative environment where their work attitude is reflective of the space they're in. Where everybody is excited about going to work, there's no dress code, the barriers are broken down. People will work harder because they don't feel like they're at work. I know that's how I felt. And it's not kids I'm talking about. It's people in their twenties, but also people in their fifties and sixties. It's the psychographic."

At TechSpace, the fledgling entrepreneurs work around the clock. Dry cleaning and laundry hang on office doors. Small clusters of people gather quietly in the café or the halls, sitting on the comfortable couches that are scattered through the space. Everyone is dressed casually, except for one group of men in suits and ties who are being escorted ceremoniously through: potential investors. And, later in the day, CNN is expected to shoot a story.

Wittmann nods. "We see an incredible deal flow, because the first thing people need is space and a presence. They can get messages or mail virtually and work from home. And they want acceleration services, services to help them grow quickly, because the hope is they graduate to bigger space here, and then we help them move up and out."

No carpeting. No paneling. No marble. "This is *their* space."

The rapid growth curve, technological requirements, uncertain needs, and erratic, often lean, budgets of the New Economy have led to radical shifts in the way the architectural community views the workplace. Compared to more traditional, old economy projects, dot coms have required solutions that have been more tightly scheduled, imaginative, and responsive to stresses of uncertainty. One design firm principal was quoted as saying "A dot com client always wants a facility that's faster, cheaper, and better." New solutions, the nature of which are evidenced by the design approach at TechSpace, were created almost overnight to address the needs of the Internet business community. And these solutions, in turn, are now being applied to a broader base of traditional clientele, spreading the sensibility. Architects are finding that most clients are developed in less time for less money. Amenities such as out-in-the-open coffee bars, team areas beyond the conference room, and open spaces are invading even the most traditional occupational arenas. Furniture designers are creating flexible furniture for the office and office-type furniture that blends into the home—computer stations in armoires, chalkboards in the kind of gilt frames once reserved for ancestral portraits. Once-basic office furniture is morphing as well, with developments such as couches that can be transformed for napping or even a night's sleep, and fun finishes like red velvet or lime-green molded plastic.

Interiors magazine, a trade publication for the design industry, quoted the vice president of a prominent West Coast design firm on the impact of the New Economy on her business. "They're making us look at the work environment in new ways," she says. "We'll probably see a blurring of distinctions between work and play, teams and individuals, formal and casual, and fixed and flexible."

Even former bastions of the old economy like banks are being impacted and infused with the New Economy's physical sensibilities as they establish their own online services. In the venerable world of banking, where a cultural mismatch might seem inevitable, instead a cultural adaptation is occurring as the lines blur between senior bankers and Internet consultants and service companies of single-digit age. At Wells Fargo & Co., San Francisco, for instance, part of the Internet banking team was actually relocated to work in new space in SoMa, a Web-friendly part of town, where the firm could more easily fit in with and attract Web developers, graphic artists, and other e-commerce talent. The division's head stated that he wanted his seventy-person team to work in a space that felt "like a dot com," a space that took the first step to "breaking down the traditional barriers that have made banks slow to innovate." Working with young startups as strategic partners, a sense of urgency and ingenuity is incorporated into the mentality of a 148-year-old institution with $200+ million in assets. This is, clearly, something that money and stability alone cannot assure.

Today the highest-profile Web initiatives are often located inside big corporations, creating an atmosphere of blended cultures. Companies like Ford Motor Co., Hewlett-Packard, and UPS all are teaming corporate vets with Internet start-ups, fusing the old with the new in a way that is sure to result in cross-pollination of purpose and paradigm.

If TechSpace is a microcosm of an environment that could not have existed even a decade ago, it is possible to observe the culture at work by dropping in on any one of the "incubatees" on the premises. I chose Rate Yourself.com — a start-up Web site that offers quizzes that help people "use the Internet to find out things related to themselves," says Amy Frome, the only nonvirtual employee.

Frome, thirty, was seated in her small, sliding-door work cubicle, identical to so many others in TechSpace, as the printer was being delivered. This start-up was so new, Frome had been working from her personal laptop. "With the computer, I can take my work with me on weekends, go to the Hamptons or Fire Island. My boyfriend, a doctor, takes his computer too." Still, this was a giant step forward in the company's development: Until very recently, she'd been working from home.

Most of the Rate Yourself workforce still works from home. "We have a virtual workforce," Frome explains. "We have thirty-five people on the staff, plus about thirty writers, but you never see them. People ask me, 'Do you keep all the people in the file cabinet?'" Frome laughs. "I tell them, 'Yes, they are very little people.' These people were hired over the Internet and work through the Internet. The writers may stop by, look at what surveys are available to write about and sign up for them. They can do a survey any time, any place. The editors come in and edit, then the survey goes onto the system. There is no paper what-soever."

The paper résumé is equally nonexistent here. Once, the way your résumé was printed, the paper stock, the color of the ink, the envelope, and, of course, your handwriting sent a message about you to prospective employers. In Frome's world, so does the virtual résumé. "I hired the staff over the Internet," she notes.

We are all familiar with the concept of Web sites and chat rooms where people tell all, but in the virtual workplace, you can give away a lot without opening your mouth. In the absence of personal interface, new measures for evaluating the person-alities of your coworkers have evolved—no water cooler neces-sary. According to Frome, the Internet can tell you more than you would think about coworkers you might never meet. "It's fascinating how people develop personalities over the Internet," she says. "You learn to look for clues. For instance, I have cor-respondence with thirty people, only five of whom I know, and even though I never met them, I know certain things about them. I send out a blanket e-mail to all the writers and just by the way different people respond, I learn about them. Certain people react a certain way that reveals themselves. Certain peo-ple are very upfront, others are inquisitive—they'll want a mil-lion details. Others take the initiative and if I suggest one thing, they suggest what about this and that. Some people open and close e-mails with great formality, others are pure business, oth-ers use capitals, others send smiley faces. You have the text of the e-mail, but there's also the speed at which people respond. Some people get right back to you instantly, and you know this because you can see exactly when they respond. Others take their time, which says something too. And the way they use punctuation tells something about them. You learn about these people this way."

Frome had just finished business school at Columbia and was

looking for something to do on the Internet. On the street, she might still be mistaken for a student, with her beige sweater set, black pants, and leopard mules. She wears no makeup and her eyebrows are unplucked and natural. But when talking about her business, Frome possesses the skills of a senior manager. "There's a trend where people are interested in learning about themselves," she says. "They are engrossed by give and take. They want to use the Internet to find out about things in relation to themselves. Rate Yourself lets people use the Internet to do that. It's a way to get a quick answer about something you're wondering about yourself or what's bothering you. We use a quiz format—the most successful sites take advantage of interactivity. You don't have to make the investment of going to a psychiatrist to find out about yourself. You don't have to leave the house. We have quizzes on almost every topic. Some of the quizzes are just for fun, of course, like 'What kind of date am I?' and we tell people this can't entirely replace a real individual consultation with a medical professional. But there are a lot of things people can learn about themselves from our site. You can even archive your test results. Our servers are secure, so your privacy is protected. You can take a quiz, store it, then come back later, say, in a week or six months, to see if you've worked on your issues and changed your score. You can even forward your score to a friend."

Rate Yourself.com allows people to conduct self-exploration in an entirely new way. Ever wonder how charismatic you are? Rate Yourself.com will tell you. What size company is the best for you to work at? Rate Yourself.com will help you guide yourself. How well do you handle stress? Are you a chauvinist? Rate Yourself.com will clue you in. After all, who knows more about you than . . . you?

Sounds pretty basic, you say. And familiar. Like those quizzes in magazines. Maybe so, but a lot of people age eighteen to thirty-four are interested. This is the first site to quantify that interest. When I spoke to Frome, the company projected it would have over a million quiz pages for the month and was growing at 30 percent a week. At even half its current growth rate, the site would be at 5 million pages within three months. Online introspection is definitely in.

And, it is hoped, profitable. Next step: partnerships. This is typical of the Baby Mogul mentality. Baby Boomers were content to take those tests in magazines as a lark and move on. Baby Moguls are turning their interests into business models. "For instance," says Frome, "someone might take a quiz and find out they are not satisfied with their body type. We will then be able to offer link to a partner gym or a diet program. We will be able to take it to the next step." The wide range of topics covered, from politics to current events to cooking to sex, allows for plenty of partnership opportunities. "And we're building an incredible database," she adds.

Where once young workers spent their early careers learning about their market, this group *is* their market, and they have created an environment that works for them. Frome understands her market because she is her own target customer: "I probably do more online because I want to experience what happens on the Internet rather than reading about it. And that's heightened my interest in it. I try to order books or music online, where before I would go in and browse the shelves. I now browse online. It's easier that way. It saves time, is faster and more efficient." When you're working long hours, that's important, she says. Although sometimes, she admits, it backfires. "I don't like dealing with the pain of returns if something doesn't fit, so I stick to ordering basic things I know.

"There's no typical day here, and I like that," says Frome. "I wish I had more time to get things done, but this is a very exciting business. You're building it, creating it, shaping it. It's very exciting when you can see it on the site, it's very concrete. Because the Internet is basically a direct-response vehicle, success or failure is clear, often within hours if not days. The paradigm of wait and see has no place here.

"A person anxious to rise or fall on the merits of his or her work always knows where they stand. It is instant gratification in the simplest form. You see if your idea has worked, and it's easy to measure the success — or not — because you either see the traffic on the site or you don't," says Frome. "And your company grows, or it doesn't. You can physically see the results. *That's* exciting."

3 SPEEDUP

In 1965, as a Yale undergraduate, a young man named Frederick W. Smith wrote a term paper for an economics course in which he proposed an alternative to replace the current air freight shipping systems, which utilized passenger routes and which Smith felt were economically inadequate. Foreseeing what he saw as the future, Smith's paper stated that what was needed was a system designed for air freight that could accelerate the traditional postal route pace, which was designed to piggyback on passenger routes, and accommodate increasingly common time-sensitive shipments, such as electronics. Smith's grade: C. Frederick W. Smith went on to stake his own inheritance, raise $91 million from venture capitalists, and found a company known as Federal Express. Smith's vision, in the face of the status quo, was an early harbinger of what would be the massive impact of the phenomenon of speedup. Like the Internet pioneers and entrepreneurs to come, he, an outsider to the system—in fact, a student with no credible experience at all in the business world—saw a gap totally missed by the economics professor at Yale and the U.S. Postal System that could be served by creating a more direct route and invented a system to serve it that was unlike anything that had been done before.

Frederick W. Smith didn't have the Internet when he thought of his idea, but he provided a prototype for the kind of thinking that ignited the New Economy. All the elements were there: concept, execution, financing, and speed. The acceleration of pace has been both enabled and caused by the Internet and evolving technologies, and by our own willingness to embrace it. This symbiotic relationship has led to placing a priority on how quickly and in what quantity we can stockpile activity and results, in both our business and personal lives, whether that is vitamins in a meal, chores in a day, courses in school, jobs in a career, even hours in a week.

Sometimes do you get the feeling that life is whipping by, faster than you can process it? That things are moving faster than they did just a few years ago? Well, it's not an illusion; they are. For those with careers, who are most of us, productivity has increased dramatically. Meaning, we're doing more, either in the same amount of time or less. A generation ago, the average person had a 100,000-hour working life—forty hours a week, fifty weeks a year for fifty years. Today we can do everything that person did in an entire lifetime career in 10,000 hours. Which theoretically means we can, for better or worse, squeeze the equivalent ten of our father's or mother's careers into our working life cycle. By 1998, the average American family worked fifteen more weeks a year than it did in 1969. (Where our parents, and certainly our grandparents, might have held one, possibly two, or at the most a handful of jobs in a lifetime, according to the U.S. Department of Labor, today the average person in the United States holds 9.2 jobs just between the ages of eighteen and thirty-four.)

Many of us, myself included, can remember being cautioned that too many jobs on a résumé sent up a red flag of undesirability to prospective employers. Too many jobs meant you were unstable, unfocused, undesirable. But let's think about where that ethic originated. The people who did the cautioning were our seniors, many of whom grew up in the depression and post-depression era. Understandably, their attitude—which was based on a genuine fear—was that you should be thankful that you had a job, and the goal was to keep it, because if you changed jobs too often or, God forbid, got fired, that would be a calamity.

Now, not only is someone with a ten-year tenure at one company seen as almost embalmed at the desk, but, increasingly, it pays to *not* stay. The technology arena—not surprisingly given the nature of the assets—was the first where the status quo culture became one of quick job changes. This behavior has reinforced itself because mobility has been rewarded. According to *Information Week*'s April 2000 survey of almost 17,000 information technology professionals, both staffers and managers who were at their current jobs a year or less earned a median of $6,000 more than those who had been at their jobs more than a year. According to *Fortune*, by 2000, the average tenure in information technology had shrunk to about thirteen months, down from about eighteen months two years prior. "Working in the industry is like working in dog years," twenty-one-year-old Aida Escriva, an IT worker, was quoted as saying in an article titled "IT Pros Find Job-Hopping Pays." Escriva had changed jobs four times in eighteen months—more than tripling her pay in the process.

The pressure to job-hop was—and is—intense in the technology sector. One senior vice president I spoke to who worked in Silicon Valley found that, even in the middle of the technology market downturn, the number of calls he got from recruiters had actually increased to the point where it was difficult for him to concentrate on his work. "Day in, day out, you're getting calls from headhunters, even when you're not looking," he said. This person had been in his job for just four months. "It's incessant," he said. "In four months, I've probably gotten forty or fifty calls. And you're like 'Wait a minute, I have hardly been at this company!' And this is after the so-called crash. And then you go to the next company, and the calls still don't go away."

"There's a feeling that there's always another job out there," says George Anders of *Fast Company* magazine. "That if you don't like your boss, you don't have to put up with it, and you can make your own opportunities. The people coming of age in this business market—the last serious business recession was in 1981 and 1982, so that's just not going to be their psyche—their feeling is, there are a lot of jobs and a lot of opportunities."

With these Change Agents being the most visible leaders, this impact is spreading. The tenure of CEOs is shrinking as well. A 2001 CEO survey conducted by Harris and Associates reported that 57.2 percent of CEOs remain in their jobs for less than four years. This is the result of a precipitous drop. In 1980, 46 percent of CEOs in Fortune 200 firms had six years or less on the job; by 1998, that figure was 58 percent. Long-termers had accordingly decreased, from 41 percent with six to ten years on the job in 1980 to 23 percent in 1998.

It's stating the obvious to point out that the ripple effect of technology itself has played a key role in this career condensation. Digital technology, mobile phones, and virtual connectedness have drastically increased productivity. Our sense of time itself has become inextricably wrapped up in technology and has evolved as technology-driven behavior has become an increasing influence in our everyday lives. With an estimated one-half of the American workforce now using computers, you do not have to work in the technology field to experience the impact of the speedup phenomenon or be a tech geek or even a high-end sophisticated corporate officer. All you have to do is order a Big Mac. Until 1996, McDonald's had opened an average of 1.55 new stores a year for the past forty-four years. By the end of 1999, however, McDonald's was opening nearly five new stores a day.

Just in time, it would seem. Even fast food is being pressured to be faster. A survey in England by a market research company called Datamonitor showed that the English lunch hour has become the lunch thirty-six minutes, with 14 percent of workers not taking lunch at all. Those who did increasingly opted for desk dining, many ordering from their company canteen via their desktop PC.

Faster access to information has impacted the pace of processing the workload in even the smallest operations — in some cases, particularly the smallest operations. "The Internet has really accelerated the availability of information," says the owner of a small, independent entertainment marketing firm in Los Angeles. "It has completely sped up my business. A proposal that took weeks is now a weekend. The Internet is a phenomenal resource to accelerate the availability of information. For instance, I had to put together a promotion for a movie, and the job involved contacting stunt schools. In the past, it would have taken me forever to find out about that — where do you even go to find out? — but I just went online.

"My business has been completely changed by the Internet. Even faxes are obsolete — they take too long to get out, and then you have to reformat the material if you're going to use it in another form. The organizations I deal with in promoting movies don't want to deal with that — they want an e-mail, so they can clip an item, paste it, and run with it. I very infrequently fax now. I can send out five hundred e-mails to five hundred outlets to promote a film, and I can do it in an instant. I still have to follow up with a phone call, but the time to facilitate the job is one-tenth of what it used to be. So I am that much more productive. And the key word is 'cc.' You don't have to fax duplicate copies like you once did. You e-mail one person and cc the rest of the list."

The pace of the online industry itself has also had an impact. It is a world in which there are two acceptable speeds of operation: fast and faster. One of the core beliefs of the category has been that the first business to enter a new market gains a "first-mover" advantage and that shortening the time-to-market development cycle keeps products more competitive. In comparison to this platform, other businesses, including old economy stalwarts, are shifting gears and fixating on speed as well, in order to keep up.

What is the impact of this speedup phenomenon on those who are working in its vortex? According to the 2000 Kepner-Trejoe survey on speed and quality in decision making, managers across the board are making more decisions in less time. Seventy-seven percent of managers believe that the number of decisions they make each workday has increased in the past three years, with 85 percent saying the time given to that decision making has either decreased or stayed the same. The pressure is clearly on: Nearly four-fifths of managers feel they miss opportunities because they don't make decisions quickly *enough!* And 68 percent say their decisions sometimes fail for lack of speedy-enough implementation. What about the rank and file? A 1999 *Wall Street Journal* survey found 40 percent of Americans said lack of time was a bigger problem than lack of money. The Gen Y2K Study™ revealed the speedup squeeze has hit the no-longer-carefree young: One-third of men and women in their twenties feel they are overscheduled.

Media is one of the first places the speedup phenomenon resonates for many of us, because it's such a ubiquitous element. We now live in the age of the surround sound bite. In the 1980s, when I was an advertising agency creative director, the average commercial was thirty seconds. A few years before that, it had been sixty seconds. Veterans were already bemoaning the loss: "Who can say something in thirty seconds?" I can remember them naysaying, in a chorus: "What can you do in a blink?" Even the number and pacing of cuts within the thirty seconds was carefully spoon-fed to the audience. It was felt that only so much information could be absorbed. Then fifteen-second commercials started creeping up in Europe. Inevitably, the first fifteen-second commercial hit the United States. As it happened, I was the creative director who made that commercial, which was a spot for Alberto-Culver. Actually, it was two spots—two fifteens, back to back. Special arrangements and dispensations had to be made by the networks where it was running. I seem to recall that we were mandated to run two fifteen-second commercials with "linked" content back to back within a single thirty-second slot, because there *were* no fifteen-second slots. And that the networks had decreed the content of each of those fifteen-second commercials had to be related—for example, one spot for shampoo, the next for conditioner—because the networks feared that viewers would be hopelessly confused with such a truncated message.

Well, the spots ran, nobody died of confusion, and, within a few years, the fifteen-second commercial became common in the United States. Today there might be twenty-some cuts in that fifteen-second commercial. A sixty-second commercial not only seems like an *epic*, it is nearly *extinct*. And now we have ten-second commercial formats.

The pace of commercials and music videos has resulted in the speedup of editing techniques across the board, literally forcing viewers to take in more information faster and altering popular tastes and expectations. People expect things to move quickly in the media—or else they are bored. Bored means channel-changing or walking out of movies, reactions avidly avoided by the entertainment industry. The hit TV show *Survivor*, as an example, does not sport a whiplash pace, but it still averages one cut per second.

Ray Gaulke has also been in a position to not just observe but initiate these changes, having held the presidency of two major international advertising agencies. "In the old days, when TV was new, it was about sponsorship," he comments. "A company could 'own' an entire show—*The Jack Benny Hour,* brought to you by Jell-O. *Death Valley Days,* brought to you by 20 Mule Team Borax. Then TV became more widespread and more popular. Commercial time became more in demand and therefore more expensive. There was the two-minute commercial and then the ninety-second commercial. As networks raised prices, most companies couldn't afford to be an overall sponsor as we had known it, so they bought thirty-second spots, then fifteens and now tens. They became a sound bite. I was looking up the word 'bite' the other day. Do you know what a bite is? It's a friction that connects things together. A friction. But messages are about content. You have to wonder—with these bites of information, do people absorb it or experience it? It's a brush, like bumping into somebody in the hallway as opposed to getting to know somebody. With the Internet, it's more so."

Gaulke raises the question of whether the truncating of media is a positive thing. "Gandhi said there is more to life than accelerating its pace," he says, landing firmly on the side of negative impact. "I think this whole compression of information came out of advertising. It came out of people being more inwardly focused and not wanting to know more. But it's also generational. Young people are supposed to be better assemblers of information. People my age depended on other people to be assemblers of information. That's why we read newspapers, more so than this younger generation. They don't want others to assemble their information, they want to assemble it themselves — they'll get some from MTV, some from the news, some from the Internet. It's a patchwork. There's a big difference in how people are now processing information."

The term "sound bite" first appeared in the *Oxford Dictionary of New Words* in 1997, but as early as 1988, George Bush's election was being called "the election of the sound bite." This compression of words into media-spoonfeedable segments matched the evolution of truncated media segments. New standards of time have emerged. The nanosecond, for instance. This term refers to the primary measure of time of a computer, one-billionth of a second. It may be beyond our capability to comprehend, but we are nonetheless sensitized to it.

I once had a conversation about speed with the great Grand Prix racing champion Jackie Stewart, a person whose literal survival, for most of his career, depended on developing highly evolved speed management techniques. Stewart, whom I interviewed to get material to write a commercial he would later record, talked about how he experienced a high-speed Grand Prix course. He said that he reacted to a kind of time-sensitive imprint of it. Rather than rely solely on seeing objects along the course route and then responding reflexively, as you or I might, his technique involved memorizing the course in a prerace run-through by counting it out timewise and then, in the actual race, responding to stimuli — such as a curve in the road — on the beat when his experience told him to respond. He literally counted out the course on a mental metronome: *One, two, three TURN four five six BRAKE,* with his mind accelerating the count faster than he could speak it. This is, of course, a massive simplification — Grand Prix auto racing is a highly complex sport involving factors most of us ordinary drivers can never grasp—but the bottom line is, years of experience had evolved and honed Stewart's sense of and reaction to time to such an extent that it altered—and sped up—his relationship with it. "What seems like a second that flies by, before you're even aware of it, to you seems like a very long time to me," he said. "I see that second in elongated segments, pieces. It doesn't fly by for me at all."

Did people always have the capability to process information this quickly? Or did we accustom ourselves to it and build on that skill, like Jackie Stewart? Do young children who grow up in a world of "bites" program their brains to a fast-track pace? Does that in turn translate, later on, to a shorter attention span—or is it the reverse, a capability of absorbing more information in a shorter time?

Now an entire generation and generations beyond are learning techniques to process and elongate shorter segments of time, literally from the cradle, which conditions them to accept and adapt to acceleration on all kinds of levels. These people have literally been in training for a speeded-up existence since they first toddled over to the keyboard.

Ron Lieber, senior writer at *Fast Company* magazine and author of the book *Upstart Startups*, says, "To me, if you're trying to understand the relationship between young people and the Internet and why these people readily adapted to an online lifestyle, which can be both working online, working in an online business, creating Web sites for an offline business, or just living online—planning activities and meeting friends online, or whatever—to me it actually goes back beyond the mid-nineties to the mid-seventies. Because that is when Atari first appeared. That was the first mass-market computer or chip-enabled technology. And what that allowed was for people as young as five, six, or seven years old to build a degree of comfort with the technology that they were then able to transfer from Atari to the Commodore to the Apple II to the IBM PC, whatever it was they had exposure to at home or their computer lab at school. There's just sort of a sheer comfort with technology that comes from being exposed to it at such an early age. And then there's the notion that video games teach you a bunch of skills, and one of them is the ability to operate at a twitch speed. Your success in a video game literally depends on your ability to twitch your finger and react quickly. And that turns out to be a pretty important skill in business, when you think about it, to have fast reactions and be able to respond to outside stimuli in a quick way, and be comfortable with that."

You can see it in the family home. The impact of time compression has entered into the mainstream of every media-savvy child's existence. By the age of seven, almost any parent can attest to the fact that their child can play a complex video game, digest a music video, and repeat a complex sequencing of lyrics, replete with cuts that fly by so quickly that the parent may be clueless as to the content.

The arc of the horizon of time has been replaced by a series of speed bumps. "It's energizing, challenging, very fast-paced," said a woman who had made the transition from an old economy to a New Economy job. "If you miss a day, you feel like you have missed a month. In sixteen months at this company, I think I have gotten six years' worth, a crash course on the Internet and what it's about."

I spoke with a woman who experienced an entire career arc in an Internet company in thirteen weeks. Morgan (not her real name) was forty years old, dressed in a dark denim jacket, a camisole, and a large gold watch with many dials. She had short, unmanicured nails, no lipstick, and a shaggy haircut. On her feet were strappy sandals, and her toenails were lacquered blood red. She was attractive and articulate, but it was nonetheless hard to imagine her as an on-air newsperson—which she was for eighteen years.

She described her career curve in the Internet quite differently: "Six weeks up and seven weeks down." She searched for a familiar analogy and found one. "Like a TV show. This was after two jobs I'd had previously that lasted eighteen years. I prepared for my TV career forever, it seemed, and it took years to work my way up in the pecking order. For this new job, I took a six-week course for $475 in how to start up a new media business. By the end of it, you were supposed to be an expert. I never even finished the course. Before that could happen, I got a job putting together an Internet start-up.

"The concept was interior design online. It had been my idea. These people had a business concept, and I said, 'Why don't you do it online?' One sentence later, I was the first employee. The CEO had never been a CEO before, didn't know what a CEO was. My job was to identify designers, sell the concepts, and negotiate the contracts. There was so much to do and so little time. When you are involved in a start-up there is not much glory, and if you are a ground-zero employee, you take all the heat. Everyone's taking a flier on everything. You all go on blank faith because there ain't no way you can confirm the unknown of how people will work in a start-up situation and handle stress as the community deepens.

"So I opened the office. Not only that, I *found* the office, put in the T-1 lines, traveled. It was fun, like turning a hobby into a job. I was inspired by the Internet and the creativity of the people I worked with. But the environment was so crazy. You're building new procedures, things that had never been done before, at the same time as you're building a new business.

"For the time that I was there, I never called anybody, barely saw anybody, didn't go anywhere, didn't think of anything else.

I was the oldest person and I thought I knew the least. Then I realized that I knew as much as anybody. It's startling. I'd get, 'Oh, man, we admire you. It's so cool—let's do a deal.' Believe me, most of the people involved in these things don't know what they're talking about. If they do, they're in a big house in Santa Barbara and they don't answer the phone.

"Thirteen weeks after I started, I carried my boxes out. Later that day someone I knew called and said, 'We need to take our business online,' and I was again the first employee." Morgan laughed. "I think I should have gone to some kind of posttraumatic syndrome clinic!

"I knew it would be a 24/7 thing all over again, and, boy oh boy, that's what it was. Of course, once the site is launched, and you see that home page up there, you never hear about the shouting matches, the 4 A.M. e-mailing back and forth, the unmet deadlines, people having breakdowns, crying in meetings. I would watch the CEO of this new company yell at people from two inches away from their face. But now I know why these CEOs get this way. The timetable is very short. You're racing for funding. The clock is ticking. You're trying to arrive at group consensus with a small internal team, which is all you have in most start-ups, interacting with outside teams—the ad agency, the Web builder, the tech people, and so on—and you're in the middle of a process you can't control unless you are literally in their face. My boss is thirty-nine years old and he is the first in his field to even try anything like what our company does. He has proven leadership in other areas—he runs an 8,000-employee worldwide organization and dozens of subsidiaries in a bricks-and-mortar business. Then he decided to try this Web enterprise to expand the business in a new way. He pushed us so hard not to meet but to massively beat our deadlines. After we launched, he hotboxed fifteen guys in one boardroom and walked out with $30 million, and we went from a pack of confused, sleepless, morally destroyed mummies to a valuation of $265 million overnight. We all looked at ourselves and said, 'How?' There were ten of us sitting here with a Web site we knew stunk. Nobody could even find anything on it! But, on the Internet, you are what you say you are. It's all about the first chapter. On the Internet, at that point, you told a story and built something just to give that story its first chapter, and then you got the money to make the story come true. Unlike everything else I've ever been involved in, the payoff came up front. We beat the market. Where else could this have happened? Beneath it all, this was a great idea.

"It's been daunting to change, but I think it's a good thing to kick myself in the butt like that. The learning curve is so accelerated. It's interesting. In my previous life, I used to think, 'If only I knew five years ago what I know now.' Now I think, 'If only I knew five weeks ago. . . .' "

This kind of acceleration allows people to speed through their careers at a warp pace unimaginable even ten years ago. It also levels the playing field. For the first time and place in the working landscape, twenty-five-year-olds are in a position of being considered as qualified as their decades-older counterparts. About a month ago, I had lunch in Los Angeles with an executive recruiter who has offices in several West Coast cities. One of her accounts was a multibillion-dollar athletic wear manufacturer. The number-two position in one of their departments was open, and she was handling the search. The department head, she told me, was six years out of school. Many potential candidates with impressive résumés in traditional marketing felt uncomfortable because they would be in a position of reporting to someone a third to half their age. This department head was not a wunderkind or an exception. More and more, this was the rule. The orderly career path — the org chart with its neat boxes and dotted lines, the progression from cubicle to corner office — is crumbling. It may have started with the Internet start-up, but the impact is spreading.

Caryn Marooney of OutCast Communications specializes in developing communications and public relations programs for Internet companies in the San Francisco area. In her career, she has worked with hundreds of organizations, spanning both old (IBM and the NFL) and New Economy, in the United States and England. In the course of developing communications and public relations platforms for her clients, which range from Internet start-ups to Fortune 500s, she has observed the phenomenon closely and dissected its impact.

"The lifestyle is fast, empowered, and opportunitistic," says Marooney. "I think the speed at which people operate is unlike anything we've ever experienced before. And those of us who work in this world have to be like that ourselves, culturally.

"In the 'old days,' there were ideas, memos, you'd bounce things around the office and off each other. You or your team think about strategies for weeks, sometimes months or even years. There'd be time to revise, refine, redo, rethink. To build. To erase and start over. Now strategic decisions can be made and acted on in a couple of hours, and you have to be willing and able to do this."

But can you make an informed decision in a couple of hours? Doesn't this sound a lot like winging it? Marooney agrees, but sees it as a positive skill. "You have to be able to walk on a wire without a net. You have to be OK with operating in a fog, constantly moving forward, and at the same time figuring out and feeling where you are."

But isn't this risky? Another nod from Marooney. But there is a payoff that makes it worth the risk. "People are willing to risk their careers and give up their personal lives for this belief. It's like, if you don't do it now, you will never do it. You just want to be part of it, play in it. The feeling is — and the fluctuations in the technology market underscore this — that there is a window, a finite window of maybe a couple of years in which you can make it. It's an immensely crowded environment. The windows of change and opportunity depend on the type of business. You need to make a profit, be acquired or go public, or make the money and then it ends. You don't want to be yesterday's idea. Too long, too much time, and you miss the window. If you're even just slightly late, you think, you'll miss it."

Another young Internet start-up founder describes it as the "tortilla effect": "There is a real sense that this is a momentous period of time that will collapse and unfold like a tortilla."

For this group, the end of the rainbow may be in three weeks, not thirty years. Everything in the process speeds up accordingly. Where in the past, size ruled, today's quotient of scale is agility. Remember "Big Blue"? That was what they used to call IBM. They were an invincible, infallible force, in their blue suits, buffed shoes, crisp white shirts, and ties. Until a bunch of grungy, geeky, T-shirted guys in garages beat them at their own technology.

Another key is the time factor involved in market pretesting, which is becoming increasingly truncated because it is becoming increasingly intuitive. Procter & Gamble, for instance, an iconic success of an old economy company, has traditionally mandated a hierarchy of research and development processes that are carved in concrete. There is no way this monolith, a profit-generating machine for half a century, could or would think up a product even today and put it on the shelves without subjecting it to the entire step-by-step process. Shortcuts: zero. This protocol does not make for speed in product development.

For decades, Procter & Gamble was the ultimate training

ground of America's consumer product development force. If you were involved in developing products, the way P&G did it, you wanted to do it. They were the mount; their protocol was chiseled in stone on the tablets. Fledglings left the company and brought those tablet teachings to the world as they cycled through their careers at other organizations. Wannabe companies copied the paradigm. The P&G way was also the classic business school model, what young people were taught going forth into the business community. They studied case histories that examined each product story in microscopic detail. Any variant approach was frowned upon and could cost you your credibility, if not your career. There was one approval-stamped approach to product development and marketing. Period. Diverting even an inch off program would have been like wearing tie-dyed shorts to a board meeting: It just was not done.

When I worked in advertising agencies in the 1980s and early 1990s, with clients like S. C. Johnson, Quaker, AT&T, Sears, and so many others, new product development was a major part of the job. This process was glacial in pace, largely because of testing requirements. Of course, this made sense, because so much was at stake. Category leaders rarely embraced the concept of risk. One seemingly simple new product that I worked on, for instance, stands out in my mind as a classic, a scaling Mount Everest of testing: Kraft Velveeta Slices. This is the sliced version of Velveeta cheese that is probably in half the children's lunchboxes in America today. As I recall, the technology for making the flat Velveeta squares took years to develop (it isn't actually sliced), and then the product concept was tested and retested, and, finally, numerous advertising executions were tested and retested. There were qualitative tests on how to position the concept; then there were quantitative tests involving thousands of consumers; and then there were more focus group tests. There were copy tests, pretests, posttests and post-posttests, commercial animatic tests, roll-out tests, and test markets. This Sisyphean approach to launching even the most seeming no-brainer product was pretty typical of every new product I worked on then, a reflection of the risk-aversiveness of the times. Who wanted to be held accountable for creating the product that put the chink in the cash cow that was the Velveeta brand?

Where once organizations tested new concepts and ideas relentlessly, using quantitative studies and worshipping at the altar of national projectability, many Internet entrepreneurs went out of the starting gate on gut. Gut and their own personal experiences. Why?

Because they could.

Robert Proctor, the thirty-six-year-old founder of the Internet Exchange, an online café chain in England and Europe, found out within eight months of opening one café outfitted with ten PCs that that was enough to attract the venture capital to expand without page one of a business plan. In the wired world, you can be your own research. Money is flowing less freely now, and, it's true, business plans are not only going on paper but going under scrutiny, but the development process has been slashed and will likely never revert to the molasses mire.

Success or failure can be immediately apparent on the Internet because it is a direct response medium. The head of one incubator company I spoke with noted that in observing the hundreds of fledgling Internet companies that passed through his doors, most either made it very quickly, or they died. There is little room for the middle ground—as has become achingly apparent. You post your site. People come to it, or they don't. You don't need phone book–size decks of research to tell you if you're attracting hits or if they're coming back. So that's another speed bump leveled.

"The feeling is that you can do anything," says Marooney. "This amazing feeling of opportunity."

Or, as Morgan puts it, "The grass was always greener in the Internet space."

4 THE BABY MOGULS

They're empowered, they're enabled, they're in demand, they're at the top of their careers. And they may have never held a job before. Not just a job in the field—*any* job. Unless they started a business before they were out of high school, that is. Meet the Baby Moguls, the natural children of empowerment and speedup.

The Internet has created a wave of access and opportunity that has not been seen before for young people in any job market. The breadth of opportunities that cut across every interest and discipline have opened the floodgates and given people entering the workforce an alternative to the traditional, hierarchical structures that featured a ladder with seemingly endless rungs to get to the top. Sidestepping this ladder, creating business models and launching them on the Internet without the speed bumps incurred by bricks and mortar, young people are opening the doors of their own businesses at an age when, just a few years ago, job opportunities might have consisted of unpaid internships or counter work at the local McDonald's.

Ron Lieber of *Fast Company* magazine explains that technological skills developed at home and school at an early age have left young people perfectly positioned to become leaders in the New Economy. In addition to the fact that, from the 1970s on, young children developed technology skills via computer games and personal computers at home and at school, the influx of women into the workforce left many children at home alone after school for the first time. "The kids would come home at three-thirty with their latchkey when both parents were at work, they'd let themselves in, and a lot of times, instead of going to watch *The Brady Bunch* they'd get on the computer. By the time they were in high school and then college and, later, the workforce, they'd developed a sense of comfort and familiarity with technology that, all of a sudden, when technology became a really important thing for everyone in the 1990s, suddenly young people had the advantage.

"That is a really critical thing to understand," says Lieber, noting that the paradigms stressed traditionally in business schools actually functioned to hold young people back. "If you think about the concept of the experience curve that was taught for years in business school—the notion that the more experience you have, the more successful you'll be—that's been a real good way over the years of keeping people in their twenties down at these companies. There was the notion that you have to pay your dues, you have to be isolated in your corporate silo, and then—eventually—you'll get to join the club and actually get to do some interesting work for a change. It's incredible how that worked. And it's not happening any more. The curtain has been pulled back and people actually understand that there is some virtue to inexperience, and inexperienced people often do amazing things.

"The temptation is to say 'Well, people just got lucky with the Internet,' but the fact is, people in their twenties were actually more experienced and more aggressive for starting and enabling Internet businesses than people in their forties because of their experiences with the Apple II, the TRS 80, and the Atari, and so on. And it's also true that people who are less experienced can create great businesses too."

Lieber notes that young people today have another distinct advantage in the business community that gives them a leg up over other segments—for instance, women in the workforce—which is access to a plethora of highly visible, highly successful role models. "Who has the better idols and icons to look up to?" he asks. "Ask a thirty-two-year-old woman, 'Who can you point to who has it all?' and the answer is, very few women. Maybe they can name two, if they think really hard. But then you ask the nineteen-year-olds, 'Who are your idols?' and they can rattle off twenty-five people under thirty who have started Internet businesses that people have heard of and who are now billionaires."

On MTV, "Underage" segments are regularly aired that feature business success stories of under-twenty-one-year-olds, giving them the cultural status of rock stars. The college kid–to–wealthy–hero–overnight profile of Shawn Fanning cut between Fanning in sweats in his dorm room ("just a year ago") and onstage in a tuxedo, starring in a montage of awards ceremonies as he was honored and applauded by young entertainment stars. A young female achiever received a similar high-profile treatment. Kids get the message through mass media: I can do it.

Jake Alpen is typical of a young person who became empowered early. At the age of twenty-five, he is ensconced as director of online marketing for the Internet arm of a music marketing company, having entered the workforce in college as a consultant—a job that in decades past would have required a substantial career platform. Alpen feels that the fact that he had an expertise in an area that was foreign to his employers worked in his favor. "I started doing free-lance Web design work. The clients I had were thinking about getting into the Internet and I don't think they wanted to invest too much in it. They were like, 'See where you can get us.' They knew I'd done sites before. So I would come in and people would see my work and say, 'Wow, we don't know anything about this!' " he says. "I think it was cool—a kid just graduated from college and doing free-lance work—and I got to do it my own way. I was entrusted with a lot of power. I did an entire sports site project for Miller Beer."

Alpen has already held three major jobs, including a senior position at an ad agency and head of strategic alliances for a Web company. He feels the Internet is an area where the playing field is leveled, so nobody at any age has a better chance of succeeding than anybody else, mainly because a deep experience base does not exist.

"Nobody knows what works yet," Alpen claims. "I love being creative. It's not like being some account executive at a place where you follow the book—you know, two plus two equals four—in the online world, as long as it equals four, let's just do it. Let's find the best way, where it's not so rigid and not so set. Let's use our brain and find the best way to get results, and let's be creative and get our energy going. That's what I love about working in the Internet. *I* get to determine what colors go into my ads, what model really works best for my company, where a lot of other places, you don't really get that opportunity to do that. That's why I've always gone toward working in online business."

David Waxman cofounded Firefly Networks, a Web site destination that was acquired by Microsoft, when he was only three years out of college. "In 1995 when the whole Internet thing hit, the Web was incredibly democratic," he says. "Yahoo, Amazon, Excite, ebay, Firefly—there were all these companies who could come out of nowhere, take on the big guys—and did. These companies just created opportunities. The Internet created a lot of jobs for people who prior to that wouldn't necessarily have had that level of career. There were all those people about whom you used to say 'Wow, he's majoring in history—what's he going to do?' A lot of people I knew in college who once at the end of the day would have ventured into investment banking or publishing or floated around until they found some niche—the Internet allowed them to find a better niche."

And there were so many fewer barriers to entry. "You don't have to build a factory or put up a machine shop to make a Web company," Waxman says. "The start-up budget to get something going is pretty nominal and fairly easily achievable. And of course, later, there were opportunities created by all that capital."

Waxman also found that the smaller, start-up environment pushed him professionally and personally onto areas he might never have ventured into otherwise, quickly expanding his experience and, ultimately, his confidence. "When you are small and there are fewer people than there are jobs, you find yourself doing things you never thought you could," he says.

At Waxman's current company, the second he has cofounded, the organization found itself speeding into a public offering without a chief financial officer in place. "There was no one to do it," he says. "The CEO had way too many things to do, so he pointed his finger at me and said, 'Go do it.' This was not what I wanted to do for the rest of my life—to me the drafting sessions are so excruciating, you have to have sort of a Talmudic sense of humor about them—but to do it once was really cool. It's about doing things you'd never do, things that are totally new, that you'd pick up on the fly, doing things that are over your head. I saw it through the first submission to the SEC—with a lot of help, of course."

It takes a certain confidence and mentality to talk about being at the helm of steering a business with investors' capital at stake through the rigors of a public offering as a learning experience. But Waxman—and those he worked with—never questioned himself or his capability of picking up the financial reins of the company. It was a critical time for the organization, yet he not only stepped up to the plate, he was anointed to do so by the person with the most at stake.

When I contrasted the experience of my generation with Waxman's to him, pointing out the unavoidable apprenticeship periods and corporate hierarchies so many of us encountered when we got out of college and entered the workforce, which in turn were barriers of their own sort to getting ahead at a young age, he was blunt in his reaction, which was to recoil at the thought. "If I had to face something like that, like you did, I mean I just wouldn't have done it. I would have done something else."

Such as?

"Like music, or something else where I could have fulfilled my creative potential."

And, it is hoped, had enough talent to pay the rent. Which, in the case of David Waxman, he fortunately did. After graduating from college and before launching Firefly, Waxman worked as a composer of electronic music in Paris for three years. After the successful sale of Firefly, he took off a year, traveled to Nepal, and then cofounded a second Web company, People PC.

"I couldn't imagine myself working for nine to five—well, really nobody works nine to five anymore—for money," he says firmly, although acknowledging that he often works far longer hours. But that's for himself.

Being your own boss. Defining your own job. Founding your own business. Making your own hours. All before you're thirty. There have always been prodigies, people whose talent allowed them to vault to the top of their profession at an early age, but, with the exception of the hereditary fiefdoms and fortunes, those who have taken the business world by storm before the age of thirty have been in short supply. Before the age of twenty, although there were a few solitary exceptions, there was certainly no single power group that could be pointed to. Today, however, the Baby Moguls are stepping onto center stage. The most visible are the media poster children, but, for the first time in business history, they are backed up by an entire generation with a similarly entitled attitude.

In August 2000 *Fortune* magazine identified what they called "America's Forty Richest Under 40," noting that "there's a whole new crop of young moguls . . . you ought to get to know them. They have a lot more money than you." Not surprisingly, Michael Dell, age thirty-five, CEO of Dell Computer, topped the list with a net worth of $17.08 billion. At age eighteen, Dell had been well on his way, making $18,000 selling newspaper subscriptions. Number 26 on the list, Joseph Chung, chairman and chief technology officer *and* treasurer of Art Technology Group, age thirty-five, is worth $621 million. While in college at MIT, Chung played bass in a rock band with a fraternity brother who is now number 23 on the list. And — oh, those pesky market crashes — Michael Saylor, chairman, president, and CEO of Microstrategy, age thirty-five, saw his stock fall 62% in one day and is still worth $902 million.

It's no surprise that many of the *Fortune* Baby Moguls came from the dot com community. The wired world gives the instant access that allows this kind of career acceleration. It provides a platform for those with the temerity and talent to start early and get out there.

It's possible that, had a medium that provided such access been available in the 1950s, the phenomenon could have happened then. Or at any time. But would it have happened? When does the window of opportunity become the transforming moment? Perhaps at the intersection of attitude and evolution. At-titudinal circumstances have to mesh with the socioeconomic surround to move the needle.

The comparison of the movement of women into the work-force with the movement of young people into the technology sector is one way to measure this theory. During World War II, women flooded into the workforce, taking the jobs the men left behind. Between 1939 and 1943, the American labor force was 75 percent married women, most of whom had children at home. Rosie the Riveter became an icon. Women did virtually every job, and the media glorified the scenario. A movie in 1943 called *Take a Letter, Darling*, featured Rosalind Russell hiring a male secretary. *Tender Comrade* extolled lady welders. Women put on pants and defined the economic mainstream, and the image of the autonomous woman quickly became enshrined. But because, overall, women viewed themselves as placekeepers rather than careerists, when the men returned from the war, the women boomeranged back to the home. Waists crimped, skirts billowed, the birth rate soared, and femininity was separated from self-sustainability. There was no supportive attitudinal — or economic — shift in place to keep Rosie riveting — not for another twenty-five years, at any rate.

The case of the Baby Moguls is different. As the Gen Y2K Study™ revealed, the younger Change Agents, those age sixteen to nineteen, were 10 percent more ambitious than their age group as a whole, and those who were into technology were 11 percent more ambitious than the rest of that subgroup. The young Change Agents were also the most competitive of those from ages sixteen to fifty, with more than three-fourths saying they played to win, compared to 58 percent of respondents age thirty-five to fifty. Regardless of where the economy takes us, can anyone imagine an entire generation of dot com entrepreneurs — and those they've impacted — reverting to the trainee paradigm?

Commenting on the tumultuous quality of the new economy in late 2000, one former sales director in a defunct dot com said, "Those with the dot-com start-up mind-set won't go back to traditional positions. Once you taste it, it's a drug, and you kind of want to go back to it." It is impossible to imagine the young Change Agents abdicating their economic position, as women retreated from theirs in the 1940s. Picturing a generation of young ex–dot commers telling the Baby Boomers, "OK, now that we've taught you how to operate the computer, you can take over. We're stepping aside. Now, how is it you'd like your coffee, sir?" is laughable. And can you imagine anyone expecting that? Yet that's just what women did at the end of World War II. (As recently as 1981, The Update: Women℠ Survey revealed, the majority of American women derived their sense of status from their husbands and children.)

Certainly don't expect it from a college kid who's running a business at age twenty that he started from his dorm room. Jeff Gut is founder and CEO of CollegiateMall.com. But he's not just a dot com phenom. Gut is already a veteran with a global old economy résumé, having been at the helm of his own businesses since the age of nine. Gut's father was a zipper manufacturer, and one day his nine-year-old son picked up a zipper off a desk, fashioned it into a bracelet, named it the Zipcord, and, with the encouragement and help of his mother, sold four dozen to a local store within a week. "It just went from there," says Gut. "Within a matter of weeks, we were selling the Zipcord in Bloomingdale's, J.C. Penney, Dayton Hudson—all the big retailers. We sold the product in thirty-seven places in three countries. It was a very popular fad. We went through the entire retail cycle. So that was my first direct marketing experience."

The fact that he was a mere nine years old, says Gut, was "part of the selling point." Accompanied by his mother, he went to trade shows and set up a booth. While he did not do the actual negotiating and business transactions, he functioned as the company spokesperson. "I guess I fell in love with the excitement and energy of starting a business," Gut says. When Zipcord ended, he was eleven years old.

For the next eight years, Gut followed the stock market. "Every morning before I would go to school, I would read the newspaper, look at the stock quotes," he says. The Internet was not a factor in his life until he got to college, where, due to accessibility factors that had not been available from home, it quickly entered into the mainstream of his, and every other student's, existence. His first year at Boston University, Gut discovered the high-speed connections on campus. He began using the campus's free Internet access for e-mail and research.

Gut realized that, like him, most college students were online a lot of the time, that this was, as he puts it, "the college culture. Out of any demographic group in the United States, students are by far online the most. They kill every other demographic in terms of doing the most online. Students today have really grown up with technology, with computers in their home, using them actively in school. This is just the way they think." Gut observed a key factor: Many students seemed to shop first online, going to stores only when what they wanted wasn't available over the Internet, as opposed to the older generations, who went directly to stores and went to the Internet as a fall-back. And students shopped at hours that did not fit retail stores that were open from nine to six. "They are in class all day, and when are they going to have time to go shopping? Very late at night, when they are finally in their rooms. Stores are not open then, they don't fit the collegiate lifestyle. Also, many students don't have cars to go out shopping."

Like many of the young entrepreneurs interviewed for this

book, Jeff Gut's latest business concept sprang from a personal experience. One day his parents came to the university for a visit. The family rented a car and spent the entire visit driving all over town, scouring the area in the pouring rain to get a few college basics—a television, a lamp. The Guts had a miserable experience, which was made "100 times worse" when Jeffrey moved off campus and needed to furnish an entire apartment. "It was a hassle, it was outrageous, and it was a nightmare," he says, still shuddering.

But a business was born. In 1998, at age nineteen, using earnings from the business he launched at age nine, Jeffrey Gut launched CollegiateMall.com, a site that provides one-stop basic shopping necessities for college students who live in a dormitory or off-campus apartment. CollegiateMall.com features everything a student might need, from a full range of futons to laundry hampers to beanbag chairs to cordless phones. Packages like "The Apartment Bathroom Pak" allow a student to equip his/her bathroom with a range of bathroom supplies, right down to the shower tote. Similar packages equip a basic kitchen for fledgling cooks (one includes a microwave). Students who have never lived on their own can log on and learn at a glance what they're going to need at school, what it's going to cost, and they can order it immediately.

Gut's first two employees were the ripe old age of twenty-six. At first, he found the age difference difficult to manage, but he was philosophical. "I think you can't demand respect from people, you have to earn it," he says. "They weren't going to listen to me just because I was their boss. And, well, there's a difference between listening to somebody and believing what they say. Getting them to believe that, OK, this is going to work. There were times when they were working really hard, as I was, and it was like—are we really going to get this thing to work? And after a certain amount of time, it's like, 'Well, it doesn't matter that he is only nineteen; he knows what he's doing so we are going to stick with this.' Success breeds credibility."

Which can be hard to come by when you are a teenage business owner. Many suppliers were at first reluctant to sell to Gut. "Some of the big electronics and furniture companies, when I wanted to sell their product, it was, 'You are nineteen years old and right now you have no customers. Why are we going to allow you to sell our product?' There were a whole bunch of reasons not to sell to me. And it was really hard to convince them that, no, this is going to work and you want to sell to me. But if one big furniture manufacturer is selling you desks, you will get the other desk manufacturers. I only needed one break, and I got one break and I kind of moved on. Still, today, I am not an authorized retailer for every company I'd like so I still face the challenge. But now that we are successful, vendors want us to sell their product." Gut also notes that by being young, he was close to the experiences and desires of his target customer. "A fifty-year-old person would have been out of college a long time," he says dryly.

Gut points to role models like Bill Gates and Michael Dell as people who started companies when they were young. "There are a whole number of people who have done that and been successful. So I think it is very real that you can start something on the Internet and make a lot of money doing it."

Young businesspeople today do not feel wedded to the ethic of having to graduate from college to make it big. Gut notes that many of the major players, like Gates and Dell, were dropouts, and he himself took a yearlong leave of absence from school to launch his business. But the spin on taking time off from the college program—which in the United States used to classify one as financially needy, desperate to discover oneself, or to be seen simply as a sort of troubadour—has evolved, thanks to the Internet.

"It wasn't like an embarrassment to me or my parents—not like, 'Jeff is leaving school!' It was understandable because of what I was doing. People respect it if you start things. I think everyone wants to be an entrepreneur. If you look at where real wealth is created in our capitalistic society, it is created by people who start things."

Like David Waxman and most of the young moguls I talked to, Gut does not have one overarching, long-term goal. He sees his career path as a series of smaller goals, and is thus rewarded by a series of achievable successes. Getting the site up and running was a goal: check. Gaining partnerships with universities was another: check. Turning a profit: check. Therefore, when Gut failed to raise venture capital, his perspective was that he failed at one thing, but that did not lessen his success. "There have been successes and failures along the way," he says, "but, overall, it has been a success."

Personal life for Gut is severely limited, as he is the first to admit. I talked to him during the World Series. His roommates had been glued to the TV set for hours. Gut was too busy working. "A lot of times, I work late and my friends and I go to a bar at, say, ten o'clock, or eleven, and we go out, have a couple of drinks, and come back. And they will go back and go to bed. And I will come back and work. I get back and I have dozens of e-mails to answer and things to take care of for the next day. There is a lot I miss out on, no doubt of that. But many of my friends have very good ideas, and the difference between me and them may just be that I act on my ideas."

Gut does not see himself ever being less than motivated. During his freshman year, he had another business idea that never got off the ground. As he remained undeterred then and went on to create CollegiateMall.com, he figures he will do the same in the future. "I have always been kind of looking for the next big thing," he says. "You know, I think I really thrive on the excitement that is generated by it."

Like most of his young counterparts, the long-term outlook does not interest Gut that much. "I think the farther long term you look, the less accurate it gets. So, what will I be doing when I am fifty? I just have no ideas."

Which brings up another new issue—what do you do for an encore when you've been the boss before you're twenty? Jeff Gut thinks about this, and he's not sure. "One thing is kind of weird for me. If I sell the business and decide to get a job, am I applying to places as a college graduate or as the CEO of an Internet start-up?"

Adam Fritzler did not have to answer that question, because he did not even have to look for his job: His job found him. Fritzler is eighteen years old and the president of a company called Nerds.com in Silicon Valley. He used to live in Arizona, where he was a high school student. Computer-literate since the age of seven, when he began by reading computer manuals, in his spare time Fritzler wrote his own software that attempted to crack the code involved in the highly secure AOL instant messaging system. He was documenting his progress on his personal Web site, just as a hobby, when he was "discovered" online by executives from a legitimate company that was trying to do the same thing. In other times, the company might have opened a job search and hired recruiters or placed an ad. Instead, their talent search involved surfing the Web for talented programmers. This allowed them interface with individuals who otherwise might not have crossed their path—like Adam Fritzler.

"They saw that I was well versed and I was the only one—no one else had been doing this kind of work," Fritzler said. The executives were impressed and hired him on the spot, via e-mail.

"I was planning to go to college," Fritzler says, "but this was a better offer. I said, 'Sure.'"

He was seventeen years old.

The executives of the firm confirmed the story. "We had no idea he was seventeen years old until we had hired him," one said. "We had agreed to fly him out meet us. We were going to send someone to the airport. And then, at that point, we found out his age."

"I think they realized I was young," said Fritzler, "but I don't think they realized I was seventeen."

At this point, the executives panicked. "It dawned on us, 'Oh my God, it's going to be this older guy picking up this kid at an airport. It doesn't look good. We could get arrested!'" They quickly made some more calls and looped in Fritzler's parents who, as it turned out, wholeheartedly approved. And they recruited what they called a "chaperon" to join the welcoming party.

One technicality emerged: It turned out that Fritzler couldn't actually be officially hired by the company until he was eighteen: "Child labor laws," notes Fritzler. Never mind, he became a consultant. Then, the month after he turned eighteen, he was officially hired as one of the chief software engineers.

Fritzler has just graduated from high school, and he plans to work at the dot com start-up for about a year. After that, he may go to college. Or not. Maybe he will go to another company, or start his own. He will be able to afford to do whatever he wants. One thing he is certain about, he does not think he could ever work in a regular nine-to-five job. For now he works from eight in the morning till eight at night. "We go live in about a month," he says. It's a busy time. Fritzler's social life is mainly online — his girlfriend lives in another state, and many of his friends are virtual. He keeps in touch via instant messaging. His community is accessible whenever he is, and the fact that he has little time to socialize and no physical proximity is not an impediment to online socializing.

But many young men and women aren't waiting to launch their visions into reality. The new urban legends that circulate around campuses are stories like that of Shawn Fanning, star of the aforementioned "Underage" MTV profile. While a freshman at Northeastern University, in January 1999, Fanning developed the original Napster application and service, a file-sharing music site. When a beta version of his site was named Download of the Week, it received over 300,000 hits at download.com, causing Fanning to realize the commercial potential. He decided to pursue Napster full time, and the admittedly controversial Napster may indeed change relationships among the Internet, intellectual property, and the moneymaking platforms of the entertainment industry. Since its launch in 1999, Napster has grown to 32 million registered users, making it the fastest software application to catch on in Internet history, and one that has served up a fierce challenge to how intellectual properties are copyrighted and protected. Picture it: The legally buttressed, resource-heavy, and ultra-powerful entertainment industry sideswiped and taken by surprise, the foundations of the industry profit system threatened by a kid in a dorm room — and not even an upperclassman, at that. If he'd walked through the door in December 1998, how easily do you think that Shawn Fanning would have even gotten an internship at a major record label?

College, once purely a training ground — and when you graduated or even *post*graduated, you simply moved on to the next level of traineeship — has become a breeding ground for Baby Moguls. Membership in the collegiate entrepreneur organization has grown to 3,000 members at nearly one hundred schools in the past three years. According to *Business 2.0* magazine, a new "undergraduate economic ecosystem" is emerging, where students attend school full time while using their student and alumni connections to "find and incubate new ideas, hire employees and raise money." Most of these new businesses are Internet-based. The educational institutions, which once frowned on such nonacademic diversion because the feeling was it took away from students' studies, have recently experienced their own sea change and recognized the student initiatives. Schools like Yale and Columbia universities and the University of Illinois have all launched variations on campus start-ups, heavily focused on the Internet arena. The student activity itself has propelled this change in attitude and new vehicles to support it. According to Greg Y. Tseng, twenty-year-old chief operating officer of Limespot, a collegiate Web portal, when he began his business activities at Harvard, the practice of running your own business from your dorm room was prohibited. In 1999 Harvard reversed the policy. Young Internet entrepreneurs profiled in the *New York Times* in the fall of 2000 noted that in the past, working out of your college dorm would have been a strain on campus resources. Today, however, a student can have a cell phone as a business line, and e-mail does not impact college operations. The net result is a kind of new focus and curriculum in the educational community—one that gives Young Entrepreneurialism 101 the same kind of weight and credibility—let's face it, more—than Modern European Literature 101.

That supportive philosophy is echoed by Dr. Chester S. Gardner, vice president for Educational Development and Corporate Relationships at the University of Illinois. "Business students for decades have had an interest in developing companies," says Dr. Gardner, "but that interest has intensified in the past decade and especially in the past five years. My office didn't exist even a year ago. And I think a lot of that is related to the Internet. Young people read about the start-up activities related to the Internet— even though it may have been oversold in terms of the actual opportunities out there."

The University of Illinois now has an entrepreneurial program within the college of engineering and the department of commerce on campus. The university recently announced the formation of Illinois Ventures, LLC, a venture capital–related organization that will screen, nurture, and cofund business concepts from students, faculty, and staff until they can get their own investors at the seed stage. The university also has established a system of business incubators, facilities with offices and lab space for start-up companies that have reasonable rents and provide start-ups with access to clerical help, fax, photocopying, contacts with accounting services, and other services.

Dr. Gardner points out that academic arenas such as Stanford and Berkeley in California and Boston in Massachusetts, which became the feeding and breeding ground for today's young entrepreneurs, began after World War II, when the government began investing heavily in academic research at MIT, Harvard, Stanford, Berkeley, and other academic environments, including the University of Illinois.

"Those regions took it a step further and began to encourage faculty and graduate students to begin to think about starting companies," he says. "But you really didn't see as many young people doing this until some people became successful, and they began hearing about this in the press. I think in the last five years the rather rapid success of these dot com companies has given more young people the courage to jump into the entrepreneurial waters. The success of other young people — Steve Wozniac and Steve Jobs — they were just kids when they started Apple — and the young people who came out of Stanford with Yahoo and Excite — those were companies that were enormously successful, and enormously successful very quickly, and I think it's knowing that age and wisdom and maturity aren't absolutely needed in order to start a company that is giving these young people the courage to go and start doing it themselves.

"Young people are feeling more empowered, have more confidence, and in large part, that's one of the reasons why our university is moving in these areas—to support that interest," says Dr. Gardner, although he admits that his own university only recently awakened to the need to provide programs for the young entrepreneur.

"Until just recently, our faculty have kept an arm's length from those activities. There was a concern that our interest in patenting software and technologies or that interests in getting involved with industry might somehow distort the academic program. But more and more, faculty are recognizing that while there are pitfalls to avoid, there are ways that we can change the culture and maintain the integrity of the academic process. We are trying to enable these people to satisfy their entrepreneurial urges but at the same time keep them in the classroom, keep them in the laboratory." Dr. Gardner notes that this population includes many young faculty members as well as 15 to 20 percent of the student body.

"I do believe that the activities surrounding the Internet have played a major role. There've always been a few young students who've wanted to start companies, but we're seeing a much larger proportion now that have those interests."

And, as in the business community, the educational arena has clearly awakened and responded to the fact that if changes are not made to accommodate the desires and goals of the newly empowered young men and women, they will simply walk out the door. Today the competitive environment cuts both ways, as schools and businesses alike are evolving in their effort to cater to and attract top talent.

Jeffrey Gut feels that the old, less than supportive collegiate environment contributed to the fact that he decided to take a leave between his junior and senior years at Boston University to launch his business. He feels that if he'd entered college only two years later, that would not have had to be the case. In the intervening time, as Dr. Gardner has illustrated, attitudes shifted, and Boston University, like the University of Illinois, has launched an on-campus incubator, the E-Business Hatchery, which introduces student entrepreneurs to venture capitalists.

Reversing their former attitude about mixing business with education—and clearly coming to the realization that business *is* education—colleges are embracing student start-ups on a widespread basis. Mark Fragga, for two years a spokesperson for the Wharton Center for Entrepreneurial Programs, sees a new scenario, where people are valued on the basis of their ideas, not on the basis of their seniority, opening the door wide for young people with fresh thinking. "A belief change across our culture in the value and capacity of fresh ideas and people to bring them into action, combined with the changes in the ability to access financial capital for start-up enterprises has created a whole set of opportunities that are new and different," says Fragga. "Whereas five years ago, the celebrated things to do upon leaving a place like Wharton were to go into investment banking or consulting—and I don't think the allure of those two options decreases, but I think a lot of what has happened is that a third option has been created. Being involved in the entrepreneurial wealth creation business became possible and also became what was lionized. That person can be a god. And it was no longer the case that that person would be a misfit who was just trying to make it go in the midst of all of his or her colleagues going the more traditional routes—now that person is one of the celebrated icons of this community. That is a big change. And that cultural change, which is broader than business school, is magnified in business school because in a lot of ways, that person who is using the resources here—the knowledge base, the things we teach in class, and also the experts of all types who are swarming around this place—that kind of a person is really pulling together all the things a business school is supposed to be about. It's fresh thinking, it's new inquiry, it's putting new methods into practice, it's creating value, it's filling a niche in the economy. And it's drawing on every discipline that we study."

Fragga notes that, if you are a student entrepreneur, you have to draw on marketing, strategic planning, figure out your accounting, manage people, finance, and draw together every piece of putting a business together. "Added to the intellectual attraction, obviously, is the opportunity to make a buck," he says. "And the celebration aspects of it—the fact that you become acclaimed for trying, and possibly succeeding, in launching a new business. All those things have just created a climate that brings the whole campus behind people who are trying to launch new ventures.

"There have been regional differences in how local business communities are responding to entrepreneurial activity in general and the entrepreneurial activity of young students in particular. Regional areas like Silicon Valley are famous for being fairly permeable entrepreneurial communities, investor communities, welcoming to newcomers. And now a place like Philadelphia is getting much stronger in doing that same kind of thing. I found that as I wrote and asked people to come to the school and share their knowledge base and help the leaders of tomorrow on their path, the response rate was remarkably high. Everybody wants to be involved with that. It's fun, it's creative, it's challenging, it has the opportunity to maybe make some money if you become an advisor to a company, it has prestige."

Fragga observes that schools like Wharton are changing their perspective as a result of the impact of the Internet. "I see it in the way courses are taught," he says. "Everything is being in a perspective of either how the Internet is changing things, or how to get small and close to your customers, how to be flexible, and still how to scale. All those kinds of issues are at the base of all kinds of things that are being done on campus. And I think that when the chairman of General Electric says that the Internet will change every job in the company, you've got to know that everybody in business is thinking about the Internet, and companies that are exploiting the Internet to do business, and how that will affect the way that things are happening.

"I see it in everything from a student's perspective, and I also know from having been on staff the remarkable number of changes and new initiatives that are going on within the school to explore the Internet, to research the effects of the Internet and uses of the Internet, to use the Internet as a teaching tool, to partner with new kinds of companies. All those kinds of things are all over the place, and a university tends to be a place that is open to new ideas anyway, or at least it should be. I think that business schools are particularly finding things that work, that are effective. There is the student entrepreneurship club that promotes all kinds of activities, helps in running the business plan competition, brings in speakers, creates opportunities for students to pitch to venture capitalists. So the students play a big role in catalyzing the entrepreneurial role on campus. And there is one move further, a lot of effort to try to create synergy by bringing in aspects of the entrepreneurial business community, so there was support from both the administration and from the students, and also from the external business community."

Business plan beauty pageants, similar to the business plan competition Fragga describes, often with corporate sponsorship, are becoming staples of many campus programs, creating the climate and opportunity for a young student to interact with the greater business community outside the university campus and also possibly to win the backing and support that could catapult him or her into business. The business plan competition held by the entrepreneurial studies program at the Wharton, for instance, drew more than 200 start-up teams in 2000, and the

University of Illinois held its first business plan competition in December 2000. In addition, corporate sponsorship by companies like IBM, Hewlett-Packard, and major consulting firms brings students, once far removed from the capitalist orbit, directly into its gravitational pull. Where, ten years ago, the most a young person could hope was to land an internship "pushing somebody else's papers" as one student called it, now these young people are Cinderella at the ball, carrying glass slippers that await start-up capital which, it is hoped, will arrive before their ventures turn into pumpkins.

But whether these ventures ultimately succeed or fail, the education process has been impacted. The time at which young people educationally intersect and interact with the concept of being an entrepreneurial culture-carrier has moved up the life continuum several decades. The die has been cast: Where their postgraduate predecessors expected to sit silently on the sidelines of meetings, often in chairs on the perimeter of the room and not even at the table, "absorbing" and perhaps ferrying (or making) the coffee, this group is educated to believe that they are on if not an experience level, then a conceptual peer level with top-tier management from the starting gate.

Gary Cadenhead, creator of the Moot Corp business plan competition at the University of Texas, has said, "In the information economy, software and technology MBA's coming out of school have distinct competencies that other people in the economy may not have. They bring a skill that they don't have to work 10 years to develop. And there's lots of money around to invest in them. The ideas, the confidence and the money have all come together."

Taking the paradigm one step further are organizations like ITU Ventures in Los Angeles, an on-campus venture capital organization that provides seed capital of $100,000 to $500,000 to entrepreneurs who are students, professors, and researchers in certain top business and engineering schools. This group uses graduate students who are paid fees to locate and nurture the start-ups.

Soon it's possible, that young moguls will not even have to *go* to college to attend and graduate from college. If the academic environment is bending to student demands to multitask out of the dorm room, can the next step be the *virtual* dorm room? There is an argument that the Internet could make bricks-and-mortar educational institutions obsolete. Could not the same professor who teaches a class to 500 students in a large lecture hall give the same lecture to thousands over the Internet?

Interactivity? With a mouse click, the student can participate in the class or activity—from anywhere. Exams? They can be proctored at preselected locations or e-mailed in. It's a totally feasible scenario that young entrepreneurs may soon be able to have their cake and eat it too—to run their business and attend college simultaneously—all via the Internet.

The concept of the virtual university was actually coined by a Victorian, Cardinal John Henry Newman, in 1852. Newman did not foresee the Internet, but he saw the concept of a universi-tyless education as a threat to the teacher-student relationship. However, every era has taken its stab at evolving the concept of education. Gutenberg's invention of printing in the fifteenth century, for instance, resulted in the removal of priests as the sole gatekeepers of information and knowledge in the same way that the Web is allowing larger numbers of people direct access to information. Today virtual opportunities are seen as educational components, and the relevance of the Web is expanding.

Numerous top universities, such as Wharton and Stanford, have set up class online, offering courses or specialty degrees. You can go to law school online or even get a Ph.D. The University System of Georgia offers ten degrees via distance learning.

Georgia Tech, Southern Polytechnic State University, and Clayton College & State University all offer a combination of virtual elements. At Jones International University, the first college to function entirely in cyberspace, courses are taught on the Web, and students and faculty meet via e-mail. There is even a cybergraduation to award the degrees.

While the head of the accreditation committee of the American Association of University Professors sided with Cardinal Newman and called online universities a threat to the "preservation of higher education itself," the corporate world has stepped in with sponsored online universities and training programs. The Board of Higher Education has given its first approval of an online college to Harcourt Higher Education, a virtual college owned by textbook giant Harcourt General Inc., and predicts that they will enroll 20,000 students within five years in a market for online education that will reach 3 million students by 2003. Corporate-sponsored universities, such as Motorola University, are predicted to flourish, multiplying from 480 to 1,600 over the next few years. As time becomes more scarce and precious, as traditional patterns become less mandatory, as a younger generation grows up on the Internet, the home ground of the video game may well become the next ivy-covered hall. And a degree from, say, Microsoft Online U may be as desirable — in some cases even *more so* — than one from an old-line, venerable institution.

The Global Education Network, a private, not-for-profit company founded and funded in part by the investment banker/industrial philosopher Herbert Allen, Jr., is offering a curriculum of college courses over the Internet, taught by a line-up of professors from top colleges, with a goal of "piercing" the walls that separate academia from the larger world to create a global information marketplace. Under the GEN model, educators would fall into a work-for-hire, rather than tenure, scenario, one that could theoretically challenge the university paradigm head-on in many of the strictly academic areas.

"The kinds of changes that corporations have undergone in the past decade will occur in higher education," says Mark C. Taylor of the Global Education Network. "The Internet and related technologies are creating the possibility of making education available to people of all ages anywhere in the world at a reasonable cost. As new competitors move into the higher education market, however, it will be necessary for colleges and universities to change the way they do business. Students raised with computers will demand different kinds of education. It is important to realize that multimedia and information technologies do not involve doing the same thing differently, but doing something very different. Indeed, the very structure of knowledge is being changed by technologies."

Taylor sees new forms of cooperation and collaboration emerging in both the business and education sectors, and the line between for-profit and not-for-profit enterprises increasingly blurring. "With the increased sophistication of communications technology, these modes of cooperation are going to become ever more present throughout the entire university." Taylor envisions new kinds of arrangements between businesses and corporations and also between public and private universities. "One of the characteristics of this new space is that competitors must also cooperate," he says. "So educational institutions will not only be cooperating with business, but they will be cooperating with each other. And there are already new players in the education market—some of these will be for profit. And faculty members will be able to enter into agreements with these other educational providers in a way that could set up conflict of interest with their institutions. But, in the foreseeable future, faculty will be working either with a university and a for-profit provider, or work part time for the university and part time for the educational provider. In part, I think universities will be driven to accept that arrangement to keep some of the faculty they most want to keep. And many faculty will want to keep and, indeed, need an educational base for most of their work.

"Online education holds the possibility of addressing the continuing problem of the high cost of higher education," says Taylor. "It's going to be possible to provide high-quality, online education to people at considerably lower cost than is the case in most private and even some public institutions." He adds, "Now, there's no doubt that this form of education will pose a threat to some educational institutions. It's not clear how brand is going to work in online education. The Harvards of the world continue to think—and with some good reason—that their brands will hold the gold standard, but it's not clear that that will be the case in the online world. To some, like lifetime learners, I think the quality and results of the course are going to be more important than the professor or institution from which they're given. What this technology makes possible is basically opening up high-quality education to anyone anywhere anytime.

"The bricks-and-mortar schools are not going to disappear in my lifetime," Taylor cautions. "I don't think they are going to ever disappear. But I think there is the potential here for there to be mutual benefit. I do think there are going to be new kinds of educational institutions that will compete with bricks-and-mortar institutions, but I also think that for more traditional colleges and universities with a certain degree of vision, there are modes of collaboration and cooperation that can actually benefit the bricks-and-mortar institutions, not only by creating additional revenue streams, but by getting the faculty out there in front of a much wider audience.

"We are talking about global education," stresses Taylor.

"What this technology makes possible is basically opening up higher education to anybody in the world, anywhere, any time. There are extraordinary opportunities here to get education to people who might otherwise not have it available, for instance, talented high school students, working people, or — I know this is controversial — prison populations. The ideal for me is a situation where anybody anywhere in the world can sit around the same table and talk about issues that matter. And, in fact, we can do that now. The technology is there, with sufficient resources."

Taylor paints a picture that is not a replication of the traditional classroom. "It's a different kind of educational experience," he says. "In some ways, I think an online course can be superior to an in-class course. One must realize that many of the courses in undergraduate institutions today involve huge lecture halls in which students come in and sit down, then take notes for fifty minutes from a teacher they can barely see. There are possibilities for better kinds of learning experiences in an online environment than in some of these large, mass-produced courses."

Today higher education is a $228 billion enterprise, and the competition for those student dollars is escalating. The existing online learning segment is also looking at a major increase, one that Taylor predicts will come from what he calls "lifetime learners" and retirees. A $2 billion business in 2000, it is predicted by Gerald Odening of Chase Bank to grow 35 percent a year, or to $9 billion by 2005.

Even the military has stepped into cyberspace education, with what has been called the biggest military education program since the GI Bill. Soldiers based at Fort Benning in Georgia, for instance, can earn degrees while serving at army posts anywhere in the world. In a test program at several bases, Army University

Access Online will provide soldiers with laptop computers and pay for the courses.

College may be the last frontier, and the time-crunched Change Agents are perfectly positioned to storm it. Young people who have grown up in online chat rooms will feel totally comfortable attending class the same way. Building on Mark Taylor's scenario of the antidote to the overcrowded lecture hall, online learning may also be the perfect antidote to not being able to squeeze in the time actually to attend classes in person, especially if you are otherwise employed. One man who got a master's degree online noted that it eliminated a dreaded two-hour commute to the actual school and allowed him to work when he wanted to.

Of course, no quantitative measure can be placed on the multidimensional experiences and the varied kinds of learning involved in physically participating in the process of a college education. However, the elite appeal of a brand-name diploma is only part of what is, for many, the end-goal commodity of a degree. For many, the fact of gaining the diploma is more significant than where it came from.

For some Baby Moguls, however, even college is way off. These are the Mini-Moguls: kids who may be in the driver's seat before they're even old enough to drive. Younger kids have always made their older brothers and sisters their role models, and today that paradigm is extending to the business world, via a gateway created by the Internet. One of the easiest points of entry is the stock market, where the thrills and rewards of online stock-picking have become a hot draw. A parent sets up a custodial account, and the child can make money decisions.

"Investing online is a very cool application," says Ginger Thomson, chief of the youth-oriented financial site Doughnet.com. A fifteen-year-old is quoted on the site as telling other teens, "By investing in the stock market . . . you could be sittin' pretty with your BMW and brand-new mansion! The possibilities are infinite."

Schools are reporting that students spend their lunch hours at computers checking stock prices. Some high schools, responding to the surge of interest, now offer clubs and courses devoted to the market.

Then there's the darker side of taking the money into your own underage hands. For the first time, the Securities and Exchange Commission is taking a close look at what kids are doing with online trading, and what they're finding is not play money. An upturn in stock manipulation by younger investors is currently being targeted, and the SEC has been more or less forced to take a position and make a high-visibility example. Several recent high-profile cases have surfaced, the most significant of which led to the first prosecution of a minor by the SEC in history.

SEC Enforcement director Richard H. Walker commented, "We were surprised and dismayed to find out he was a minor, though we've been increasingly finding violations by younger people without business backgrounds. The Internet has become a staple of young people from grade school on."

The young person in question, Jonathan G. Lebed, was a fifteen-year-old who according to authorities used the Internet to manipulate the stock market. Lebed and a sixteen-year-old classmate had started two Web businesses, designed to help others develop and advertise their own Web sites as well as advice on issues like how to take a company public. But by age fourteen, Lebed was taking bolder steps, and within a year he had pocketed $273,000 in allegedly illegal gains via a scheme the SEC called "pump and dump." This involved buying up obscure penny stocks, hyping them via up to 500 messages per stock on various Web bulletin boards, and dumping them as soon as the prices rose as a result of the hype. The advice was simplistic, but it worked. One Lebed comment, "The most undervalued stock in history," resulted in a next-day spike in value for an obscure stock from $1.38 a share to $2.00. Lebed, who had bought 18,000 shares, turned a tidy profit.

"While he was sitting in math or science, he knew he was making his profits," said Ronald C. Long, the United States Securities and Exchange Commission's district administrator in Philadelphia, where the case was prosecuted.

Long told me that, in his personal opinion, "It is frightening. In and of itself, it's not a bad thing for young people to learn to be responsible for their future by investing themselves. The idea that people at an earlier age are getting some financial knowledge and financial awareness is a good thing. It's not good, at an earlier age, that people are engaging in securities fraud."

Long sees a distinct link to the Internet, and it's the dark underbelly of information access. "The problem is, the wealth of good information on the Internet is at least matched, if not exceeded, by a wealth of bad information," he says. "I can't say for certain, but I can guess [Lebed] didn't learn 'pump and dump' in the backyard or in the school playground. Almost certainly, he learned that in an Internet chat room, where you do see this." Long holds parents accountable. "When parents allow their children to have unsupervised access to the Internet, I think you only allow them to be exposed to the possibility of being caught by the spell of the evil side of the Internet as well as the good side."

The evil side?

"The evil side is the attitude that there's a quick way to make a buck here and that there are gullible people out there. The Internet is full of Web sites whose sole purpose is to tell you how to take money from other people." As a result, Long notes, the SEC itself has gotten involved in surfing the Web and what he calls "a lot of cybersurveillance."

What kind of a kid was Jonathan Lebed? Industrious and ambitious, for sure, like so many entrepreneurs in their early years. In eighth grade, he got up at 5 A.M. daily to watch CNBC for stock tips, which helped him lead his team to a fourth-place national finish in a national stock tournament. His schoolmates found him very smart, a bit off center perhaps—he eschewed a backpack for a black leather briefcase—but cool. He was involved in civic causes—if they helped his own cause. It bugged Lebed that his hometown of Cedar Grove, New Jersey, did not have high-speed Internet access, so he turned up to lobby at town council meetings to upgrade the local cable TV system to provide it. At those meetings, an observer noticed what some might have seen as a less humane side of the young teen. When the council debated the problem of wild turkeys on the local roads, Lebed's comment was "Personally, I don't care if they get squashed like bugs."

Ronald Long suspects that the nature of the Internet itself could also contribute to the viability of victimization by young people, a scenario where those taken in by a pump-and-dump scam are just more turkeys on the road. "It is anonymous," he says, "so they think the victims are anonymous, they don't really exist. But there *are* victims for this kind of conduct. And it is conduct that is absolutely harmful to investors."

Securities fraud is a whole new arena for young people, one inauspiciously opened up by the Internet. "This was a young person," says Long. "But we're a civil agency and we couldn't ignore what he was doing. A young man who throws a baseball through a window is responsible for that conduct, and this is clearly at a higher level than that. The opportunity is absolutely there, but it's also an opportunity that can only be there if parents fail in their parental role."

Long views the Lebed case as "a wake-up call" and does not hesitate to point out a larger and even darker implication. "On one level, you have to say, thank goodness this was only securities fraud. Imagine the same level of freedom, the same lack of supervision, in some other, more personally harmful things that this young man might have gotten involved in on the Internet. It runs the gamut. Society has seen recently what's happened when young people have engaged in antisocietal behavior that's initially promulgated and learned on the Internet."

Lebed settled a civil suit brought by the SEC, not acknowledging any wrongdoing, by repaying $285,000; he was also allowed to keep $500,000 that the SEC deemed profits not made on illegal trades. One of the most striking facts of the entire case, at least to some observers, was that when Lebed was fourteen years old, he had been warned by the SEC about his online trading activities. Arthur Levitt, the chairman of the SEC, commented after the settlement, "If I'm a kid and I'm pulled in by some scary government agency, I'd back off." Jonathan Lebed was a different kind of kid.

Lebed's court proceedings were covered by all the major media. He was the subject of a cover story in the *New York Times Magazine*, his picture glowering from the front cover like James Dean with peach fuzz. At his high school, following the settlement, Lebed was a hero and role model to his peers. One classmate commented, "He kept his cool. It didn't faze him too much."

Long notes, "Hero worship in our society today seems to be drifting toward people who in another time and place wouldn't be heroes."

Regardless, there is a growing undercurrent among the very young that can no longer be viewed simplistically. As a sixteen-year-old junior from Lebed's class said: "If a fifteen-year-old kid can make $273,000, anything is possible."

5 THE ENTREPRENEURIAL EPIDEMIC

The most-asked question among the New Economy community may be, "What's your business model?" This is because there are very few precedents—people are inventing their own as they go along and are searching for answers, like people feeling their way in a fog. Ask yourself: What kind of people would put their careers on the line to become involved in a business that almost nobody knows anything about, something for which there is no precedent, something at which very few businesses today are actually making an above-the-line profit and that could fail as easily as succeed? These are not your gold-watch corporate lifers. No, we are talking about the high-wire walkers of the business world.

Most of the entrepreneurs interviewed in this book started young—in some cases, practically fetal. Remember nine-year-old Jeffrey Gut and his invention that became a craze, the Zip-cord bracelet? Lisa Sharples, cofounder of the now-defunct

Garden.com, is a female version. She says, "I took an entrepreneurial approach to everything my whole life." In fifth grade, Sharples started a business with her best friend that involved quilling, an antique craft. Her father got the young partners business cards, her mother hauled them and their wares to craft shows. By seventh grade, Lisa and her friend had made $2,000. "I had to put half in the bank," she says. But did she buy Barbies with her windfall? Hardly. "With the other half, I bought a drafting table, my own phone—and a pair of earrings." In college, Sharples started the women's golf team. "I was terrible at golf, but it was the point that women weren't having a chance to play. Of my current partners, all three of us are entrepreneurs."

"I was always an entrepreneur," says Corey, at twenty-eight the veteran of three New Economy ventures. "In college, I set up my own hat stand during the Michigan baseball games. Eventually I expanded to two stands and hired three other students. We made a ton of money!"

The mother of Mark Oldman, one of the founders of the Internet career guidance site Vault.com, told a corporate seminar that when he was six years old, her son refused to go to summer camp because he "insisted he had work to do." The "work" consisted of sitting home, looking up companies in the phone book, putting on a deep voice, and getting product samples sent to the house.

The Internet makes it easier than ever to be an entrepreneur, and at a younger age. When he was in third grade, my son came home from school with a disk in his backpack. He explained that on the disk was his Web site. Everyone in the class had made his or her own Web site. Immediately he announced that he wanted to launch a golf site for children. Other kids would come to him over the Internet to read his golf tips, which he would sell. He hadn't yet figured out the e-commerce part, but he was sure he could.

They used to say "Only in America." Now it is "Only on the Web."

"The world used to be divided into crazy entrepreneurs who were outside the system and the corporate system—and now the entrepreneurs are the system," observes Donny Deutsch. "So being a member of a club and working your way through an organization and having an allegiance to an organization is clearly not the gold standard now. The days of people pledging their allegiance to a company and being there for thirty years and being taken care of and then walking away with their gold watch are over."

Every era has its sprinkling of entrepreneurs. And there have no doubt always been closet entrepreneurs, who longed to blow up their cubicles and break out of the rank and file but never actually crossed the line. Donny Deutsch was one of them. Early in his career, Deutsch, now one of the entrepreneurial deans of the advertising industry, worked at an advertising mega-agency. "I will never forget, I hated it!" he says.

"I remember going in . . . I was an assistant account executive, and I would go into my cube, and I would stand on my chair and look over the top of the cube. The confinement of being in something like this and not being able to see what is around! So I think now that this ridiculous symbol is me, age twenty-one, standing on my chair so I could see over the cube and talk to people—because I couldn't be cubed. . . .

"My very first day on the job, I was working on a coffee account. I was called into the office of the head guy. He had a huge office, bigger than mine today, and I will never forget, his entire office was lined with coffee cans. Every wall. Hundreds of coffee cans from all over the world. And he was sitting there saying 'Nobody knows coffee better than I do, I have been in this business for fifteen years.' And I could see a thought bubble over my head, 'I do not want to be where this guy is tomorrow.

What a schmuck!' I'm sure he was a lovely guy, but—that is when you know. When you look seven levels above you and not only do you not have an aspiration to be there, but it is not even a matter that you are going to get there faster. You don't want to *be* there. You *know.*" Deutsch went on to join his father's modest ad agency—where he turned up the heat and super-charged it into the largest independently held ad agency in America—and eventually to start an Internet advertising agency himself. In December 2000, at age forty-three, Deutsch sold his company, for over $250,000,000.

Like Donny Deutsch, a certain proportion of entrepreneurs no doubt had the good fortune to inherit both a family business and a proclivity to run it from their parents, which they then built on and made their own. However, the Internet for the first time provided an affordable virtual platform for an entire com-munity of entrepreneurial spirits. Suddenly you didn't need a family business, or even a business. Or an office.

In old economy business models, there are many very real barriers to starting a business, even if you are fiercely inclined to do so. There was the cost, for one. You had to have the money to pay for office space and furnishings and to invest in some kind of inventory or supplies for a service to sell. You may have needed employees. Insurance. Financing to even get off the ground. And it took a long time to see if your risk paid off.

Marketing paradigms have also been by overturned by the Internet. One of the most dramatic examples was the success of the movie *The Blair Witch Project.* The movie itself was pro-duced outside of Hollywood for about $35,000 by relative nov-ices, without the traditional Hollywood lures—stars and special effects. Unlike traditional entertainment marketing, which fo-cuses on an advertising buildup that leads to a film's release date, *Blair Witch* relied on the far less expensive venue of the Internet.

A Web site, launched a year before the film's release, featured unused footage, "journals," and news items of the legend and mysterious disappearance of the characters, which led to word-of-mouth mystique. Posters, ads, and commercials, the traditional advertising arsenal, were deployed only minimally. It wasn't needed, with the Web site pulling in 115 million hits. Having seeded the hype, the filmmakers sold *Blair Witch* to Artisan for $1.1 million following its debut at the Sundance Film Festival. The film went on to pull in $140 million, trouncing the top-heavy Hollywood system.

In other words, if you're inclined to start your own business, you can see a clear and achievable way to do it. The allure is powerful: You don't have to have a lot of money to put up a Web site. You don't need a staff. You don't need an office, a pencil, or a wardrobe. You never want to get out of your robe? Who will know? Work naked if you want. Here's the point—flick on your laptop, and with a few keystrokes and mouse clicks, you can be in business. You don't even have to sell anything or make anything.

How? Well, here's an example of the way it's supposed to work. Let's go into business together. What do you say, partner? What? We have no money? No problem. We're going to do it right here, in this paragraph. Zero risk. We don't even need office space. After all, who's going to see us?

You start—pick an interest area. I don't care what it is. Any topic at all. Next, let's add up our only expenses: a book on how to make a Web site and the fees to put our site on an Internet server. Can't figure out how to build the Web site yourself? If you have a teenager at home who knows how to build a Web site, use him or her and advance to the next step. We are going to launch a chat room by asking people to tell us what they think about whatever subject you have chosen. Let's name our Web site "Chats R Us." Ask a question about your topic and post it on CRU. We are now in business as a chat room. Go to other chat rooms on similar subjects (aka our "community") and tell people there is something very exciting going on over at CRU. Do this a lot. (Hey, it worked for the *Blair Witch Project* and Jonathan Lebed.) If enough people come to it, we've got a data base that's probably worth something to somebody. That somebody may be a venture capitalist or a potential partner. If nobody comes, what have we lost? Our sweat, maybe, but not our skins and certainly not our fortunes. We've bought time while we figure out the next step, maybe how to get e-commerce or advertising partners. And we've learned that we can accomplish something ourselves. This is about psychology as much as it is economics.

Simplistic? Admittedly. Realistic? Absolutely. And if you understood the basic principles behind this nursery story, you can be sure, so did thousands of other people who have a stirring in their soul to be in business for themselves. Or even simply to say something for themselves.

One of them was Esther Drill, founder of teen site gURL.com. In a matter of three years from its creation in 1996, gURL rose from the woodwork of the Web to national prominence as the Web site of choice for teen girls, now including over a million members who communicate with each other daily about issues that are important to their lives. The site has won numerous awards, including the prestigious Webby. A book created from the content and advice offered gURL to gURL on gURL.com debuted in the top 50 on the Amazon.com top-100 sellers' list.

Many of the entrepreneurs I interviewed came from entrepreneurial backgrounds. Drill, wearing no makeup and downtown New York's ubiquitous black, was one of them. "My father has his own business," she says. "He was a general contractor, and I grew up with him working, going to the office, seeing him make his own living. I appreciate what it is to be your own boss. I also liked being very involved in all aspects of the business, which you can do when you work for yourself. I find it fulfilling not to be categorized as one thing. Being able to have a say in everything was really satisfying—whereas anything else I thought about doing cut me off from other things."

Drill started her business totally from scratch. "I had no business background and neither did my partner. I just felt strongly that I had something important to say. I started out wanting to share my own stories as a way of showing girls that everyone goes through trauma, through multiple perspectives—and can laugh at it. We hope we will help change things for girls at a time when they are trying to change how they think about family, themselves, and how they think about things." Prior to gURL, she had majored in math and Russian studies ("Something that I haven't done at all") before graduate school at New York University's Interactive Telecommunications Program. She had worked as a book buyer in an independent bookstore. She and gURL's cofounder, Rebecca Odes, had wanted to start a magazine, an idea that "always seemed too insurmountable." The Web had more appeal "because there wasn't this preexisting canon to live up to. gURL.com was a labor of love." So they started gURL as an online "zine."

Internet entrepreneurs become quickly immersed—many used the word "obsessed"—with their goal. For the first three years, Drill worked "nonstop, ninety hours a week. We used the grad school labs and stayed there till 2 A.M. I couldn't have any other conversations. If I met somebody for dinner at, say, 8:30 or 9, they'd ask why I was so late. And it wasn't late for me at all."

The open-endness of the opportunity is what appeals to Drill. "In a regular business, there still is a ceiling," she says.

Not here.

Elizabeth Talerman, thirty-six-year-old CEO of Agile Industries, a fast-rising Internet advertising company, began her entrepreneurial career at age eight when she signed on as an underage Avon lady. The daughter of a photographer father who was deaf and self-taught, she also sold seeds door to door from a catalog. Her parents encouraged her. On the first day of school, other kids got pencils with their names on them. Talerman's pencils had sayings: "This above all: To thine own self be true." And: "Procrastination is the thief of time."

Talerman claims she was a born entrepreneur. "It wasn't ever about the money," she insists. "I know that from when I was very little I always wondered, 'How can I get people to buy this?' There was a lot of gratification in selling to someone else. It was about the strategy, not the sales."

For many people, landing a great job is the ultimate in career satisfaction. For the new age entrepreneur, however, it's not enough just to have a great job. In fact, almost all the people I spoke to had impressive, exciting jobs before they started their own businesses. Many described their former positions as "the world's greatest job." Still, no matter how stimulating the job, if it involved working for somebody else, it was universally perceived as "not exciting enough."

Talerman is typical. After graduating from Harvard, she worked as the director of marketing for Harvard Business School. "I was bored. I created some marketing plans, and I knew that's where they would go, but I also knew it would take five years. I knew I had to go to an ad agency, because they had different curves." Talerman detoured into consulting, where she worked twenty-hour days, "learned I was really smart, but crashed myself," then joined Ogilvy, a top advertising agency. "My two and a half years at Ogilvy were the Harvard of ad agency experiences," she says. "I was well positioned—I was head of worldwide brand strategy for the IBM team—and I was around people who made me think harder than anyone ever had." This included her future partner, who, after a successful pitch, hugged Talerman and said, "This was really fun. We should start a business."

Fortuitously, a friend in the entertainment business called and needed a Web site for his father, a legendary singer, and the two prospective partners tested the waters by making a joint pitch. They didn't get that job, but they got something better — motivation. "That gave us impetus to quit our jobs," says Talerman. "Ogilvy offered to fund us, but they wanted 70 percent of the business."

No deal.

"I'm not interested in working for anybody but my clients and my creative people," says Talerman. For her, like many entrepreneurs, it's about the process, the parts of the job that many hierarchical bosses prefer to delegate. These entrepreneurs run their businesses as if they were hands-on mechanics of high-performance cars, more interested in the tinkering than the driving — while resisting the thought of anybody else at the wheel. Talerman, for instance, is not interested in the mechanics of being the boss or running the business. "I don't care about running a company," she says. "I care about being a good market strategist and having it transformed to communications so someone out there finds value in it. I love what I do and the chance to be smart." The sense of excitement Talerman feels, the buzz she gets from her own business, is another hallmark of these entrepreneurs. "Every day, I go to sleep thinking 'Is it real?' " And if the business gets too big, Talerman says, and if she gets too far removed from what she loves doing, she will walk away and start over. "Neither my partner nor I has a penchant for running a big or a public company. After twenty-five employees, you start having meetings about meetings. That's when it's time to sell the company."

The Internet has been a magnet for young entrepreneurs because it opened the lid of a Pandora's box of new niches that these opportunistic souls felt they could fill. Sometimes the way was lit by their own experiences, but another route involved simply identifying a need and finding a way to fill it. No experience? No problem. Frequently nobody else had experience either.

Such was the case with Mark Selcow, cofounder of BabyCenter.com, the leading Internet information and commerce company specifically serving the needs of expectant and new parents. After graduating from Stanford Business School in 1993, Selcow, who describes himself as a "wayward premed," went into the biotech industry. After about seven years, he decided to "reinvent" himself. In other words, after years of training and preparation in the healthcare and biotechnology areas, he walked away. "I made a complete industry change into something I knew nothing about," Selcow said.

It wasn't an entirely blind decision, however. "I decided to pick an area where there was a combination of a real problem and a kind of platform change occurring; specifically, the appearance of the Internet as a consumer medium." Selcow saw a parallel with going into the field of biotechnology, such as genetic engineering as a tool with applications across a range of different areas. After trying several different ideas on for size, Selcow, a thirty-one-year-old bachelor without so much as a marriage prospect on the horizon, decided on the baby business. His partner, a former Stanford classmate, actually contributed the genesis of the idea because at the time, he and his wife were trying to start a family.

"If the Internet hadn't happened, we would never have gone into the baby business," Selcow asserts. But the partners figured that the Internet could provide welcome solutions to what Selcow called a "point of pain"—and he wasn't talking about labor. Selcow and his partner reckoned that it was common sense that couples would have difficulty picking the right stroller or car seat. That new mothers and fathers, too, would have lots of questions—that experts and other parents could help answer. That they would be up at odd hours, looking for solutions and products. That many mothers might even be housebound for a time. "This was a platform change in an area where there was a deep information problem."

They had their concept.

"We just dove in and started BabyCenter.com," said Selcow. "We quit our jobs in the fall of '96, raised a little money, and recruited our core team in 1997. And I reinvented myself from a biotech marketing person to an Internet person. We didn't know when we quit our jobs what it would be. But we had a pretty firm conviction that whatever we quit our jobs for, it had to be something where we could surround ourselves with passionate people and work on something that we could really be excited about. Besides, we could see that most of the stuff that was online in this area was very poor quality. We just assumed that if we delivered a good-quality product it would be used."

Used? In 1999, BabyCenter was named by *Red Herring Magazine* as one of the top 100 companies in the electronic economy. The company merged in July 1999 with the then-leading online toy retailer, eToys, to create what the company calls "the ultimate online family destination."

After the merger with eToys, Mark Selcow and his partner moved on to future challenges. Challenges they plan to create for themselves. "We are working on new business ideas now," Selcow says. There will be one major difference. "I think I would like to work not seven days a week, twelve hours a day," he says. "If I can work six days a week, twelve hours a day, I would be perfectly happy. I am looking to round out my life."

6 TWO HANDS, TEN BALLS

Remember juggling? Well, forget it. It's over. Juggling is for sissies with only two hands. Change Agents don't juggle—they multitask, at the speed of the Web. As one said, "The ability to do eight things at once is incredibly useful when trying to do eight things." The Internet has made it possible to live a lifestyle where you actually *can* do more things simultaneously, and Change Agents are taking full advantage, ordering cat food, previewing movies, making travel arrangements, and checking weekend weather, all while juggling two phone calls and a Palm Pilot—and maybe a baby. Becoming immersed in multiple information sources and visual stimuli has prepared Change Agents to handle multitasking in a way that their predecessors could not, and it is a capability that allows the compression of experiences and the multiplication of careers and lifestyles that are changing the patterns of how we live and work.

"We have a desire to do as much as we can," says Abbi Gosling. "Actually, I think women are better at multitasking. I find that the ability to do eight things at once is incredibly useful when trying to *do* eight things. What am I doing at the same time? Keeping an eye on seventeen projects; being responsible for real estate, legal, and hiring for our company; buying our apartment; picking the movie my husband and I will see tonight; handling the phone and e-mail. Sometimes I have to stand back and say to myself, 'You fucker, you're multitasking! Focus!' A hallmark of my relaxation time is single-input sessions — a book, a movie."

Lisa Sharples said she tries to do everything at once. "That's what I like. Having a lot going on. I get bored quickly. I can't sit still. When I read a book, I read a chapter and get up. This weekend it was 110 in Austin and you couldn't go out. So I reorganized all my drawers. I'm running my company, I am the mother of a three-year-old, and I'm trying to adopt from China, all at once."

Multitasking is as old as humanity, but the word as it is used today began as a common technical term pertaining to multiple functions performed by a computer. In 1966, according to the September 1968 issue of *Datamation*, multitasking meant "the use of a single CPU for the simultaneous processing of two or more jobs." The term has since clearly seeped into the mainstream, another example of how technology has become the incubator for evolution of the (increasingly) commonplace.

Literally every person who fit the Change Agent profile whom I spoke with was a multitasker par excellence, but none more so than Steve Klein, who exemplifies not just the multitask ethic but a lifestyle on the rise.

Down the road, past the orchards and the fruit stand, past County Line Road and the church with the graveyard, down the gravel road and past the pond with the ducks and canoes, Steve Klein can be found standing on the terrace of his hundred-year-old brick Pennsylvania farmhouse, checking out the cucumber crop. He is probably wearing beat-up khaki shorts, wire-rimmed glasses, a wrinkled, dirty T-shirt, and sandals. The farm is "in the part of Pennsylvania that is not on the New York axis," and the Mason jars are lined up on the weathered wood table, ready for the pickling process. An antique tractor and a '52 Ford laze in the shade of an ancient-looking barn. Klein gives the highlights of the gated kitchen garden across the lawn: "My dahlias, my peppers, my beets, my basil. Over there is sorrel." A rooster crows, and as Klein moves inside to cut tomatoes for a snack, the sheep in the adjacent pasture bleat on cue.

"Hey, Bill," he calls to a ram with monolithic, curved horns. "Why do I have sheep? They produce manure for fertilizer, and wool, and they keep the pasture mowed, and if I were a real sheep farmer, I'd eat their young." Klein grins wickedly. "The sheep are real multitaskers."

Although not the first farmer in history to discover the multiple merits of sheep, it could be said that Klein's multitasking capabilities are right up there with his livestock. At forty, he has multitasked his way through several successful careers, beginning as a student, which, in a way, he still is.

"When I was sixteen, my dad threw *Crime and Punishment* at me and I loved it. I still read a book a week and a ton of magazines," Klein says. He graduated from Columbia as an English major in 1981 and landed a job at Grey Advertising as an assistant media planner. "At first I was in awe. I said, 'Oh my God, all these people know what they're doing.' Then three days into it I realized these people are idiots and this is basic math. My boss is a complete moron. So I became a pig for work. Whatever business came in, I wanted to work on it. I stayed for four and a half years. It wasn't that challenging. So while I was at Grey I got involved in a friend's record company."

In the Change Agent tradition, Klein's family background was entrepreneurial. "My dad started his own business. He cuts cardboard. You know when you buy underwear there's that sheet of cardboard? My dad started this when I was born, and growing up my model was that the highest-integrity job was the one you did yourself."

As soon as the Internet started, Klein taught himself the computer language HTML. "I like to know the job at the bottom of the totem pole. Early on in the New York Internet community, there were about fifty to a hundred of us, and we were involved because it was fun, not to get rich. The thought was 'Hey, an individual can publish!' "

By this time, Klein had worked his way up in the ad agency world to media director of a medium-size but showcase shop. He knew the value of media placement, and he coupled that with his growing interest in the Internet, which led to an idea. "I contacted the people at Yahoo and told them all I wanted was to own keywords. I saw keywords as a potential advertising medium. They thought I was crazy, but I kept calling them back and pushing it. I can't tell you how many times they shot me down and I had to call back and try to convince them that this could work. Finally they said they would sell me keywords at $1,000 a word for a month, mainly to get rid of me, I think. I immediately called my brother-in-law and told him we had a golden opportunity. We scraped together as much money as we could and bought keywords like books, travel, music, food, coffee . . . then we resold the word 'books' for $3,000 a month. I was the first person to buy keyword-sensitive banners on Yahoo. I'm proud of it. Fifty years from now, when someone brings up a banner on the Internet, I'll be able to say I was the first person to do that."

Klein made enough money on that deal that some people might have thought he would cash out. Many people *would* have cashed out. But, he says, "It's fun for me." He then moved on to create a travel page that had links. "We built one of the largest travel pages out of this barn." He indicates the ancient red structure with the requisite hayloft, rusting equipment, and mice, noting that he had done all this Internet work in his spare time, while still running a major ad agency media department. But now it was time to take it to the next level.

Klein's next move was to leave the ad agency to start his Internet media company, iBalls. "I started it out of my pocket with an equity deal. It was profitable after three months," he says. The company grew to have a database of 2,500 sites and 109 clients before he partnered with a "behemoth" to form his current incarnation of the organization.

Steve Klein's perception of success and status is common to many entrepreneurs linked to the new economy. Let's put it this way: There's no Rolls-Royce in this man's garage. "Morgan Stanley said, 'Cool, you can take your money and buy a boat,'" Klein recalls. "But I don't want one." A week after his company went public, his bike died. "Then I did buy a new bike," he admits. But his car has 250,000 miles on it, and, in New York, he still lives in the same tiny studio apartment he had in college. "Status to me is owning your own hours," he says. "Freedom. And not having to work with people you don't want to work with."

Like so many other Change Agent entrepreneurs, Klein says he is challenged by the challenge, not the money.

"I'm hyperkinetic," he admits. "I need to be doing a lot of things at once. I have to multitask. I trade a lot of stocks. I'm on the boards of a lot of companies. On the farm, between the barn and the weeds, I say I have to plant the seeds. In my garden, I have thirty things growing. This weekend I played in the garden, came in, went online, spent five hours instant messaging, and played Yahoo cribbage in another window simultaneously. Sometimes I play two games at a time. As a kid, I was considered lazy, but that's because I wasn't challenged."

No doubt.

Four days a week, Steve Klein presides as chairman of iBalls ("Sixty employees, zero turnover") from loft-space offices in Tribeca. The rest of the time, he is a Pennsylvania farmer. The two worlds, however, are not as far apart as they seem. At the farm, Klein often finds himself "on my porch, barefoot, with a cigar, a headphone, and a laptop, doing business through e-mail while talking to a client. Farmboy dot com. My deal was always that Fridays I work in Pennsylvania. Clients can call me out there. It's the day I schedule client calls, paperwork, computer work." He supresses a chortle. "But I had an 800 number so when clients called, it sounded real. I've been working virtually for ten years. It works. I can work anywhere in the world. I had a conference call in Hong Kong. I was instant messaging from an Internet café at 11 P.M. in Hanoi. It makes the world really small."

In the iBalls office, an oasis of calm and quiet above the bustle of Greenwich and Canal, Klein injects the presence of the farm when he cooks his monthly "Chairman's Breakfast," complete with eggs and herbs brought fresh from his farm. Klein stands in his rumpled shorts, one eye on a huge flip chart checkered with a grid with thirty orders for eggs: scrambled, fried, omelette, herbs (his home-grown dill, for instance), cheese, whatever. Klein cooks them all in an open kitchen that he kept and had moved when the space was remodeled. Occasionally an early visitor in a suit, wandering in to make a presentation in the adjacent conference room, will be startled to see the chairman flipping omelettes — or washing the pots and pans by hand. (The senior vice president of marketing mans the dishtowel and dries.)

"To me, it's all about the senior person doing the cooking," Klein explains. "Most senior people don't give a damn. People who grew up in the business with me, I can understand some of them think it's weird. They grew up in a world where management was treated with the ultimate respect. But I like to cook. Why not be able to come to work and do what I like to do? I've always done it. I did it at the ad agency—I had Farm Day and I grilled chicken and baked twenty-five apple pies for the whole media department."

When it comes to real-world tasks other than cooking, however, Klein far prefers to operate online. "I've done everything on the Internet that there is to do," he says. "I've bought everything. I buy at online auctions—tin globes, an old tractor ad. I've played chess and cards. I had a cyberdate. She was a doctor; she was nice. I've hacked other people's sites. I've bought groceries. Bought tickets. If it's there I've done it. I even let somebody take over my screen at one site, just to test it out.

"And I don't shop for clothes," Klein says. "Everything I'm wearing I got online at J Crew.com."

To Klein, downtime is only another opportunity to do more. "I like to travel," he says. "I went to Egypt and took a boat down the Nile. I learned ancient Egyptian history in four and a half days. I like learning. To me, when you stop learning, you die."

A continuous learning curve is a key leitmotif to almost every Change Agent, illustrating the findings of the Gen Y2K Study.™ For most of the Change Agents I spoke to, it was a platform engraved in their experience since childhood. Steve Klein describes it: "This business is one hundred percent learning. You have to learn. My father would say, 'What did you learn today?' If you didn't learn something, life wasn't fun. Creating a new Web site is fun because you're learning what people want, what motivates people. It's a treasure trove of information and learning. It's not about the individual. When I look at what's happening on a Web site, I don't see individuals and what they did. It's groups, aggregates. To me, that's what's fascinating. I like knowing stuff. Data. Some of it is completely meaningless—I admit it—but to me, it's alive."

The dishes washed, Klein pads over to his desk, which is standard issue steel, out in the open, not even in a cubicle. He has a spectacular view of the Hudson River. On the desktop is a bunch of dahlias from the farm in red and yellow and a stack of empty cardboard egg cartons. He turns on his computer.

"Come on!" Steve Klein snaps his fingers at the computer screen impatiently. He is a guy in a virtual Maserati, revving his engine at a red light in cyberspace.

7 FULL ENGAGEMENT

What am I *not* obsessive about?" asks Renny Gleeson, running his fingers through his short, spiky hair as he wolfs down lunch at his desk overlooking the Statue of Liberty, Ellis Island, and New York Harbor. Tourists to New York City make beelines for this view, but Gleeson's desk faces *away* from it, into an institutional-green wall and a door. To him, the more scenic vista is his computer monitor, the link to the world of his market — teens. The iTurf offices in a high-rent, modern high-rise are worlds removed from those of the start-up it was just a few years ago. But you'd never know it from the receptionist in frayed jeans and platform sandals and the prominently displayed snapshot collage from a recent iTurf party, which looks reminiscent of a college bash, albeit with a hipper wardrobe. Gleeson himself was wearing his usual summer uniform — a baggy blue shirt over a T-shirt, jeans with rolled cuffs, and, on his feet, backless slides with rubber soles.

Renny Gleeson personifies the Change Agent in full engagement. These types might term it obsession, but it's more accurately total immersion of mind, soul, and body; a fusion of emotion, focus, and activity.

"Where are the boundaries? The new terrains?" asks Gleeson. "That's one reason why the Internet is so important to me. I don't want to be the guy who missed Woodstock. I feel like I'm part of a defining moment, and I'm creating the terrain."

This echoed the sentiments of many Change Agents I spoke to. "For a lot of us, it becomes an obsession," said Caryn Marooney. "You're never doing enough, you're never thinking enough."

"We are a fully engaged workforce," commented another Change Agent. "We are excited, totally into what we're doing. We are not going to be like our parents and work medium hard till we're in our fifties. None of us are going to get downsized — we're going to flame out."

The obsession usually starts early and continues into adulthood. Some were immersed in music by grammar school. Others literally lived for sports. Many were Mini-Moguls, trading the playground for running their own businesses by the time they were ten. One man happily admitted to an obsession with the band KISS. "I grew up with them since I was four years old," he said, proceeding to recite the basic principles of the KISS philosophy of existence. "And that is really where a lot of my thoughts come from. I love them, I am obsessed with them."

One Internet executive I interviewed, just three years into the field, spent his younger years directing his passion into athletics, training for the shot put three hours before school and three hours after. The athletic club he belonged to was a hundred miles from his house, and three times a week his father drove him there to train. As he grew up and became a businessman, the obsessiveness refocused on his work. Today he finds nothing unusual about putting in eighteen-hour days, six or seven days a week.

Some obsessions were darker. One young woman who co-founded an Internet company was a recovering alcoholic. Her job helped replace her alcoholic obsession. She observed, "You can avoid all kinds of stuff when working like this. We keep putting off life. . . ."

Carley Roney of TheKnot.com says, "I think it has to be a certain level of obsession. I have an obsession with my subject matter and an obsession with my industry and an obsession with our business. I can be sitting at home on a Sunday afternoon and see somebody walking by, and I wonder if that person is getting married. Everything you see, you see through the lens of your business."

To people like Renny Gleeson, the rationale that pays off the obsession is the landmark nature of the initiatives they are involved in. "There are ups and downs," he admits, "but nobody can argue that the Internet isn't a fundamental force in changing society. I think it's an important thing."

So important that it has become Gleeson's life, but not in the way that his parents related to their work. "My father and mother were both entrepreneurs," he says. "He was the president of the company, she was the vice president. They had eloped on Dad's motorcycle and all that stuff. They were nonconformists." Gleeson's father had been a systems analyst for the air force, a mathematician who had gotten into computers early on. Later the senior Gleesons became involved in alternative energy and moved to Maine, where they reconditioned old dams. They did things like living in summer rentals in winter and winter rentals in summer, to keep expenses down. When the family moved to a particularly poor area, Gleeson "made a conscious decision in fourth grade not to adopt the slang that would designate me as from that area." One of his first goals was to get out. He picked a place that was about as far out as you could get: outer space.

"I was interested in art, but I got involved in math because I wanted to be an astronaut," says Gleeson. "I got involved in computers quite young. We had the original Pong game when it came out. I got my first computer when I was twelve, what they called the 'Trash 80' model from Radio Shack. I got into the games." That might have been enough for some kids, but not young Gleeson. He didn't want just to play the games; he wanted to *create* them. "I found out there were books you could buy to learn Basic. The problem was, in those days, you had to turn off the computer at certain points, and if you didn't save it absolutely right, you'd lose everything. So I'd write thirty pages of code, only to have it all disappear." Then he'd start all over again.

Gleeson went to MIT, where he double-majored in physics and art/art history. "I couldn't do just one thing that wasn't math, I had to do two," he says. In a class called "Sleep, Dreams, and Health," he had the good fortune to sit next to a beautiful and brilliant eighteen-year-old. Since it was "a no-brainer class," Gleeson took his eye off the books. (Eight years later, that young woman became his wife.)

After graduation, Gleeson decided to be a painter and got his MFA at the University of Pennsylvania. He then bounced from a year in Paris, where he went to study art, but ended up in a job as a video editor at NBC, to Bear Sterns back in the United States, where he sold junk bonds. From there, he worked on games at a CD-ROM company. (He created a game on ancient Rome.) Next, he moved to the interactive arm of an advertising agency, where a client recruited him. To some, this might seem like a lot of bouncing about, but, to Gleeson, it makes perfect sense. "Where I am is a conflagration of a lot of skill sets — math, physics, history, creative. For instance, at the CD-ROM company, I utilized my history and art background as well as my experience in technology and math."

This interlacing of aptitudes and skills is a typical hallmark of a Change Agent. Think about how people used to get ahead. In the 1980s and 1990s, much career advancement stemmed from *networking*, which involved creating, maintaining, and tapping into a system of contacts who, when called upon, could help you get ahead. Mentors played a big part of this, a system that has been around since feudal times. For Change Agents in the new economy, this system has been replaced by one you could think of as *patchworking*, a self-contained, lateral application of a series of skill sets and aptitudes, in which the individual relies on himself or herself. Rather than linking with some outside contact or network, what propels the Change Agent's career is the deployment of these internal skills, in a fully engaged, totally focused manner, and it is one reason why job tenure is becoming increasingly truncated—no single job can hold the patchworker.

"I was doing something different five years ago, so why not five years from now?" Gleeson asks with a shrug. "It's important to have a skill set you can bring to the table—creative, conceptual, quantitative. If you'd asked me five years ago if I'd be sitting behind this desk today, I wouldn't have predicted it." Patchworking is perfectly in keeping with the multitasking ethic, and, if the work style of the Change Agent has one "killer application," this is it. The assumption is that you, and you alone, can make it happen, by a combination of sheer skill and will. With this mind-set, it is not a very big leap to feel that you can run a company today, not tomorrow—and do it.

"My whole background is in assuming that nothing is outside the realm of possibility," says Gleeson. "You throw yourself at a problem, and eventually it will be solved. Logic matters in this. The building blocks are important. I'm not as random as it seems—each piece does fit in with what I've done. But you don't go looking for it. I could take the Zen attitude—that for which you are prepared, does it come to you or do you come to it? For me, it's been a logical progression but, at the same time, totally *not*."

Full engagement means being 100 percent in the moment, and if the moment is the job—and not necessarily a career-related job—the job *becomes* the moment. Or as long as it takes. "I'm obsessive about everything," admits Gleeson. "Things I'm working in, it's a hundred percent. If I'm doing it, it's full bore. When I was painting, it was twenty-four hours a day, working with polymers and resins that were the most toxic of their kind. When I was at Bear Sterns, that was all I did, all I talked about. I got in there at 7 A.M. when the markets didn't open until 9, just so I could be there. At CyberSites, another place I worked, which was a start-up, I was there twenty-four hours a day. And working on a start-up means you get in and stay until whatever you're working on is done, or you're so exhausted you have to leave. It wasn't uncommon for me to leave at 1:30 A.M., including weekends. When I started at CyberSites, my wife—then my fiancée—wasn't in the city, so I would work from the time I'd see her until the next time I saw her again. She eventually worked in a similar environment, for a network of sites, so she understands and in fact she is the same way."

But where does work start and life begin? "The problem is, work can go infinitely. You're never gonna be done. On a Web site, technically, there's no end. Your audience is on there twenty-four hours a day. One of our sites has chat room monitors here till 3 A.M.

"I have an addictive personality," admits Gleeson. "I tend to be obsessional about things in general. To me, to do an all-nighter to do something is not a big thing. I have to adjust my expectations when I'm working with teams, because I know other people have personal lives."

What about personal life? In spite of his long-term, committed relationship, Gleeson put much of it on hold until they got married two years ago. But he's obsessive about his personal life as well, he says. "I order books, electricity, tickets, food, music, everything online. We comparison-shop online. For vacation, Pam and I wanted to disengage, to get outside. We went to Wyoming to relax. Monday was the six-hour kayak trip. Tuesday was the twenty-two-mile hike. Wednesday was the eight-hour rock-climb—my first rappel backward off an eighty-foot cliff. It helps put things in perspective. I need to work on what I should manageably obsess on." *Manageable obsession.* Gleeson does not see the irony in this. He sees the reality.

Then there was the cat.

The Gleesons are thinking about having a family. Realizing that it is not desirable to work 24/7 if there is a child at home, the couple decided to put their little toes in the water and try out the concept of having a warm-bodied third-party presence in their lives that required care. "We borrowed a cat," says Gleeson. "She happened to be very old, and one day she fell over. We didn't know if she'd still be all right when we got home, and we were both very worried. We thought about it all day, then we both rushed home early and ran in and grabbed the cat and kissed it. I guess that's what it'll be like when we have kids."

"I was very impressed." Pam Lloyd, Gleeson's wife, laughed about the cat incident. "Renny actually called me and said he was thinking of something else besides work!"

I visited Lloyd at the Web company where she worked, Urban Box Office. Three months later, this company would abruptly implode, but, at the moment, it was an epicenter of the urban-cool ethic. A conglomeration of ten Web sites, the place seemed as if an asteroid populated almost entirely by Hip Hoppers had crashed to Earth on the site of the midtown New York premises. Shaved heads, funky hair, stiletto boots, cargo pants, Hawaiian shirts, combat shorts, and jeans jackets were the norm as we squeezed down two floors of aisles crowded with desks and boxes so densely stacked it seemed impossible not to trip. The halls were shiny Plexi, the mind-set urban funk. The sites within the network ranged from one focused entirely on hairstyles to sites on Latin culture and fashion commerce, and one devoted to discovering new musical artists online.

"We're on the verge of our fourth round of funding, so it's a tense time," Lloyd had explained. She actually looked more Preppie than Homie, as if she were a refugee from Martha Stewart, where, in fact, she had previously worked.

Like her husband, Pam Lloyd is a Type R—for Renaissance. She majored in archaeology at Yale, then moved to New York and worked two years at *Art Forum* magazine. From there, she segued to an Italian newsweekly, where she worked as an editor and photo editor. She cofounded a magazine called *Outdoor Gear*, then applied to Wharton business school, which she attended from 1995 to 1997. "My intent was to stay in the media," she said. "But at the same time, the Internet was starting as a media. I did not fit the mold at Wharton. I think they considered me an 'interesting student,' like a test case. I was wearing leather pants to finance class, I didn't come from Wall Street. But there are lots of people like me in business now. I think things have changed in a very short time."

When Lloyd graduated from Wharton in 1997, there were not many jobs in the Internet. She was editorial business manager of *Martha Stewart Living* for two and a half years. "I did the numbers for the IPO," she says. "Then, by '98, the Internet world was exploding, and Martha got into it."

Lloyed found herself working with a small group who were

launching Martha's Flowers Online. "That took 80 percent of my time for a year, and I learned the perishable commerce business," she said. It was an experience of total immersion. "I learned things like flying things overnight from Holland, warehousing. The roses were picked in Bogotá on Wednesday and in your home on Friday. I worked with the Web designer, I learned about how to represent the shades of the colors of the flowers online, and then selling through the editorial content to the consumer. Actually, not just selling but educating through the pictures and the how-to descriptions. I learned about flower qualities, that, no, there aren't just two kinds of roses — and how to sell them online. It was amazing. It was a complex and enormously challenging business, an e-commerce model to get feet wet in, and I was up to my eyeballs."

Lloyd felt she was a kind of a pioneer. "At that point, the Internet wasn't perceived as all that friendly. The strength of Martha Stewart was that it brought softness and beauty to the medium — which was rare on the Internet. And that it was so rich in information. That's what the Internet is all about. To me, it was enormously exciting and three-dimensional. Since this whole area was not only new to the company but new to me, it meant activating most of your brain.

"There was no job description. It wasn't like you woke up and said, 'These are the twenty things I'm going to do today.' There could be three hundred, and you'd never done any of them before. It was refreshing. Of course, there was enormous pressure. I was yelled at all the time, but it was exciting and new, and either the business didn't exist, or you were to be involved at that depth. It was like a start-up within a larger start-up.

"I got to thinking about the Internet as a media, and at that moment, I transformed myself from Magazine Girl to Web Girl. There were enormous differences. The Internet is a visual medium, Web based, with data collection and expressing a point of view from a 'page.' We call screens pages on the Web, and that's no coincidence. TV screens aren't referred to as pages because it's a false belief that they represent a deep kind of thinking." Lloyd gingerly massaged her hand. She had carpal tunnel syndrome on her right index finger from clicking the mouse.

Lloyd's job at Martha Stewart, on the surface a diametrical opposition, was in fact the ideal ramp-up for Urban Box Office. Lloyd's description of her transition from the perfectly ordered world of "That's a Good Thing" to the Hip-Hop craziness of her next job illustrates the critical role of Engagement, with a capital E, to the Change Agent. At first, Lloyd had felt stimulated by the Martha Stewart environment. But, literally as soon as she had absorbed it, mastered it, and lost the feeling of challenge, she felt a letdown and the stirrings to move on.

"We started in an 8,000-square-foot loft with cement floors, warehouse windows, and just a bunch of desks, and it was like a scene from *Blade Runner*," said Lloyd, still excited by the memory. "People dressed like messengers. I had three cell phones on my desk, because we didn't even have phone lines. It was like working in that movie *Boiler Room*. There was one actual phone for every seven to ten people, and when it rang, everybody would just dive for it because whoever got there first got the call. It was quite a scene — everyone constantly Black-Berrying each other, just to find the meeting, our poor assistants screaming 'Pam! Line One!' all day. There were people on scooters and RollerBlades zooming through the office — and hundreds of amazing-looking people scooting around on their roller chairs, with eighteen electronic devices: their beeper, three or four cell phones, a BlackBerry . . . we'd all sit down for a meeting and everyone was beeping and clicking and buzzing the whole time. The first time I saw it, I walked in, took a look around, and thought, 'I've got to work here!' "

Lloyd had no door, no assistant, no office, no phone, no perks.

"This coming from Martha Stewart, where I had a gorgeous corner office and wore my nice Prada shoes to work! But that doesn't make it important, or interesting, or exciting. It's about the quality of work, the quality of people you work with, and being rewarded. You can give me air conditioning or twelve phone lines, but at the end of the day, if it's impersonal or hierarchical, it's not worth it. I say, if you complain about the phones, go back and work for Disney or something. I'm not saying you don't need creature comforts — I'm not going to work in an alley! I know this isn't a pretty office, but no one cares. At Martha Stewart, I loved walking in and there were tulips in the hall, but that doesn't mean everyone was happy.

"Here there is no doubt that this world is more intense. At the magazine, I put in time, but here the hours are longer, the complexity is by the power of three. People's roles are less defined so their roles cover more landmass. That's positive. If you're in marketing, you're in the whole world of it from trafficking to Internet research to data collection. Even if you're twenty-three, your responsibilities are a page long. Compare that to if you're an assistant at Condé Nast — you do three things and you're stressed out and it takes you all day. Here it's not ever dependent on your experience. People are younger and have less experience and are doing it all. A lot of mistakes are made, but it's about street smarts. Even in 1990, I had my Yale degree and no one cared. I was still considered a 'little thing.'

"But here we have a twenty-two-year-old head of online guerilla marketing and he's one of the most important people. I don't mean to focus on age, but at the end of the day, whether you're twenty-eight or thirty-eight, the company doesn't consider it a risk. They're looking for street smarts, passion, excitement, and the start-up mentality. There's structure, but a sense of accessibility, openness, and mutual respect up and down the ladder because there is not a rigid hierarchy."

To Lloyd, the key is that she feels like she is part of something that matters. "I think there's empowerment," she said. "It's cutting-edge, going into the urban market, talking about the digital divide, and to serve an audience starving for this particular content and be the only one delivering it is great." She likened it to the paradigm shift in another great frontier—travel. "Going to India used to be the most exotic thing. Now everyone is jaded. We may not be going to the moon or curing cancer, but there's an enormous amount of pioneering going on. No one else has an office like this, résumés like this. On weekends, I sit back and think, 'God, this is incredible.' "

Like Steve Klein and like her husband, Renny Gleeson, Pam Lloyd feels that she is not just doing a job, she is making an indelible mark. "I know that in twenty years, I will look back and say I did something important."

This sense of landmarking, setting a personal stake in the ground, is a key reason why Change Agents are not only willing but driven to make the effort it takes to be fully engaged. Nobody but a drone would allow their lives to be absorbed, for the lines between work style and lifestyle to be so blurred as to be nonexistent, if they thought they were simply to be a cog in the wheel of commerce.

Or would they? Plenty of us grew up with working parents who spent so much time on the job, we barely saw them. My own father, a steel salesman, worked all day, came home at 6:30 at night for dinner with the family, then frequently left the minute we put our forks down to go back out to entertain clients. "The guy from Fisher Body (or wherever) is in town," he'd say as he headed back to the garage, and I knew I wouldn't hear the garage door again till almost midnight. But I know for a fact that he was not passionate about his job. Even though he headed his own company, it was just that—a job. He was a self-employed cog, but a cog nonetheless, and remained so until the day he retired. He had no illusions of a role in the bigger scheme. The golf course—now that was something he could get passionate about.

Not so in the Internet space. These people are fully engaged. Their work ethic includes a fusion of emotion, passion, and commitment—and a strong sense of adventure and destiny that go beyond the clock, the company, and even the paycheck. "At this point," said Pam Lloyd, "what's driving me is the excitement of being in the forefront. I've always been obsessed with popular culture, and this is just where it's at." The tales of lucrative stock options involved in Internet start-ups do not stir her. "It's not about the stock options. I know very few people in the industry who have actually made it big time. The super big guys, but nobody else. This isn't like the gold rush, it's like going West. Wild and woolly."

Like many in the new economy, although Lloyd's career path has not been a straight line, she does not feel this makes her any less purposeful. "My lifestyle may have changed, but I think I would have taken the departures I have taken no matter what I did," she says. "Renny and I have known each other since we were eighteen. I think that says something."

Working in the Internet world has, however, impacted the way Lloyd lives, and she finds her life increasingly oozing into the Internet space. "Our actual lifestyle has shifted," she admits. "I spend ten hours a day on e-mail, but I still run around the rest of the time. I go to meetings, go through materials. I love going to the store. When you work on the Internet, shopping takes you out into the real world. I like cooking—although Renny is a Power Bar kind of guy. I don't think he needs food. Outside of work, I'm a normal Internet user. I go online for news, gossip, I like weirdo sites, gaming. I just bought plates online.

"We socialize with people from the office—parties, dinners, bars. The people we work with are interesting—the environment attracts different kinds of people. There's a guy in my marketing group who's a Hip-Hop DJ and an Indian sheik. I love that. That's the whole deal. So many of our friends are in this life-style — although my closest friends aren't. One is a writer who works out of her home." Lloyd paused, searching for an example of normalcy that has become alien to her. "She makes breakfast."

Lloyd did not see her lifestyle as a sacrifice, perhaps because her work and life are so blended. "My personal priorities are very high and getting higher," she said. But there is one nagging thought. "Kids do throw in a bender." After mulling this over for a minute, she brightened. "But there's a woman here who had a baby and was back in two weeks, and she's happy. Still, I know I'd want to be with that little baby. Renny and I just look at each other — here we are, two smart people. Can't we think of a so-lution?"

That solution will be increasingly important to anyone living in the Internet space. The obsessive, 24/7 mentality that was born of limited resources and a beat-the-clock mission may have been a required mind-set to move the needle to where it is today. But it has left some of the foot soldiers emotionally stranded in cy-berspace.

Doug Hall, founder and chief executive officer of Richard Saunders International, an executive consulting, research, and new product development organization that has worked with hundreds of companies, from Pepsi to Disney to AT&T, is an expert on creativity, productivity, and the genesis of new ideas. "There's been a lot written about the fine line between genius and madness," he says, and then asks, "Do you need that level of madness in order to shake yourself loose from all the rest of the things that may stand in the way of the process?"

Maybe it's madness, but maybe it's also a passion, an emotion that is inflamed by the psychic rewards of work. This is a dy-namic that had a parallel in the women's movement. Today the bulk of the new economy workforce have never worked in any other environment. In the freshman workforce scenario twenty years ago, the first Update: Women Survey revealed that the majority of women moving into the workforce said that they would continue to work at their jobs even without pay, because their self-esteem was so positively impacted. I just pulled out the questionnaires from that survey to review them. Although the respondents were required only to check boxes, the margins of the pages were covered with handwritten notes with respondents tending to pour their hearts out about their passion for their work. The executive women were the poster girls for this movement, but they were few and far between at that time, and the vast majority who were expressing this extreme positive feedback had jobs like school bus driver, beautician, administrator, even toothpaste tube filler. Fast forward to today. Add an incredibly aspirational social aura and the still fresh opportunities to cash into the two-comma salary club, situations unimaginable by the women of twenty years ago, a large percentage of whom were swimming against the status quo and actually derided by their peers and their mates, certainly few of whom ever expected to see even six-figure incomes. The madness starts to make sense. Or at least you can see where it's coming from.

"It is obsessive-compulsive behavior," says Doug Hall. "This is a raw addiction. It's about limitless clicks. You never can get to the end."

For Peter Katz, veteran of three Silicon Valley ventures, it's all about passion. "Young entrepreneurial types like their lifestyle. They feel passion for what they do. That's why they do it. One of the reasons I've been with as many companies as I have is that they've all fueled a passion in me, not because I felt I want to make millions out of it. I hope to make a good living— but I'm doing it because I totally enjoy what I'm doing."

8 LIFE MEETS WORK

Once upon a time, there was work and there was life, and rarely the twain met. If you didn't leave your work at the office, you took it home in a briefcase. Work was almost a physical thing, a creature, an entity—sometimes a monster you wouldn't want intruding on your *life*. The briefcase would thump onto the table in the hall by the front door. There it would sit, big, ugly, and intrusive. An interloper.

"My father, who was an art director, used to come home with these big packages," recalls Donny Deutsch, sketching out a huge, unwieldy shape with his hands. And there was an attitude about work that really didn't jibe with the pleasantries of the rest of your life. "When my father talked about tackling a challenge at work, he'd say"—Deutsch grimaces—" 'We've got to break the back of this thing.' That was the way people thought about work."

Work was . . . well, *work*. Putting hours in the work bank was like doing time or a prison sentence. Like hard time in the big house, your career status was measured in the years you'd been at a company: one to five; three to ten; a lifer. All jobs were relatively interchangeable. Who ever heard of the guy next door going off in the morning to a sexy job, unless you lived next door to, say, Steve McQueen? There was little charisma to be had about the office, or any form of work. Everybody pretty much looked alike, sounded alike, worked alike. There were few business media icons outside of the scions of inherited family fortunes. No one sector of the economy was a particularly provocative place to be. Rather than providing a venue to quick success, work was a structure that was fixed on keeping the young entrant on a long and predictable path, along with hordes of his or her peers.

As Deutsch puts it, "Other than for the very, very top captains of industry, work was not defining."

Of course, work still is *work*. But the edges have blurred, as life and work mutually seep across each other's boundaries. Technology has created the virtual briefcase, allowing work to be accessible almost anywhere, any time. Your work can be whenever and wherever you log on. When I had my own business, working on the phone, fax, and Web from my home office, some days were so busy, I never had time to get dressed. My partners had times like these too. We called them "nightgown days." (We were all women.) Working in your nightgown—a concept once possible only for ladies of the night. But my house lacked a video conference room, so who knew? You could send an e-mail stark naked, for that matter, and not attract any attention, as long as you weren't standing in the street.

This was first-stage boundary-blurring, the creation of a new way of working and adapting it to your lifestyle. Then there's stage two, where work and life are one, the emphasis flips, and it's a work style. *Fast Company* magazine, for instance, calls itself a "workstyle magazine." Senior writer Ron Lieber says, "One of the things we've figured out at *Fast Company* is that trying to draw a line in the sand between what is work and what is life, or lifestyle, or after work, is not possible anymore. There aren't those sorts of clear distinctions anymore. *Fast Company* and the Web have sort of grown up together. We consider ourselves to be a magazine about work, and how work has certainly been greatly impacted by the Web. It's probably had more impact than anything in the past four or five years. It's hard to avoid talking about it, thinking about it."

During our conversation, Lieber pointed out that, at that time, both of us were at our respective homes, yet both of us were working. "How you can draw a line and say that one place and one thing and one way of thinking and being in the world is work, and then there's a whole other group of things that's not work is sort of foolish."

In Europe, one of the wrecking balls of the digital divide is a chain of cafés called the Internet Exchange, where, in countries such as England and France, the cost of a personal computer is often prohibitive, anyone can come in off the street, get a cup of coffee or tea, and plop themselves down in front of one of the dozens of computers that are set up in a casual, almost homey environment. There they can log onto the Internet Exchange's proprietary portal and become part of an online community even if they do not own a computer. Robert Proctor, the company's founder, understands the need to connect because he feels it himself. "Everyone works differently," he says, "but if the working environment wasn't part of my social environment, then I couldn't do it."

He has always been a cubeaphobic. "Those poor guys who go to work and sit in those boxed-off cubicles and then go home — ugh! I just need to interact with people. I love coming up with ideas, and I am working with people who think the same way. When we get together and we have a few beers, the interaction and the ideas that come out are just great. It's exciting stuff."

The work/social connection is so important to Proctor that when he hires senior managers to join his 400 employees, a key concern is social fit. "I guess I know that any of them can do the job, that they have the skills. But a huge portion is—are they going to fit into this company? It is just such a manic environment that it is important. You have people who are coming in, many of them join based on my personality or the senior management's. They will be working below market rate to do sixty-five hours a week, to come in Saturdays and Sundays. That is a huge factor. So there are a lot of very funny, very smart people in this office."

Proctor feels the Internet business environment itself is obliterating social strata between the old and new economies. "I think that chucking those two sets of people together is really interesting," he says, noting that the Internet Exchange, because of the nature of its business, melds both virtual virtuosos and traditional forty-year real estate veterans. "To see our [seasoned] property guy interacting with an eighteen-year-old Web developer—and at the end of the day, they are both trying to achieve exactly the same thing for the company."

At many New Economy companies, staffers bring dogs to work, and it is not uncommon to see baby gates on offices for the dogs. One dot com founder says, "We work hard and we ask people to work hard, so we want to make the work space as accommodating as possible. One of the things is they can bring their dog to work. People from old economy companies ask me, 'Aren't you concerned about this?' But I can't imagine not being able to even have a dog just because you work. If people work a twelve-hour day and if they take ten minutes to take the dog for a bathroom break, it's a good thing. Everyone has a specific set of things to get done, and if they get it done, they get it done. If they spend three hours surfing online, then they'll work three hours longer. We don't anally watch people come and go."

A vice president of a dot com company that is ramping up to go public put it this way: "You see the people who are there till nine at night taking a break at around five, and what do you see? They are gathered around the obligatory foosball table or Ping Pong table — and believe me, my company does have one. They cut out little faces and tape them to the foosball characters and they have our Web sites around the table and there is a whole league they have established. What this is is an outlet for stress but also a building of camaraderie. Never before has an industry been so dependent on getting people to adopt your ideas — or to all adopt the same idea — whether it be the mission of the company or a mission of a division — so that everybody is working toward a common goal."

In such environments, socioeconomic lines blur. In a country where class lines are drawn in indelible ink, the Internet Exchange, where Lord Astor's son is the media director, has thrown together offspring of the titled, people who left school at fourteen, and highly educated brain-trust types. "It is a different mind-set," says Proctor. "It has nothing to do with a demographic. Who cares? What does it matter?"

Donny Deutsch has a view that "very often, businesses that are built around creations and creating something are models for convergence, because creativity doesn't stop. You know if you trade money, that stops when you go home. But when you are creating and birthing things, that happens around the clock whether you're doing it yourself or with other people. With this new economy and all the things involved, yes, work is life and life is work. That's certainly obvious, because of the technology itself which allows for it. But even more so because work and a work endeavor and the creation of these new businesses and economies have a certain cachet that work never had before. Other than the early business stars, the Carnegies, the Mellons, the Fords, for the next forty or fifty years after that, you didn't have these kinds of icons of business, with the exceptions of a few business leaders, like Ted Turner. But with the emerging technology, you have dozens and dozens — from the Steve Cases to the Bezos to those people we see on the covers of magazines every day of the week, or so it seems. So work and the workplace and working became much more of a definer of where you stand in the world, where you were, a good thing, a fun thing. It is who you are and what you do and how much money you make and how effective you are — much more a part of our overall system of where you stand in the world."

Suddenly work is aspirational. And sexy.

"Today's business leaders are the rock stars of this new generation," Deutsch states. And he should know. A staple of his industry trade publications and in the business press, Deutsch found himself migrating into the glossies alongside the likes of Puffy Combs, Russell Simmons, and Denzel Washington. His engagement was a lead item in the *New York Post* "Page Six" gossip column. A business rock star? As Deutsch sees it, "What a rock star has is the ultimate aspirational perfect lifestyle — there is tons of money, you are in the inner social circles, you love what you do, there is adulation from those around you. So, no, a great young business leader today does not walk into an arena where twenty thousand people are screaming for them and young girls are throwing their bras at them. It is much more subtle than that."

Like the Deutsch/Russell Simmons et al. connection?

Deutsch can't suppress a grin. But, looking out through the glass walls of his perfectly hip 130,000-square-foot office space in New York City in a crisp pink cotton shirt and black denim jeans, he is certainly an example of some sort of business star power. Still, the irony doesn't escape him. "I mean, what is goofier than that? It is hysterical. But there it is—I can now call and get into any restaurant I want. I hate it when I refer to myself, but that is an example of what the media does. So, not myself, but the really visible business people today are really the ultimate aspiration for a lot of people. It would be a fascinating poll on the Internet—to ask young people who would you rather be, the guy who is head of Pearl Jam or Jeff Bezos, or pick your similar person. You know, you couldn't even play that game twenty years ago, because frankly, you couldn't serve up the business name."

Working in the new economy has provided inner rewards that add to the convergence factor. In spite of sixty-hour workweeks, Abbi Gosling, of Agile Industries, finds her work "incredibly relaxing." According to Gosling, "For fun, my husband and I help with each other's companies. It's a very seductive medium."

The Internet allows you to occupy personal and professional worlds simultaneously. "It has an impact on socializing and the way people make plans," says Esther Drill, of gURL.com. "With the way people communicate with each other. You feel more connected on a regular basis. People are instant messaging each other and they feel like they're in the same place, even if you are in New York and the friend is in Brazil."

And you have more control over your environment. "It leaches over into weekends," she admits. "But we hang out with each other and we'd all rather do business with people we like," says Gosling. "When it's your own company, you can fire the clients you don't like.

"For me," says Gosling, "there is very little distinction between what I consider work and what I consider life. I get up and I go to work, but that's just a representation of the physical place I'm in. I talk about work all the time. This is the most fascinating and the hardest thing—and the most compelling and most satisfying. It feels like having a child, but without the deep emotion. That's part of the impetus for me."

Another impetus may be the fact that the Internet and your coworkers may be the only accessible social outlets when you are working New Economy hours. These people are not nine-to-fivers. They are 24/7ers. "I work sixty hours a week on a good week, a hundred on a bad week," says Elizabeth Talerman of Agile Industries. These kinds of hours have become standard for a start-up, where the stereotypical image of the loft space worker who is up all night and goes home only to shower and change clothes began. This media-driven, romanticized image has, in turn, had a ripple effect and sparked a new kind of work ethic that has spilled over into the old economy. When you don't go home for days at a time, you actually need concierge service. And if concierge service keeps you in the office longer, it has value on both sides.

One of the first things I noticed when I joined an investment bank was the hive environment—a lot of people were practically living in their offices due to the intensity of the hours. Dry cleaning hung on cubicles. Young people carried bundles of laundry down the hall, as if it were a dorm. (There was a dry cleaner/laundry on the premises.) There were also check-cashing services, a manicurist and beauty salon, a barber, and, across the street, a company-related medical facility. Once I broke the heel off a shoe. That's when I learned there was a shoe repair on the premises. People ate breakfast at the twenty-four-hour cafeteria, or ferried entire meals up the elevators to their desks in Styrofoam containers. It was not uncommon for young associates and analysts to pull all-nighters, then shower in the company gym in the basement and go straight back to their desks. Many times, when my group added new members, we had to send the keyboards from the former occupants of newly assigned offices back to technology services because they were encrusted with what appeared to be the moldy remnants of an all-you-can-eat buffet. "Chili," diagnosed one tech guy with a shrug as he disconnected yet another keyboard–turned–science project. He tucked the offensive piece of plastic under his arm to take it away for a hose-down. "These people live in their computers. You can't believe what we find in these things."

TheKnot's Carley Roney, for one, would believe. "For a long time, it was totally normal to go home at midnight and go straight to sleep. To eat dinner in the office every single solitary night for a year."

The heat is on, but it is not driving many people out of the kitchen. According to the Gen Y2K study, two-thirds of men and women in their twenties and thirties said that even if there was something else they wanted to do, they would not leave work. One reason may be that, due to the Internet, they can now do many things at work that, in previous years, would have required leaving the premises, whether that was ordering a movie or a pair of shoes. And half of all men and women in their twenties said that they expected to work from home at some point in their career.

There are, however, warning signs on the horizon. Actually, the evidence is stronger than mere signs. There are clear indicators that the wired world as a social whirlpool is in danger of pulling some of the younger participants under. Just as the Internet serves as a social outlet for adults, it provides the same platform for teens. In the Gen Y2K study,[TM] Gen Y teens age sixteen to nineteen said that computers are the major way they connect with others. Six in ten girls as well as boys agreed that the primary way they connected was online. The same young people who said this, however, had a discomforting but logical correlation — they were also less likely than other kids to feel they had a good relationship with another person. Computers can be the bridge to stave off the loneliness and sense of separateness that is normal at this stage of life: Connect with a click. And perhaps they are part of the reason it can become difficult to move beyond the click.

It's always encouraging and tempting, especially for young people, to think that there is a new way to make friends or tap into a social flow. But a closer examination of the Gen Y teens in the Gen Y2K Study™ who used computers as their major social outlet revealed that they are more likely to be stressed, overscheduled, struggle with depression, and feel pushed too far. These are the kids who say they feel they are on the brink of explosion. To them, the computer goes beyond being a hook-up mechanism to becoming a valve to let off steam, a virtual way to vent. While serving the important function of keeping teens from feeling isolated, the computer also paradoxically *keeps* these kids isolated and contributes to them bottling up their emotions to the point where almost half of these teens say they feel pushed to the limit.

"Our research has shown, in study after study, that kids who feel a sense of belonging feel healthy," says Richard Saunders International's Doug Hall. "Belonging is critical. We ran five separate studies, and the very first factor that came up each time was belonging. Kids are becoming so addicted to these machines because that's where their sense of belonging is. But they have left the land of the living. Their only sense of belonging is on the computer. They are part of a group, but there is no sense of responsibility for being part of that group. Online, everybody gets heard equally. Nobody can scream louder. Kids are empowered because they're connected, and what you've got is a cybergang. They find the equivalent of a street gang online. But when you're dealing face to face, it's dysfunctional."

Of course, the Internet is far from the only contributing factor in this scenario, but it is one to be reckoned with as families make choices in raising children. Beyond the family, we need to consider these issues and their impact as young people move into the mainstream of society. Those already there are struggling to come to grips with the world they have created.

"We've created a network of refugees of the Internet," says Richard Kirshenbaum, co-chairman of kirshenbaum bond & partners, a creatively driven advertising agency that has an Internet subsidiary, dotglu. Kirshenbaum, along with his partner, Jon Bond, has observed changes in how people communicate. "There is less time in business, things are moving faster, and then what you get are a group of weary people who can actually concentrate on fewer and fewer things," says Kirshenbaum. "I can communicate with four hundred people with the click of a button, yet at the same time, I see these people walking the streets looking blank, like misplaced refugees with no place to go."

Today the Change Agents struggle to find the balance and proportion that any of us seek in our lives—but their lives make their task even tougher. They find themselves looking at the analog world as if through a pane of glass, their noses pressed up against it somewhat nostalgically. And they take steps to reach back into that world, to stay connected in the most everyday of ways, perhaps because when you exist in a rarefied atmosphere, the mundane and everyday are the bridge to reality.

For example, Carley Roney purposefully takes the subway to work, even though it is less convenient. "Because if you live in this little track of taking your car to the job and you work with all these young, smart people, then you just sort of lose track of what the complexity of the world really is," she says. "And riding the subway, hearing all these different languages, seeing these different relationships—I like that experience. It makes me remember."

Reality—the new nostalgia.

Abbi Gosling makes quilts, cooks, and, as she puts it, loves "to do the whole domestic thing."

Steve Klein puts up vegetables and rides a bike everywhere.

Richard Kirshenbaum has observed this scenario. "People are so into the earth and the best that it yields. When you're dealing with technology, in a certain sense, there's a dehumanizing factor to it. If you're in front of a screen every day, or you're raising money, or analyzing data—whatever you're doing, I think that at the end of the day you want to do the opposite. You want to, so to speak, get your hands dirty. So on one level, you hear about people having an interest in a vineyard in Sonoma, and they want to trek through the vineyard, or everyone has a wine cellar. Or they have a personal sommelier at their party and make the connection that way, which people are actually doing. But because of the speed and pace of life and business, the new luxury is macaroni and cheese. When it comes to what is considered luxury, it's having the time to sit in bed and watch a cheesy movie on TV and have macaroni and cheese. On the other hand, there's a sense also of, who can go on the most daring white-water river rafting trip, or who can take the most exotic trip to Asia that requires bringing the most medication? It's 'Well, I had a medicine chest that they injected me with when I went to India.'

"There's less touch in the world of the Internet, and I think that's one reason why places like Starbucks are successful now," says Steve Klein. "They serve a basic need to touch human beings."

You can actually hear the difference. Compared to traditional offices, one of the first things you notice when you walk in the door of most Internet-related offices is how quiet they are. Sometimes all you hear are the sounds of muffled clicking, like thousands of crickets in the yard on a hot summer night. "Well, maybe once in a while you might hear a beep from an instant message," allows Steve Klein. "But a wired company is a quiet operation, because all the communication is done electronically." As a result, Klein thinks, simple connections like shopping, cooking, or just walking around take on a heightened level of importance. The simplest expedition is savored, and if you crave human proximity, there's always a table at Starbucks.

Perhaps people who are operating on a level of high engagement in their work find solace in the simple, the uncontrived, and the most basic of human connections, which have nothing in common with technology and everything in common with respite from the complexities of a crowded mind: observing the world from a bicycle or subway; tasting the juice of a sun-ripened cherry; putting your baby to bed. Yet the very nature of a work ethic that crowds the edges of their lives can make these seemingly simple and abundant pleasures elusive. Younger people immersed in the new economy would be the most susceptible, but, because of their age and relative life inexperience, they are less able to achieve the balance necessary to integrate these respites on an ongoing basis. There is talk of balance, but the reality has been all or nothing—total work or total escape; the eighteen-hour workday or the trek through Tibet.

For some of those immersed in the Internet space, the answer is an attempt at proactively protecting their personal spaces, which is not always effective—a clear downside of merging life and work. When these aspects of your life are blended, creating lines of demarcation can be rather like trying to drawing a line on water.

Carley Roney and her husband and business partner David Liu, for example, resolved to partition off a safe harbor in their personal life when they became parents. They began with an edict that they would not have a computer at home. "When we were at work, we were going to stay at work, and then when we would go home it would be pure home time. There would be no invasion of work," says Liu. The result, however, backfired: "Unfortunately, what it wound up doing for me was that I was spending most of my time at work."

So they broke down, got laptops, and brought them home. "You often find me working with the laptop downstairs in the dark, so I don't wake up my husband or daughter," says Roney, noting that they have a very open floor plan.

Prioritizing comes easily for no parent, and Roney and Liu are no exception. "It is by no means easy to be a mother and an entrepreneur," Roney says with a sigh of resignation. "I think that is one of the hardest things. I mean, your child will always come first, but you even hate yourself for the fact that anything comes close. You sort of sit there and think — at six o'clock at night I always think, oh, I should go home. But then I think, if I stayed another hour, I could go deal with this and talk about that. And I can't. There is no perfect balance between the two. It is a constant struggle. Because you really have to care about your business, but I'm also really not into having someone else put my daughter to bed every night either. That doesn't sit right for me. I would much rather go home, put her to bed, then stay up till 2:00 A.M. working on my laptop. I always wanted to have both, and it took me a long time to realize that you can have both, but you can't have both perfectly. You know, there is no having it all. You are going to give up something. Growing this business and being a mother taught me about how to focus on things that are really important. I wanted everything to be perfect and realized it could only be good most of the time. And that is hard for someone who has mainly built her life around doing the best that is humanly possible."

"Now it is about trying to come up with a little bit more of a balance," says Liu.

A footnote: For my interview with Liu, I had to go back to his office twice in the same day. The first time he did not arrive and the meeting was canceled; the second time, that same afternoon, he was forty minutes late. He apologized profusely, but, Liu said, he had a very good reason. He had been stuck at his house, having DHL lines installed so he could have high-speed Internet access from home.

9 FASHION FORWARD

Fashion is an evolving reflection of culture, and it is interesting that, as often as it seems to change, the really major changes—as opposed to the trends—have been inspired not by the industry but by socioeconomic shifts. The designers, in turn, interpret these shifts. Today the Internet—as opposed to Paris designers—is the key fashion influence of our times. And, unusual in a fashion trend for at least a century, men started the trend. In fact, they are more impacted by it than women.

The necktie, a staple of the nonagrarian male wardrobe since the eighteenth century, evolved from a lacy bib worn by men over their collars to associate themselves with prestige and wealth. Ties have been not just a staple but a ritual of male dressing. Anne Hollander, a fashion historian, was quoted in the *New York Times*: "Ever since the Middle Ages, powerful men of the West have covered their throats." As anyone who owns a dog or cat can tell you, showing your throat is a basic sign of vulnerability in animals.

Fast Company's George Anders says, "You no longer have this nineteenth-century British dress code where gentlemen of letters were expected to wear clothes that could not be worn to plow a field, just to say, 'I am not a farmhand.' We are beyond that now. You can wear clothes that are comfortable and you no longer need to have people wear neckties just because neckties are a way of saying 'I sit at a desk all day.' "

When the five-day-a-week dress casual mode rolled across the country from Silicon Valley to Wall Street, the pressure was on the men, who suddenly found themselves tieless. There was a slight undercurrent of discomfort, even panic at the thought of the loss of their uniform. What surefire accessory was a guy to reach for when fumbling through his closet in those predawn hours?

For the past hundred years or so, in order to give a powerful impression in business, a man needed that buttoned-collar shirt and knotted tie, the pattern of which often communicated a silent message, such as his club or former school affiliation. It was instant branding. Even the knot of the tie carried a message. The Duke of Windsor, a fashion icon in his era, started a mini-trend with the Windsor knot, which at the time was radical, but was quickly copied by those aspiring to be upper class. In the 1980s, when women moved into the workforce, they mimicked men, with crisp little shirts and floppy silk bow ties at the neck. However, the empowerment of the Internet has spread to fashion, because it is a medium in which information and its holder is equated with power.

"When you've been to information mecca, you no longer need to wear the veil," says Dr. David B. Givens, director of the Center for Nonverbal Studies in Spokane, Washington.

Tie sales plummeted, and today, more than 70 percent are

sold at a discount; meanwhile, sales of men's casual wear, such as polo shirts and khaki pants, jumped as much as 300 percent, even as prices of these items are climbing. How far has the business casual look spread? In the United Kingdom, 58 percent of men's clothing sales are now classified as "smart casual." Even the royals are dressing down. At a fashion gathering in The Netherlands, Prince Claus ripped off his tie and dashed it to the ground at the feet of Queen Beatrix, calling it "a snake around my neck." Once the epitome of business formality, the American Federal Reserve has adopted business casual standards for days when no outside meetings are scheduled. And during the press conference announcing the appointment of the new chairman and chief executive officer of General Electric — at that moment, the most highly valued corporation in America — both the chairman and his predecessor wore open-necked blue shirts. When the papers ran pictures of these two industrial icons the next day, they also showed shots of the two out-of-luck executives who had been passed over for the job: Both were wearing suits, white shirts, and ties.

Perhaps they should have listened to Prince Claus.

It seems it is now officially OK to show your throat. Thanks to the Internet, a fashion revolution had begun that not even the combined talents of Calvin Klein, Donna Karan, Tom Ford, Barney's, and the guy from the Men's Wearhouse could have created.

Cindy Lewis, publisher of *Harper's Bazaar*, says, "The Internet generation has influenced and relaxed the dress code at work. They are responsible for moving the needle on the times." The impact of the Internet pace, Lewis feels, is part of the reason that even the tightest-laced professional men and women are trading their three-piece suits and dress-for-success Armanis for a pair of chinos. "Everyone has realized that the pace of work is so intense that they have turned to fashion to bring into the workplace a sense of ease," Lewis says. "Because you are what you wear in many cases. And no one has taught us this better."

Marilyn Levey, a fashion marketing consultant with clients that have ranged from Federated Stores to Neiman Marcus and Laura Ashley, has conducted fashion focus groups with thousands of consumers in all economic and age segments across the United States. "It used to be, a young man graduated from college and went straight to Brooks Brothers and bought his first suit and white shirt," says Levey. "And I think all the original Internet millionaires were for the most part in math and engineering, or computer sciences, as opposed to content—that was the origin of the Geek Chic. The typical Geek Chic outfit was jeans and a T-shirt, the de rigueur of Silicon Valley. That's how it started."

The (at the time) decidedly unchic workstyle of the Internet start-up community, rather than a chic designer, incubated its own fashion trend, which, in turn, filtered up to five-day-a-week casual on Wall Street. Filtering up is not unusual; many fashion trends start at the street, Hip Hop being a notable recent one. Top fashion designers like Tommy Hilfiger have been the first to realize this, and trend-setters like Nike even employ "street teams," which are somewhat akin to the undercover, plainclothes force of fashion, to comb the underbelly of the streets, spot the incipient trends, and report back to their staff designers, who reinterpret what kids are wearing on street corners for the upscale market.

But Geek Chic was born of being wired, not of hanging out. I discussed the phenomenon with Diane Silberstein, publisher of *Yahoo! Internet Life* magazine, a woman who spent the first half of her career in the bosom of the post-Vreeland years of the voice of fashion authority, holding top positions in magazines such as *Vogue*, *Glamour*, *Allure*, and *Elle*, then made the leap from the glossy printed page to the virtual fashion community.

Impeccably put together in the latest of Prada-touched business casual, Silberstein has a two-sided perspective. "The Internet look is very casual, almost like an unmade bed look, where it is a badge of honor not to be as well groomed or as polished in your dressing," she said. "It is the look of 'I have stayed all night at the office,' or 'I worked until 2 A.M. last night—aren't I terrific?' This is a world where people expect to be working a minimum of twelve-hour days—8 A.M. to 8 P.M. is more or less the norm. If you are in by 8, 8:30, you are there till 7:30 or 8 at night. And I don't care what office you call at what hour, you can almost always find someone there, and of course there are the technology people who are on call twenty-four-hours a day."

The work environments as well as the work habits of Internet companies have impacted the way people dress. In many cases, walls may be missing, but lifestyle elements such as food, recreation, pets, and various cultural mirrors are integrated into the mix.

In Austin, Texas, where the temperature often soars into the hundreds, the pendulum has swung from dress for success to dress for self. "It is 110 degrees, but they used to expect a woman to wear a suit and stockings," says a woman Internet executive. "When I started in portfolio management, a woman checked the dress code as she came into the company. Today it's dressing down and accepting people who look different, act differently, and have a different approach. Our work space is a converted warehouse. We all work hard and expect people to work hard, so we make the space as accommodating as possible. I wear Birkenstocks and shorts to work."

Jack Sansolo comments, "You have a hot start-up Internet company, they are all sitting on the floor, they are up all night and they have no real hours, no desks, no real office space—that is the kind of stereotypical grunge thing you would think of."

Diane Silberstein feels that the Internet-start-up rush paved the way simply because it was just that—a start-up rush. "You were looking at a tremendous amount of companies where there have been corporate cultures being formed from scratch," she points out. "The whole premise is that the first thirty people in an organization form a culture. How do you dress if you are one of four people on the ground level, sitting around a dining room table—which is the way my previous company started—writing your business plan? And then how do you dress as your company grows? When you have moved from the dining room table to the Greybar Building in Grand Central Station with meetings with investment bankers and venture capitalists to expand globally? You are seeing corporate cultures that are evolving and being developed while people are coming and going, trying to adapt to a culture that is in change."

Start-up hours, Silberstein states, are still a mark of status, perhaps these days not even relating to a start-up but of being in the flight pattern for the IPO, the funding, or even the bailout, or just staying alive. In a volatile economy, it becomes a matter of working even harder, longer, and smarter. "That is the fashion look," she says. "Status is 'I was here till eleven last night, went home, had a nap, took a shower, and came back the next day'—not 'I spent hours at the beauty salon, left at five, had dinner with friends, and had a good night's sleep.' "

Perhaps we're reinventing status, where it comes from and how we display it. In the 1998 fielding of the Update: Women™ Survey, we found that women, the traditional fashion leaders, had become much less brand-oriented; and they had become more independent in their thinking—less than one-fourth said they cared what others thought about them, compared to almost half twenty years ago. Overlay this attitude onto the New Economy mentality and you've got a bunch of people who are not going to be slavishly following the next dictates from anybody's runways.

Recently a fashion magazine featured an article on the twenty-something, Seattle-based wife of an Internet multimillionaire who loves clothes. Her personal shopper spent days scouring the designer collections for outfits. The shopper's mission: find clothes that looked anonymous, giving absolutely no clue to their pedigrees. It was fine if the clothes were astronomically expensive; the expense just had to be invisible. Hidden luxury is a hallmark of the well-dressed New Economy woman, who has no problem parting with the money but would not be caught dead with her logo showing. As one young executive put it, "I will spend more on a white T-shirt than most people spend on a dress shirt."

Diane Silberstein laughs. "That messy-looking haircut may very well be a $300 haircut."

For the fashion magazines, whose birthright has been to take the lead in commanding women (and men) as to how they should look, this cannot bode well. *Vogue* returned with a brilliant counterstrike on what appears to be the Witness Protection Program approach to fashion: vintage clothes. With a vintage outfit, who knows where it came from, or whether its origins were a vintage boutique in West Hollywood where Cameron Diaz shops, the Goodwill, or your grandmother's attic? It's non-status status, taken to a newly creative level—create your own. A Web designer may recycle his T-shirt after he slept in it; a fashionista will recycle Halston.

"Women of the New Economy still have the same desire of women everywhere to be pampered," Silberstein notes. "It is very empowering to make your own statement, to create your own look."

Expressing your individuality through dress is rampant among the women of the New Economy space and is another way of expressing an empowered attitude. Where the women who invaded the working world in the 1980s first tried to clone the look of the men, in their dark suits and business-correct bow ties, and then tried to power their way through the glass ceiling in broad-shouldered *Dynasty* power suits, the women of the New Economy have never been afraid to show that they are females.

Agile Industries' Elizabeth Talerman says, "I wear tight, long-sleeved jersey tops—our [loft] space is cold—and fitted shirts. I love sexy shoes, high heels, mules. I am a brain with blond hair attached to a pair of mules. My mules are very girlie. I want to be seen as a woman."

But does she ever encounter credibility problems because of her wardrobe choices? Talerman scoffs. "You mean, would I be taken more seriously in an Armani suit? I don't think that's a problem. Otherwise the Dallas Cowboy cheerleaders would have gotten ahead of the rest of us."

And the men are not being left behind. "I still dress like when I was a kid and wanted to be a rock star," says one twenty-five-year-old Internet marketer who works for the online arm of a traditional company. "I wear whatever I want. Yesterday it was baggy parachute pants with a sweater, the day before orange pants with a sweater, and when I go out, leather pants with a metallic shirt."

As the business models and technologies of the Internet have moved into a more mature phase, which could be called Beyond the Start-up and After the Market Correction, so have the fashions. Flexibility is increasingly important. "Two days a week I work out of the house," says one virtual executive, "so I wear sweats and T-shirts. Two days I am in the field, so I wear a suit with a jacket, tie, the whole nine yards. One day a week when I have meetings, I wear khakis and a collared shirt."

"Dress codes are now more relaxed in fashion in general," says Diane Silberstein. "It is no longer necessary to have a suit on to meet with an important client—you can wear a good pair of pants and a fabulous sweater and still carry it off. People feel much more freedom working for an Internet company, and the expectation walking in is not that you are going to be dressed up to the nines. I am dressed up in the office when I walk in in a sweater and skirt. Although, trust me, if you are a man at a dot com and you are going to lunch at the Four Seasons with a banker, most likely you are wearing a jacket and tie—dress codes have relaxed across the board. Take the lines that used to do the little blue suit—a line like Liz Claiborne, which is very accessible to the masses. If you look at Liz Claiborne's merchandise mix in the stores today, you see very little of the suit. Tahari is a bridge line that used to do only suited looks. Today they can't survive on that. They had to do a look of a pant, a tunic, a funky evening look, an office-to-night look. Lines that were traditionally suit lines are also now showing sport and weekend. I think this is partly because of the Internet impact, because the Internet took us from casual Fridays to casual five days. That now permeates other industries. And then if a big blue chip company does it, others will say, 'I want my company to do it.' So the Internet became a driving force for many other companies, because whether you are a real estate leasing agent, an architect, or in a New Economy company, these days you are a provider of technology."

Jack Sansolo notes, "You don't have to sit on the floor to be a good marketer in an Internet company anymore. Bill Gates is not so anti anymore. He is in suits and his hair is cut. Even he has changed. I think of it as mainstreaming. So many of the technological advances now are fine-tuning basic things. Sixty-five or 70 percent of the American population now has Internet access. You are talking mainstream now. I assure you, they are not just nerds. And, you know, mainstream people have other concerns in life. For them, it is not about the technology. It is about how does the technology work in my life."

Technology has now gone full circle and has evolved into becoming a fashion accessory in its own right. "Your cell phone now comes in how many different colors, how many shapes and sizes, how many different materials? Look at the different beepers, the cases for the Palm Pilots, and the chic laptops without hard edges and in colors. And on and on," Sansolo says. "So what has happened is the technology itself has been integrated as part of the fashion statement. The technology has been adopted by people who aren't sitting on the floor. So immediately, what you have is a transformation of the association of what you look like when you are with that technology. A nerd sitting on the floor isn't going to worry about a Coach leather case for his cell phone. So the technology becomes fashion accessories as we have integrated it into our lives."

Sansolo recalls "the old days, when you had a black phone with a black dial and that was it. Then they started introducing colors, then shapes, and on and on. So what happens is beyond the technology now. The technology is there and the next step is the consumers' needs and wants—and how can I integrate it into my lifestyle? How small can you make it? How thin can you make it? How light can you make it? And what color?"

And beyond. Silicon Valley and New York's Seventh Avenue have literally converged to produce jackets that make cell calls and play MP3 tunes, digital jewelry that connects wearers to the Web wirelessly, pocket pens that send e-mail, and other wearable computing devices. "Computer intelligence is spreading out into smaller and smaller capillaries of society," says Michael Hawley, professor of media and technology at the Massachusetts Institute of Technology. "It's now reached the level where it's wearable." This evolution is a result of the shrinking size and price of electronic components.

Only a few years ago, these microtechnologies were relegated to areas like defense and industrial science. Today, household names like Levi Strauss are getting into the game with items like "smart" jackets with speakers in the hood or collar. Levi's and Philips Electronics have announced a collaborative venture to produce water-repellent jackets that come equipped with a sewn-in voice-activated phone and MP3 player and a single exterior remote that controls both. Wires threaded through the nylon lining emerge from the collar, where they hook up to earphones and microphone. When you want to make a call, the music automatically fades out. The wireless arena has also allowed wearable computers and peripherals to seep into the blue-collar arena, where workers are now able to access processing power equal to that of desktop computers via voice-activated or wearable keyboards and displays strapped to chests, wrists, arms, helmets, or hats. It's only a matter of time before these elite wearable technologies become the mass-market staples of tomorrow, available to every consumer. It is the demand launched by the Change Agents that will push technology into our wardrobes.

Role models have undergone a similar evolution, as the Internet evolves into Phase Two. "Take a typical film," says Sansolo. "Before, when you wanted to show new technology and how it was transforming the world, you had to focus on the nerds, because they were not only developing it, they were practically the only ones using it. But now technology has integrated, and who do the films show being involved with it? Tom Cruise." He laughs. "Well, anybody, really. Because the technology has integrated as part of life now. It is no longer something off on the fringe. It is dead center, and it is associated with use. And it is associated with *hipness*. And looking good and feeling good and all those things."

But what about the *übergeeks*, like Bill Gates? A brilliant individual, but not many people would confuse Gates with Tom Cruise.

Diane Silberstein points out, "If you look at any recent interviews in a business magazine, you see Bill Gates in a suit and tie, you see Larry Ellison in a suit and tie, you see all the big names out there, the rock stars of Internet fashion. Jeff Bezos from Amazon is perhaps the only one that is not in a suit—but he may be wearing a blazer. It's the maturing of the Internet, next phase. Internet businesses are just so much more thoughtful today, and that's reflected. It is no longer a business of people sitting in someone's garage, brainstorming. As New Economy businesses grow and develop, the CEOs and the founders realize they can't get away with that just-rolled-out-of-bed look."

The Change Agents are moving on. Which has led to a number of interesting contradictions. Take, for example, a fashion moment that is becoming an urban legend in its own right. An Internet business group has a meeting with investment bankers or venture capitalists for a post–start-up round of financing. The "geeks" show up in suits and ties; the "suits" show up in khakis and shirt sleeves.

Full circle.

10 SHOP TILL YOU VIRTUALLY DROP

The role of the Internet in shopping is critical to the psychology of the community because it allows literally anyone with a credit card — or a parent with one — to participate in the system and become, in a couple of clicks, more empowered than ever before in how they spend their money. And you don't even have to spend money to become a more informed shopper than you probably have ever been, because the research capability about what you are buying allows you to have the capability of being better informed than ever — and information is power in any marketplace. At your command, the merchandise is delivered to you, whether it be a box of Pampers, a bunch of orchids, or a LearJet. The shopping process is simplified, sped up, integrated into your life. Shopping is also critical because it is the point where many people who do not work in or otherwise touch the Internet space will first intersect with the Internet.

In 1981, in my book with Laurie Ashcraft, *The Coming Ma-*

triarchy, we wrote: "Consider video shopping, which displays merchandise and relevant details on a television-like viewing screen and lets shoppers place their on-line orders by punching in merchandise, credit and delivery codes." I suppose we would have used the word Internet—if we had heard of it. But at this point, nobody had home computers—or even office computers, the exception being a huge corporate mainframe you never saw and certainly never used unless you were an engineer. The Internet was still waiting to be conceived. No doubt, a certain segment of the population who either invented or studied technology knew the day was coming, but most people could hardly imagine it. When we made the "video shopping" prediction on a TV talk show in 1981, the audience responded as if we were describing a fanciful episode of *The Jetsons*. And not even the most forward-thinking fashionista could imagine a day when the geeks not only provided the technology to access chic but were the epitome of it.

As I write this, twenty years later, the holiday season is approaching. I check out my list. Gifts to buy: 30. Gifts bought: 0. Time to shop: 0. Hours available when stores are open: 0. Martha Stewart complex: over.

Guess where I'll be doing my shopping? And maybe you were pointing and clicking right along with me. Being a creature of habit and lover of stores, as recently as last year I wouldn't have considered it. But suddenly online shopping has become downright tempting. If you're not sure where to click, all you have to do is leaf through those online shopping supplements that are bundled with the magazines or the online shopping magazines themselves. Or click on the Web site of your favorite brand or store. And you don't need statistics to prove that, if you've grown up ordering music CDs online, you are not going to be even one-tenth as intimidated as I was to jump into cyber gift-giving. Even the lesser holidays are going increasingly virtual: In

February 2000, according to Ernst & Young, over 11 million Americans made Valentine's Day purchases on the Internet.

In the face of a plague of dot com extinctions, business models with profit potential, especially those with brick-and-mortar brand affiliations, are the standing species. Still, Forrester Research, Inc., reports that younger consumers do not even distinguish between a retailer's online and offline stores; the two forms of shopping experiences feed off each other in a symbiotic way.

Shopping is one of those primitive life-forces that refuses to die, like the roach, or one of those baseline animal forms that survived the flashier but hothouse dinosaurs. The explosive growth of e-commerce and Internet shopping has not abated and has, in fact, spawned a virtual shopathon. The virtual store is always open. According to Simmons Market Research Bureau, the year 2000 saw a 65 percent increase in the number of people who shopped online. And it is estimated, according to CSFB Internet Research, that e-tailing sales will more than triple in the next three years, from $83.5 billion in 2001 to $273.9 billion in 2004, in spite of fallout and consolidation that has left many retail dot coms littering the failed start-up landscape. This in itself is a milestone, but the human impact is not about the ebb and flow of bricks versus clicks and the comparative merit of their business models, but the new kind of consumer who has emerged from the process, a consumer with a revised set of expectations and behaviors. And this, in turn, has spurred new and more sophisticated products and services on the Internet that will, in the end, evolve and endure.

What kind of person shops online? If you think it's a bunch of kids surfing for CDs, you are mistaken. Although the heaviest concentration of Internet shoppers are between the ages of twenty-five to thirty-four, a *PARADE* magazine study conducted by Greenfield Online in 2000 found that most Internet shoppers were actually Baby Boomers age thirty-five to sixty-four. Contrary to popular belief, the study found that the online shopper was not a young, tech-savvy male but a forty-two-year-old individual almost as likely to be female as male. The technology shopping revolution had gone mainstream. "Middle America is driving e-commerce, not some digital elite," said Lamar Graham, PARADE's technology editor. What started as a young, male-driven, techno-phenomenon has given Baby Boomers a new lease on shopping.

Some Baby Boomers, like Jennie, an executive in her mid-forties, are into it for what she calls replenishment. "The Internet makes it easy if you know your size and your brand," she says. "You wear a certain size of Calvin Klein underwear; you look up a Web site that features it; you point, click, and order a six-month supply. Or you see a certain Gap leather jacket in an ad. You go to the Gap and they don't have it. So you go home and go on Gap.com and order it in your size. But you've already seen it, touched it, maybe tried it on, but not in your size."

Convenience converts a lot of time-pressed people to the Internet-shopping lifestyle. Elissa, a marketing executive, was a veteran of linen-tablecloth dinners, complete with candles and hand-rolled (by her) truffles. She had always been especially proud of her holiday repasts, when the groaning board usually meant that, with the days of shopping and preparation that went into them, she was the one doing the groaning. But last year Elissa was simply too busy to enter into the usual cookathon. "I looked up and it was two days before Christmas," she says. "But I didn't panic. I bought my Christmas ham online at the last minute. My mother said, 'How sick is that?' But I bought what-ever else I could online too. I did buy the lettuce at the market—one that was in Grand Central Station, on my way home. I wanted that to be fresh. But an online delivery service probably could have delivered that to me, if I'd wanted."

Even the once-diehard experiential store shopper, the upscale customer, is crossing over. *Harper's Bazaar's* Cindy Lewis understands how the lure of online shopping extends to the upscale customer. "It's a different thing for people to do it in the convenience of their home — they don't have to find a parking space, they don't have to get dressed, they can do it any hour of the day." Lewis had a personal online shopping epiphany while in Paris for the fashion collections. "As regards my shopping habits," she says, "I will always be a creature of habit. And I especially love department stores. However, there have been times. . . ." She breaks down with a confession. "I was in Paris when I got that second wind and got over my jet lag at somewhere around three o'clock in the morning. I went online and did my e-mails, and when I was tired of doing that I went into one of the luxury sites and I thought, 'What the hell, I might as well buy that barware from Baccarat that I've been procrastinating over going to Madison and 54th Street.' And I did! Even though Baccarat is French and I was in Paris, because I knew I wouldn't even have time to get there, let alone lug it home."

Many people who work with the Internet pace find they simply prefer the way transactions happen online. They are in a groove with the pace, the methodology, and the directness of working at their own speed, without the interference of other humans, such as salespeople and checkout lines. The head of a Los Angeles online advertising firm told me, "I order my groceries on the Internet and they deliver it to me, and they show up at my house, and literally, I am so lazy that I have it delivered when my maid is there because I don't even want to put it away. I don't care about the coupons — the only thing I care about is that it is convenient. It saves me time. I don't want to go to Ralph's and sit there for two hours. That bugs me."

Steve Klein, the sheep farmer/Internet executive, has a similar perspective. It's not so much that Klein loves to shop online, it's that he finds the alternative is totally alien to his psychology. "I can't *stand* shopping in stores," he states. "All this inactivity in stores — it's like zero pace! And I don't care if stuff fits me or not, but I can't stand human error. I don't shop in stores for clothes." He gestures with a shrug to this day's iteration of his uniform — cotton shirt and khakis, courtesy of jcrew.com.

Steve Klein had a major wardrobe crisis that forever cemented his beliefs. He had been chosen to appear as a contestant on the *Who Wants to Be a Millionaire?* show. Although he was confident of his skills in the knowledge area, one of the preshow requirements threw him for a loop: The producers told him to bring a pair of dark pants to wear on camera. (Regis never wears khakis, they pointed out.) "I had to stop at Eddie Bauer, a real store," Steve said, the inconvenience of it all still lingering in his voice. "I bought the pants on the spot and went to wear them out to the show — and the security tag was on! I told the people in the store that if I won and Regis asked me what I was going to do with the money, I'd tell him I wouldn't have to steal pants. This is exactly what I hate about shopping in stores."

Actually, the people at Eddie Bauer have been listening — and watching customers like Steve Klein very closely. To them, Klein and everything he thinks about shopping in stores represents not a complaint but the future. Eddie Bauer, which as of 2000 had 600 brick-and-mortar stores standing, is no stranger to dealing directly with the consumer. The company began direct marketing when it got into the catalog business in 1946, and today they send out about 10 billion catalog pages a year. Eddie Bauer was also among the early retailers on the Internet, where it has been established since 1994, and has been closely tracking the evolution and impact of the Internet consumer. It has documented an explosive trend. In 2000 alone, the company noticed 80 percent growth in its apparel category online.

At Eddie Bauer, Jack Sansolo analyzed the composition of those who shop evolve from early triers to mainstream. "The psychographics and demographics have really shifted back and forth, depending on where the person is in the curve," he says. "At the very beginning, the first customers were a psychographic segment, those who were enamored of the technology, and they would do anything the technology enabled them to do. These were basically the nerds. And then that was immediately followed by a demographic which were young people who were also enamored with technology and all the new technological components of their lives. But then it became bimodal. You had your young people and then, all of a sudden, your older people. And the older people weren't so much of a demographic as a life-stage thing. They had more time, and shopping online turned out to be convenient, entertaining, involving, a nice pastime thing to do at home.

"But now it is flattening out. And what we are seeing now on the Internet is that it is not simply a transfer of the home shopping experience from the catalog to the Internet, it is getting new people to shop from home. That is the first big change in terms of who is shopping. It is no longer the catalog versus the Internet—there is a whole new category of people. So there is something in the experience itself which is expanding the population that finds it an attractive way to shop. People find the technology itself interesting and involving—that is the first thing. And the second thing is, this is a generation of people who are very oriented to that technology and shopping is simply adding one more thing to their desktop."

These technology-oriented Change Agents are pushing the shopping envelope to yet another level. Name your pleasure, it can be had—anytime, anywhere. Shopping online has evolved as far as the imagination can stretch. Who in the world would buy a jet online? Or, for that matter, a set of Porthault sheets? James Finkelstein, president and CEO of LuxuryFinder.com, a luxury portal, points out, "You have people all over the world who don't have access to the great brands and are used to shopping for them in New York, or Bond Street, or Paris when they are on holiday—or they may just have a lack of time. We have sold jets online, and we do that fairly regularly. We put up T Anthony and in two minutes, a woman bought twelve suitcases, then came back a few days later for the equivalent. I thought she was moving the world, but it turned out she was buying gifts. In less than a year, we have doubled our sales every three to four months. This holiday season, we expect to do eight to ten times the business of last holiday. The Web is doubling every year in terms of e-commerce. The U.S. consumer who is online made an average of four online purchases in 1997, six in 1998, and thirteen in 1999. They spent an average of $237 in 1997 and $1,200 in 1999. Ernst & Young predicts that the online luxury market will be $70 billion by 2004." Finkelstein sees the Web as evolving into simply a vehicle for the changes it is enabling. "As it becomes more integrated—on your screen, your wall, your Palm Pilot—it will be such a part of your life, integrated into your life, just another outlet."

Which has raised expectations accordingly.

John Maienza, a designer whose work has been featured in *Architectural Digest*, works in California, New York, and France. He is among those who have noticed that the expediency of Internet shopping has had a halo effect on offline expectations. Maienza has several clients who have been successful in Internet ventures, or, as he puts it, "Well-off dot commers from Silicon Valley who have decided they're missing out on life after the IPO. They move to San Francisco, buy a big home, and hire a designer." These clients, having lived the Internet pace, now expect that the rest of the world functions like the Internet. One typical Internet client, owner of a 6,000-square foot-home in San Francisco, had been too busy tending to business to furnish the house, which had remained mostly empty, except for "a bed, two beanbag chairs in front of a state-of-the-art large-screen TV, and a bottle of wine. Period." The client wanted the entire thing furnished and decorated immediately, meaning in a matter of days, if not sooner. "After the IPO, there are reentry problems," says Maienza. "They've got their four hundred thousand shares, but they don't understand that there's a process. They just want to know how fast and how much. Dot com people have always worked at lightning speed, and they expect the same thing out of the rest of the world. You've heard of those Web sites, Decorate.com or whatever? Well, they think that's me, with dialog. I have to tell these clients, 'Excuse me, I am not a Web site! You can't point and click me!'"

Actually, they could have gone to a Web site, pointed, clicked, and furnished. Unlike a home decorated by John Maienza, the results might not end up in *Architectural Digest*, but they'd get instant gratification—and a place to sleep and sit.

"On LuxuryFinder.com, you can go to five furniture places in five minutes," says Finkelstein.

"Go to the Eddie Bauer site," says Sansolo. "You want to buy a bed? Look at not just a bed but a bed with a sham and the pillowcases and the quilts and the comforter and the sheets— the whole thing right there, one click away. You don't have to say 'I want these sheets and this bed.' You know, people want it put together for them in a way that makes sense—one click, the entire thing. That's what the designer is saying: They want it that easily now."

And, if they can get it that easily now, what is to come? If there have been two phases of Internet experience, the first being adoption, the next, mainstreaming—the third, just on the horizon, is customization.

"The whole idea of personalization online is making a huge difference," says Sansolo. "The next phase is going to be 'How do we adapt it to our individual lifestyles?' Internet penetration is now something like 70 percent of the American population. And 40 percent shops online. You are talking mainstream now. And, you know, mainstream people have other concerns in life. It is not about the technology. It's about 'How does the technology work for me? In my life?' "

Customization means personalization—an online experience that is tailored to your specific needs. The first step: "You have shopped before, so when you come back, the home page welcomes you personally. It knows who you are. It can make available your purchase history. You like blue sweaters. You wear a small in a sweater and a twenty-eight in a pant. Then the next step beyond that is ready technically, but there are concerns over privacy and use of data. And that is, when you click on, the home page that you see is different from the home page that the next person sees, and the navigation is different, based on your shopping behavior, your psychographics, and your demographics and attitudes to things."

For instance, let's say you are a businessperson, very concerned about time and style. Your home page would lead you to six outfits that are stylish, in stock now, that work in a business setting. Let's say that your friend, on the other hand, is more concerned about style. She wants the latest, the newest, the most "in." So she clicks on and is welcomed back with the news of the six hottest items in the fashion world or the top sellers of the site. The site's database is custom-tailored to the user. "This is the ultimate in personalization," says Sansolo.

Another word for it is individualization. "It is individuality," says Cindy Lewis. "Really, it is encouraging that. Because, you know what? You are defining everything on your terms. When you are going to shop, when you are going to access information, what you want to buy." Addressing this trend, *Harper's Bazaar* is pioneering a first-of-its-kind link from the ad pages of the magazine to the interactive experience. ShopBazaar.com enables readers to access immediate information from the printed advertising page, so if, say, a woman sees an ad and wonders about literally any aspect of what she spies, she can go online and fulfill her curiosity and answer her questions. For instance, a reader might spot an advertisement that interests her. Once logged on the site, with the click of a mouse, she will be able to find out all the information that exists about the shirt or the jacket or the skirt or the shoes in the ad, simply by moving the mouse along the picture and clicking—the type of fabric, the range of colors. A mouse click on the model's neck will yield information about her fragrance. And, if the reader chooses to take the next step, she will be given the most conveniently located stores or boutiques. She will be directed to the personal shopping department of the store or boutique. The next day she will receive an e-mail or a phone call from the store. Or, if she opts to take the less high-tech route, she can simply complete the transaction and place her order online. Lewis thinks this kind of retail progression and linking of the online and offline world has happened largely due to the time crunch. "People don't have time to figure it all out," she says. "And the choices have become so abundant, they're confused. They are looking for service."

How far will the database take us in the name of better service? Jack Sansolo outlines a progression in which the very first time I click on a site, it will reveal an almost scary in-depth knowledge about me, culled from a database that is, in fact, already publicly available on most Americans.

How public? A friend of mine, who is an Internet "newbie," decided on a lark to enter her father's name and see what a data search would turn up. She was convinced the answer would be nothing. After all, her father was a person who was not a name in any household but hers. Moreover, he had been dead for more than twenty years. Within seconds, however, she was astonished to see her screen filled with information about her (very) late father, including his name, address, social security number, the correct home phone number of the family home where she had grown up—and, she was shocked to see, precise information from her father's death certificate.

And that's twenty years after you're dead.

Today it is entirely plausible at any minute that I would click on a site for the first time, and that site would already know not only where I live and what I do, but that I was in the PTA, or a book club, or any number of personal details. This is the Big Brother aspect of the Internet that frightens a lot of people. But it is, in fact, entirely doable. "The data is there, the technology is there," says Sansolo. "Although we don't do anything with anybody's data unless they request it."

This is information empowerment, brought down to the most personal of levels, and, if information is power, leverage and impact that no previous group of human beings short of the CIA has been able to access, much less act upon. With the delivery systems in place and the technology evolving, the in-control attitude of the young Web-enabled generation is on target to become supercharged and escalate to a new level of power and aggressiveness. The privacy concerns of the Web "unfamiliars," the Baby Boomers, will be swept away by a tidal wave of not just technology but confidence in the medium that has incubated an entire generation from the time they were old enough to turn on the computer. When you're seven years old and your nighttime reading is not *Goodnight Moon* but the computer manual, it's not likely you're going to grow up to sit like a wallflower on the edges of the online orgy.

How this new power will be used remains to be seen. But the highly aggressive, even violent, psychographic indicators of today's mid- to late teens point toward if not a confrontation, a reinvention of many cornerstone social and economic platforms.

The easy access of information on the Web has torn away a

wall of unassailability that previously kept many of us from doing many things. We've seen how a fifteen-year-old scammed investors in a pump-and-dump scheme. At the time he was born, if you wanted to buy a stock, who could imagine that you could punch a few keys and have access to almost the same research as your broker?

Traditionally, change in the area of financial behavior has moved about as quickly as watching lead turn into gold. Mutual funds, for instance, had a fifty-year gestation period. The introduction of the credit card took hundreds of millions of dollars (in 1960s' dollars), and major losses were sustained by the banking industry before consumers started to carry them and merchants started to accept them. With the Internet, in a space of less than a decade, it has become possible to do things like comparison-shop online for a mortgage, abbreviating and easing a process that can be, as every homeowner knows, incredibly time-consuming and even painful. The information is there, at the fingertips of the mortgagee. The speed of the success of on-line financial services has been stunning. "We have seen the Internet give birth to major, major financial institutions that were barely blips on the radar five years ago," says Jim Marks, an investment banker at Credit Suisse First Boston who specializes in financial services. "A lot of people don't realize how important they have become. E Trade, for instance—if you look at its customer assets and compare it to deposits at banks, E Trade would be the tenth largest bank in the country today. AmeriTrade would be about the twentieth largest."

Marks attributes much of this to "the democratization of information." He observes, "Four or five years ago, the information resources that sat on an investment professional's desk were vastly superior to those of the retail investor. And at this point, that is not true anymore. I mean, it is basically equal, and it is almost humorous to walk around the research floor and see how many people are using Yahoo Finance to look up basic information, rather than the $300-a-month information terminals we have hooked up. It's amazing." Marks thinks this is because the Internet companies are much more responsive to people's information wants and needs. "They understand the presentation a lot better, and it is simpler and easier to use—and basically, the content is just about the same."

And so one of the major, underestimated contributions of the Internet has been the leveling of the playing field. You, your broker—or your eighteen-year-old, or your eighth grader—all have access to the same information.

For better or for worse.

11 CONNECTING THE DOTS

In the office of Razorfish, a major Web design company, a young woman works intently in front of her monitor. To its side she has taped a Polaroid of a smiling guy, identified with a caption on a Post-it: *virtual b'friend*. They had met in college, she told me, moved apart for their jobs, and now carried on an on-line commuter romance. He lived in Texas, she in New York City. Still, through instant messaging, e-mailing, and the sharing of files and music over the Net, they were able to be in almost constant touch, without actually touching or even speaking.

Isn't it romantic?

This couple and many others think so.

The Change Agents are reinventing romance. At first, it might seem that nothing could be more antithetical to romance than a computer—the epitome of high tech versus the pinnacle of high touch. How can sitting at their respective keyboards, often in different states, bring people closer, much less together? You have to understand that the Internet is, to Change Agents, as much a part of the social landscape as the fern bar was to the Yuppies. In December 2000, a follow-up online study of Gen Y Change Agents by Nickles & Ashcraft revealed that 48 percent said they talk regularly to online friends in other parts of the country, and a third had regular dialogues with online friends from other countries. It's clear that the impersonality and anonymity of the Internet have a paradoxical effect in that these attributes inspire and motivate young people who are reaching out in search of making human connection on a deeper level.

In any relationship, the first step has to be one person meeting another. When you meet a stranger in a typical social situation — say, a crowded room, cocktail party, a bar, a gym, or even walking the dog — your entire self is in many ways exposed and open. Everyone can see what you look like, what you are wearing, and hear how you sound. Your clothes say something about you. A judgment may even be made based on the breed of dog you are walking. Maybe notice will be taken, one way or another, about what you are eating or drinking. And, on both sides, a lifetime of social conditioning kicks in, including safety nets and barriers built up since the first rejection.

Defensive mechanisms start early, partly because to reach out in even the most innocuous way is to leave ourselves open to a very personal rejection. Recently an eleven-year-old boy told me that he had been "dumped" by a girl last year (their entire relationship having consisted of talking after class) on Valentine's day because he put one of those little candy hearts on her desk that said "You're sweet." He probably won't be so open again for the next twenty years — except, maybe, online.

Forget the candy hearts. On the Internet, people feel freer to be much more open, often immediately upon making a connection. One woman said, "I start by e-mailing back and forth with someone, and my entire criteria is how articulate are they and can they make me laugh, because if they can do it there, then maybe I have a shot in person."

Another woman, in her mid-thirties and the war-torn veteran of a lifetime of traditional meeting and dating, put it this way: "I think that in some ways it is less risky than real dating. I think if I'm out and I'm approached by someone face to face, I'm less likely to open up because of all the chatter that's going on in my head: 'What's he going to think of me?' On the other hand, with the Internet as a first contact, I have a feel of whether I want to start or continue a conversation with a person. Because you don't see that person physically at first, people let their barriers down. And if someone doesn't write you back in an e-mail, it's not as personal."

Conversely, the anonymity of the Internet can be misleading. Sara Frost (not her real name), an Internet advertising executive, is one who has had some negative experiences in that regard. "There are people who are so eloquent and so free when they write to me online, and then I sit down with them, they're quite awkward. That's been a big disconnect. I think the Web makes people feel like they're in a space alone. I feel like there's also a false sense of intimacy that occurs sometime after the third or fourth e-mail exchange. I've seen that people imbue words with all kinds of meanings when they write them and read them that may not be construed if those words were spoken, and I think sometimes people can build their own meanings — they can fictionalize what's going on. I've had a few really amazing writing relationships that turned into nothing when I was on the phone with somebody or met them at dinner. And the anonymity coupled with someone's subjective interpretation can blow things out of proportion. You can literally invent a fictional character in your mind."

Frost has had people become angry with her because she's made a joke or written something that has been interpreted as snide, when that was not her intent. "And I had a guy I had exchanged e-mails with literally find my number, call me, and tell me he was completely in love with me and that he was coming from England to see me. I told him, 'You can't be in love with me, you don't know me!'

"He said, 'But you've been writing me.'

"And I said, 'But you don't know who I am. I share with you selectively. You don't have a holistic picture of me, nor I of you.' "

"I always looked at it as a copout," says a young, single man. "It's like, 'I put this wall up in front of me and then I am going to talk to people.' It's kind of like drinking, when you go out to a bar and drink a lot of alcohol so you can talk to somebody. It's like the same thing, except there is no alcohol involved."

Pictures can be a double-edged sword. Many of the people I interviewed who were interested in finding a relationship on the Web began simply by exchanging written messages, but, as they became accustomed to the medium, moved on to making it a policy to look at the picture of the person they were interested in before making contact. In the same vein, these relationship-seekers did not, at first, post their own pictures. Then, as they became more comfortable, they typically changed their mind and did post a picture.

This was what Sara Frost did. "Now I don't meet anybody that I haven't seen a picture for," she says. "Because I do have a sense of aesthetic—there's men that I find physically attractive and men that I don't. And the Web affords me the luxury of using it like a Chinese menu—leaving what I don't want and only taking what I do. It's sad, I suppose, but . . ."

She noticed that posting her picture changed the kind of response she's gotten. "Before I posted a picture, people really focused on what I wrote. I had a lot of responses from people about my writing, and people would read things into it and think that I was, say, superintelligent, or very poetic and artistic. Then the minute I mentioned football, a bunch of guys started using sports slang—they key into one thing. When I put my picture online, I got a lot more responses very quickly, and people were not as focused on what was in the writing."

For some, the Internet is a virtual masquerade ball. "I've heard stories about people who lie, who say they're six foot three and they're not, or send pictures and they're not them," said a gay man. "People go crazy when things like that happen! And the person will say, 'You know, I have this picture and it's not you.' And they will say, 'I know—but I really wanted to meet you.' That doesn't really fly."

Sara Frost's online exploratories to connect with potential romantic partners has changed her entire social pattern. "Before, I used to focus on dating and meeting people when I went out and about," she says. "But now that I've been cyberdating, it's like *You've Got Mail.* Every morning, I literally use the Web to replace going out to meet people. Every morning, I race to my computer before work, and plug it in, and see—did I get anything? Did anybody write back?"

E-mail relationships give participants something unique to look forward to and add a new kind of interlude to their lives. It's a bit like having a brightly wrapped candy appear in front of you in the midst of an otherwise routine day. Frost says, "That's probably one of the nicest things that will happen in my day, to see an e-mail like that pop up."

When a relationship clicks, Frost has found the Internet can play yet another flirtatious role. She has gotten to know a man who lives across the country. "And our relationship exists largely because of Amazon.com," she says. "After we met, I went to his house and we wound up having wine, and I noticed he had no wine cooler. And so the next day, I went online to crateandbarrel.com and had one shipped to him. So not only do we e-mail, but we use the Web to gift each other. We send each other gifts all the time. He loves really interesting music, and he just sent me a blues CD. There is probably a gift once a month, in a box, with a card."

Many people who have a mission of finding a partner, like Sharon Karson (not her real name), find the Internet helps streamline the process and shields them from the more undesirable aspects of the in-person aspects of the search. "If, ten years ago, somebody had told me I would be meeting men this way, I would have told them they were crazy," says Karson, a consultant who designs training programs around technology. After years of working nonstop and having what she calls "no personal life," Karson, at age thirty-five, left the corporate mainstream, set up her own business, and made a commitment to find a relationship. However, she found instead that it was increasingly difficult to meet anyone. Friends suggested she try Internet dating, and after an initially skeptical reaction, she stuck her toe into the virtual whirlpool. "I just did it to see what would happen," she says. "I created a profile and put it on a couple of sites, and before I had even finished putting up the entire profile, I got an e-mail! And I thought, 'Hey, this is kind of fun.' It turned out, I ended up going out with him for a couple of months."

Karson finds the process of online meeting-and-greeting enjoyable. And she finds it preferable to the analog alternative of the bar scene. "A lot of people are in the same boat," she says. "They are busy, they want to meet people, but they don't want to go and hang out in bars."

In creating an online profile for the dating sites, Karson found she edited the way she presented herself somewhat. "My profile was pretty much a combination of a little description of myself and kind of how I see life and some of my interests. And a little humor. You have to be honest, but at the same time, you have to put a little spin on it," she says. She also acknowledges that posting your picture online can impact the results of your efforts. "I didn't have a picture up there, and a little while ago, I thought, why not, let's see what happens, because other people did have their pictures up. I can't tell you—in the past two weeks I got about thirty e-mails. And you know what? That made me feel really, really good. You have to be attracted to people, and this lets you get it right out there," she says. "If you don't like their picture, then right off you are not going to be bothered with those people." She does not see this as superficial. "Not any more than responding to someone, or not, at a party or a bar."

Beyond the picture, more subtle social cyber-clues are emerging. Recent Internet research reported in the London *Times* revealed that men and women's communication styles differ on the Internet, just as they do face to face, and that, in fact, e-communication between the sexes mirrors the interactivity of conversation.

Not surprisingly, then, participants in Internet dating sites use them as an adjunct to their offline dating behaviors. In Karson's case, when she is dating someone seriously, she will take herself out of circulation. Likewise, when she met a man she liked on her dating site and they started going out regularly, she put her site profile "on hold" as well.

The initial attraction over the Internet is not, to Karson, a replacement for actually meeting them, but she feels she does get a feeling for what they are like. "The e-mail gives you a flavor, it can tell me about them, you can flirt. You can flirt via e-mail or with instant messenger if you have America Online. The way people ask you questions is really interesting. I think that because you can't actually see the other person, you can ask direct questions if you want to. More direct than in person.

"I think that if I am out and I wanted to approach someone face to face, I would be less apt to do so because of the chatter going on in my head—what does he think of me, oh no, I can't do that . . . that kind of thing. Whereas with the Internet, that first contact gives me a kind of feel whether or not I want to start a conversation with this person. And I think just having that information out there on a profile helps the selection process along. It takes some of the risk out because that person is not face to face with you. And if someone doesn't write you back in an e-mail, it's OK.

"I had one guy from another city who was asking me things like 'Tell me about your first kiss,' and 'Tell me what you were like as a little girl.' And 'Who is your favorite superhero?' As I was doing this, it was so refreshing that it made me start reminiscing about certain things that even I had forgotten about. And it was a pleasure to share that. So it was like a new way of probing for information and sharing yourself at the same time."

Karson feels that the Internet can reveal a level of depth but, at the same time, allows for a certain selectivity. "He sounded like an interesting person, a passionate person," she says about the man who asked about her favorite superhero. "When I receive an e-mail like that, I will go to the site and look up the guy's profile. But he didn't have one. So I e-mailed him back and asked why not. He answered that he wanted to look for people with similar interests and passions and then pick and choose who he wanted to share himself with. I thought that was really interesting."

Sharon Karson follows what is a fairly typical Internet dating protocol: "I have these steps. I will put the effort into e-mailing and then if I like the person and they like me, my next step will be to do the instant messenger thing to see how they are. After that, I would like to hear their voice, so then we will graduate to a phone call or a couple of phone calls. And exchange pictures, then maybe decide if we want to meet. I treat it like traditional dating. You still have to get to know a person and it still takes time. Regardless of the Internet, everyone has their great points, everyone has their hang-ups. In the end, it's about having a relationship, not spending all your time online. I would hate to have an e-mail marriage."

But for some couples, like Abbi Gosling and David Waxman, who met online and married, an e-mail marriage — or one that is lived largely online — is reality.

Gosling and Waxman met online through cybercircumstance. Her company is in New York, while he is a virtual nomad, working in San Francisco, launching an office in Paris, and coming home to New York for weekends when he can. She contacted his company on the Internet while researching Web sites for a client, found his name listed as the creative director, and contacted him because she felt the person in that position could answer her questions without being crushingly technical. "My client wanted a collaborative filtering agent, and the only one at that time was by David's company," Gosling explains.

The two exchanged a business e-mail, then another. But something in their mutual words shone through and caught each other's attention, as surely as, in the nonvirtual world, a couple might feel a spark in a glance across a room full of strangers. "His writing had a whimsical quality," Gosling recalls fondly. "That was resonant. That's one of the things about e-mail," she adds. "It's so fast, you can banter. His site had instant messaging, so we could chat."

"Abbi is charming and she writes really well," says Waxman. "Gradually the e-mails became more familiar."

"After about two serious e-mails, things degenerated into sarcasm." Gosling laughs.

The e-mails flew fast and furious, and the two developed what Gosling calls "an epistolary relationship." She sees the Internet as a positive vehicle for the return to the importance of the written word. In romance, she sees it playing an almost Jamesean, go-between role, once again allowing emotions to unfold in crafted words, as they once did in letters exchanged between two people who were attracted to each other.

"The Internet is a very seductive medium," says Gosling. "As a society, we've gotten out of the habit of taking the written word seriously, since we've become so visual in the past twenty years."

"Before we met, we put a lot of effort into our letters," says Waxman, confirming his wife's opinion.

The couple finally did exchange phone calls, then image files; then they met, fell in love, and married—although it is unclear how much of the falling in love happened in person and how much happened over the Internet, with an entanglement of words, things said and unsaid. This much, however, is clear: One would not have happened without the other.

During the long stretches when they are on different coasts or continents, Abbi Gosling and David Waxman still communicate by instant messaging. The messages, like the relationship, have evolved, and resemble any married couple's communications. "Now the messages are more like 'Feed the dog!' " says Waxman. "But we are in contact at least ten times a day, probably more than most couples. We talk on the phone, and we send and forward mails to each other. She can always be on my screen, so even if we're not in the same place, it feels like we are."

He attributes the fact that he and Gosling are able to enrich their relationship by staying in almost constant touch, wherever they are, to the Internet, which can play another paradoxical role in providing an ongoing virtual link to lives of people who are, in the real world, geographically apart. The loved one's virtual presence can be constant, a part of the ongoing day-to-day activity, even without their actual presence. "The technology affords a lot of that to happen—it's less of a disruption," explains Waxman. "E-mail is unobtrusive."

In the gay community, relationship issues are also being

adapted to the Internet. Todd Abrams, founder of Alternative Marketing, a firm that has marketed extensively to niche markets and the gay community, notes that gays were among the earliest to embrace the Internet. "Gay people were able to find out what was going on in their local towns and also what was happening in different cities as related to their interests. Gay people, for instance, like many Americans, do a lot of travel research on the Internet—where they can get active reviews as they apply to gay people. So the Internet has become a phenomenal way for gay people to meet one another and connect for a lot of things—not just for gleaning information, but also to meet people.

"Computer ownership and Internet usage is still disproportionately high among gay people, compared to the population at large," Abrams says, relating this to the fact that the gay community consists of many individuals who are early adopters and Change Agents.

"One reason is it's a very anonymous thing," says Abrams. "I know people that prefer it. It depends on the level of intimacy that you're looking for. In some ways, it's less intimate. For me, picking up a telephone is much more intimate than sending an e-mail. And a lot of people have intimacy issues. I think e-mail is quicker and has less intimacy. And, from a gay man's point of view, online you can create anything and be anything that you want. You can be any person that you want to be, because, unless you're looking for someone to connect with offline, they're never going to meet you. They can't hear your voice, they don't know what you look like unless you choose to send a picture. You can create an entire persona.

"But a lot of gay guys have met on the Internet, like a lot of straight people—and fallen in love. But while many straight women are looking for Mr. Right, many gay men are looking for Mr. Right Now. The reality is that many men meet sexually over the Internet. As a matter of fact, it is the hot way that gay men connect and date, particularly those who don't live in the major markets, or [who live] in areas where it is difficult for gay people to meet others, like rural areas. It is a terrific device for connecting and for love and sex and romance. I can relate to this through the gay world; a lot of gay people have met through the Internet and hooked up and dated and fallen in love—and so have a lot of straight people."

On the other hand, Abrams sees the shorthand of cybercommunication as a boon when you do not want to say too much. It offers the ability to be in touch on a responsive level without the commitment of actually having to have a conversation. "It's almost like when I'm doing business with people, I don't like calling people because sometimes I find it to be invasive and people don't really want to talk. I think, for instance, that there are tons of people who won't even pick up the phone anymore. They basically live through their e-mail. Whether or not they capitalize on something, that depends on the level of intimacy they are looking for. I think that for me, and for the vast majority of people in this world, it is perfectly fine to just e-mail them and send off a message. It's a way of keeping in touch without having to expend too much effort. It's also a qualifying thing. You are sitting there and you can say, 'Oh, I e-mailed you. I didn't return your call, I didn't really have to extend all that much, but I did make the effort to contact you. Like an electronic Post-it. It's also cheap. You really don't have to call long distance. I mean, if you think about it, you can send out five hundred e-mails for nothing. So it's a brilliant invention."

Like Abbi Gosling, Abrams sees the Internet as a paradoxical medium in that it is a medium of distance, yet it is becoming a force in initiating and promoting the return of the written word. "It reminds me of years ago when they used to write letters," he says. "Which is funny when you think about it. When they invented the telephone, they were like 'Great! We can talk and talk!' Now it appears that people don't really want to talk, that they like writing letters, in the form of these little notes. And once you write it, the letter doesn't take two weeks to get there or however long Pony Express or even the mail took. Now it can be read instantaneously, and they can respond. So it is an improvement."

In spite of this, Abrams feels that the Internet is a not-always-unwelcome barrier to intimacy. "There is less intimacy, and I think for a lot of people, it is in fact more comfortable that way. I think that a lot of people have intimacy issues."

The crucible of the impact and potential of cyberrelationships may be the online dating sites, the leader of which is Match.com. Click on to their site, and you'll be greeted by a photo of a bride and groom who met—where else? The headline reads "A click of the mouse, and you're on your way to a life filled with happiness." Those interested in the romantic details can scroll through and read how the bride used the Web site to find her soul mate: She subscribed in January 1999; they started dating in October; he proposed in January 2000; they married on October 13. (See the wedding pictures, which include celebrants at the reception dancing joyously.) The site offers everything from advice to tips on dating to discussion of gay dating issues to a chance to sign up for a Caribbean cruise, meet fellow members, and, theoretically, share a totally analog piña colada.

Who buys into this? According to Match.com, on their site alone, almost 2 million people do. Since its launch in 1995, the site receives traffic of 65,000 unique visitors daily and registers some 25,000 new members per week. Fifty percent of the site's members have gone beyond the virtual experience and have met a fellow member face to face. Match.com has confirmed more than 650 marriages. And at least twenty-five people have been born into this world who would not exist if their parents had not met on Match.com.

As the time crunch and comfort with the virtual world increase, it is certain that a growing segment of the population will exist solely because of online matchmaking or courtship. Making this, perhaps, the ultimate incubator.

12 CYBER CRADLE TO VIRTUAL GRAVE

ertain basic rites of passage mark the ebb and flow of life, and the rituals and customs surrounding them have been woven into the fabric of existence from the beginning of recorded humanity. One indicator of the domino effect of how the Internet has entered—and moved toward altering—the lifestyles of its participants is a snapshot of the impact on three critical rites of passage, two of which are inescapable to us all: birth, marriage, and death. It's also important to note that those who not only invented but first accessed and, ultimately, altered the protocols of these rite-of-passage arenas were people in the Internet community. The themes that evolved had one key thing in common—a sense of connecting at one of the most important junctures of human experience. The Internet emerged as the back-fence advisor, the protocol expert, the open arms for a broken heart, the ever-present ear when someone needed to be heard or remembered. It morphed from the sympathetic ear when a young woman first missed her period, to the wedding planner, to the place where a child could be memorialized and anyone could visit. The depth of emotional involvement in the virtual world underscores the fact that the Internet is already very much more than a place for e-commerce, encyclopedic information, or casual chat room connecting. Its most underestimated power may be something with no dollar value — a unique fusion of anonymity and intimacy.

At first glance, for example, BabyCenter.com seems to be about shopping for baby stuff. Which it is. A parent or prospective parent can purchase thousands of items for babies and toddlers online through the site. The connection, however, goes far deeper than the credit card. And it can start even before the sperm and egg are introduced.

BabyCenter.com's preconception bulletin board features hundreds of entries, starting even before the final reproductive decision is made — "Thinking of Conceiving" — and ranging to categories from "Actively Trying" to "Detecting Ovulation," "Lubricants and Conception" and "Ready for a Baby, But My Partner's Not." There are bulletin boards for "Gay and Adopting" and "Single Parent Adoption." Medical conditions are included, such as "Polycystic Ovary Problems" and even "Trying after Miscarriage."

The site takes a phased approach, so visitors "graduate" along the baby continuum from conception to pregnancy to birth to newborn to baby to toddler. There is something for almost every circumstance or point of view. Your baby is a junior Einstein? There's a bulletin board for those with "Gifted Babies" on the site. Colicky? Check in with "Dealing with Colic" or "Surviving Teething." Feeling like a bumbling parent? There's even a "Bloopers" bulletin board, where other parents share their misadventures, such as the mom who tells in graphic detail how she found herself the target of wayward poop while on the wrong end of a diaper change.

"We have a very active bulletin board. People can post their questions and get dozens of answers," says cofounder Marc Selcow. "There was a demand for the information, and we really did solve the problem. People started flocking to us and then they started talking to one another."

Selcow points out one reason why an Internet company has been so successful in taking on an intimate role that had traditionally been held by the woman's mother, close friends, obstetrician, and pediatrician. "Moms of today's generation get less valuable information from their parents than ever before, because the volume of information about parenting, nutrition, discipline, behavior, about medical aspects, has swollen in the last generation. So, invariably, more conflict than there is valuable advice can come out of talking to your mom. Number two, obstetricians and pediatricians are intensely busy. They are effectively primary caregivers, which means they are overwhelmed by the number of patients they have to see in fifteen-minute increments. And pregnant women, certainly new moms, often have inhibitions about calling their doctor; they don't want to seem like they don't know what they are doing, and they don't want to bother the doctor. It became clear that people today needed to augment that. The feedback we got for BabyCenter.com was that, for many people, we became their primary information source. People were actually asking us almost frightening questions, even questions like how to deal with a health scare, such as a hemorrhage. We got questions from young moms who were taking drugs during their pregnancy and they weren't turning to anyone else, they were turning to the Internet. They were turning to us."

Site visitors with critical medical questions are immediately told to seek the advice of their personal physicians or, in some cases, sent an urgent e-mail suggesting that they go immediately to the emergency room. But to address health and everyday medical issues, BabyCenter.com has a medical advisory board of physicians that consists of, according to their press materials, "leaders in all fields relating to new parenting, including obstetrics, pediatrics, family medicine, midwifery, mental health and parent education." Advisors have included the famous T. Berry Brazelton, M.D., and Penelope Leach and an experienced editorial team culled from top parenting magazines.

Three years after its own conception, BabyCenter.com had 2 million unique visitors a month and began expanding into the United Kingdom with a site uniquely designed for new and expectant parents there. On a monthly basis, BabyCenter.com reaches more pregnant women than any other medium, including all the parenting magazines combined. In terms of pure product sales, the site became one of the largest baby stores in the world after just one year in business.

"I think we managed to hit it right on the head," says Selcow. "People really wanted a place where they could find information. They wanted it anonymously, they wanted it in the middle of the night when they were up feeding, they wanted it whenever they had a question. Take the first trimester, before many couples have even told anybody they're expecting. There is only so much support they can get when they are keeping their pregnancy private." How personal and private can the connection to a Web site be? BabyCenter.com actually registers a huge spike in usage at the point of four and five weeks into the pregnancy, "When women discover their period is late," notes Selcow.

Then, it naturally follows that, when the time comes to start equipping the nursery and the baby, BabyCenter.com gets the order. Because it's already part of the family lifestyle, and it's been there long before the new mother got on the mailing lists at the hospital or what Selcow calls "those damn things that drop catalogs on your door when you come home from the hospital, because you signed up at a parenting class.

"We know about these women, confidentially," he says. "We've been talking to them on a weekly basis since week five of their pregnancy."

Every week, member parents receive a free electronic newsletter from BabyCenter.com that is specifically tailored for the challenges of that particular point in parenting time. "We can see them through age three," says Selcow.

And beyond. BabyCenter.com recently launched a follow-up site called ParentCenter, which reaches parents of children age three to eight.

"I think it all boils down to what I call the 'Oh, shit!' moment," says Selcow. "The moment when you realize your life is about to change forever and you are in this thing and you think, 'Oh, shit! What do we do?' There are a few moments that represent a substantial change in your life where information is valuable, things you value dearly are involved, and you are willing to dig and look and investigate and gather information. Having a baby is certainly one of these moments. And getting married, planning for a wedding, is another."

Carley Roney and David Liu, cofounders of TheKnot.com, the premier wedding site, would agree. Certainly another key flashpoint for the Internet as an evolutionary incubator is the wedding, a universal rite of passage that could, in theory, be a mere paperwork formality, but which has for most of us become a process so emotional that it seems antithetical to everything the Internet represents.

Any wedding, however simple or elaborate, involves two emotional people and thousands of years of tradition. Emotion and technology; tradition and change — two pairs of antithetical concepts. Tradition and change are historically opposing forces — as any bride and her mother, struggling to find a common ground for the wedding plans, can attest. The bride wants a small wedding; her parents want to invite business associates. The bride and groom want to get married barefoot on a beach; her mother had in mind a gown with a train and a church. The bride wants to invite people by fax; her mother is appalled. The bride and groom want their dog to officiate; her grandmother feels faint. The couple-to-be are the same sex . . . And so it goes. But, with the Internet, traditions that have been hallmarks of the wedding process since the first bride waltzed down the aisle have taken a radical shift into cyberspace and, with them, brides, grooms, and their families and — in a shift that is closing the loop — traditions themselves are evolving as well.

It all started with two people who fell in love.

In 1993, when David Liu and Carley Roney decided to get married, they had problems. "I was an educated person," says Roney, "but I had no idea whatsoever how to plan a wedding." Blonde, crop-haired, slim, and sleek, Roney is clearly a no-nonsense type, but the airy, somewhat retro lime-green colors and molded plastic chairs combined with lacy, decidedly non-utilitarian bouquets scattered throughout her company's loftlike offices reflect a woman's yen for romance with a modern twist. Which is exactly the sensibility that she, her husband, and their two partners created when they founded TheKnot.

TheKnot's theme line is "A refreshing, new approach to the bridal business," and so it is. The large, community-style office area, where women in tailored pantsuits and men in chinos and shirt sleeves share space with Hip-Hop techies in backward baseball caps is broken up by stacks of wedding-suitable gifts. An editor jumbles through a shoebox full of assorted engagement rings of every shape and cut imaginable. "They're imitation," she explains. But important. "We wear these to bridal shows. If you aren't wearing an engagement ring, nobody will pay any attention to you." On TheKnot's Web site, a bride does not have to sort through a box, or even set foot in a jewelry store; she just has to click on "Ringfinder." Retrofitting the ritual premarital tasks to fit today's brides and grooms is the linchpin of TheKnot's purpose.

"When David and I got engaged, we had a lot of issues," recalls Roney. (Mark Selcow would call these "Oh, shit!" moments.) Roney is the kind of person who moves and talks at warp speed. Decisive, authoritative, and charming, I first saw her at a women's Internet conference, where she held her own with roster members who included Hillary Clinton. It's hard to imagine Roney being confused about anything, but in planning her own wedding, she found she'd met her match. "David and I were planning in a hurry, in a city where we didn't know anything, didn't know where people had weddings, hadn't even been to any weddings there. So much of people's knowledge is based on other people, and we didn't know enough people at that time to tap into that. And David was largely responsible for the planning, and he was completely out of the loop."

"No way was I going to be caught dead in some bridal shop or thumbing through one of her bridal magazines," says Liu, immaculately groomed in a tailored tweed suit with open-collared blue silk shirt, still shuddering at the very thought.

Roney adds, "He probably wouldn't have taken advice from *Bride's* magazine anyway. Tell me, what man would? And it just seemed to us that *Bride's* was a little bit old-fashioned and tired and that it wasn't what I considered our wedding was going to be."

On top of this, Liu and Roney were a multicultural couple, trying to piece something meaningful together from a mixture of heritages and traditions. "Help was nonexistent in the bridal world," says Roney. "Forget it!"

"You felt somewhat left hanging in the wind," admits Liu. "When we were planning our wedding, Carley was working full time with very long hours, like a lot of women today, and I was the one with more time because I was free-lancing, doing entrepreneurial jobs. So a lot of the day-to-day stuff fell on my shoulders. You realized—all the media about weddings was geared to the bride, the fiancée, and her mother. The sole source of authority was the mother of the bride. But the reality was, more and more, the demographics were changing. People were getting married older—like we were a little older than the norm. And given that situation, many people were either contributing to their own wedding or paying for it, which in fact we did," says Liu.

"When it is your check and your money, you want to have some say and you want to make sure it is done properly. Still, you could have been with your fiancée for eight years, but you probably haven't thrown a dinner party for 150 guests that you had to provide entertainment for." Roney, for instance, was working as a photography curator for the 150th Anniversary Exhibit for the Smithsonian when she and Liu got engaged. Organizing 150 years of photography did not faze her, but she was flummoxed by making her own wedding plans.

Clearly, many millions of other brides and grooms had faced their own issues and in-laws, gnashed their teeth, shed a few tears, walked down the aisle, and written it off to the monster known as Having a Wedding.

Not Roney and Liu. They saw an opportunity. "From our personal experience, and also from a general analysis, weddings just seemed to be the most perfect fit for an online business. You spend money and you spend money on a deadline, and you are desperate and starved for information," says Roney. She and Liu figured it was a good bet that lots of other couples were having problems like they'd had planning their wedding. They were right: 2.5 million couples a year, to be exact, are finding the concept of TheKnot appealing enough to join. A business concept was born. "Nothing new had been launched in weddings," Roney notes. "This was different from everything else out there. We thought the concept of weddings for the real world would be a good idea. The real information and sort of like your friends giving you advice, rather than some snooty old lady or protocol expert."

Today Liu and Roney, who call themselves "The post–Emily Post" ("Emily Post wouldn't know what to do with half the questions we get in a day!"), along with the two other founding partners, are at the helm of what could be seen as the Amazon.com of the wedding industry. Half of all brides today visit TheKnot — to plan their wedding, set up a wedding Web site, chat with other to-be-marrieds, preview wedding wardrobe options, ask questions, find out honeymoon information, or register for gifts.

Grooms, once almost total outsiders in the wedding planning process, visit TheKnot too. The online world is comfortable to them — certainly in comparison to a bridal consultant's office, a florist, or a fitting room — to find out everything from their role in the wedding, to that of the best man, or how to plan a honeymoon. "It's not all flowers and doves and pink," notes Roney, recalling David's experiences. "We accept women and men equally. We don't just assume that the bride is the one picking out the flowers. It could just as well be the groom. Never mind the fact that guys like to do things like make wedding Web pages and do the budgets — or the bride might do this too. The point is that this whole interactive aspect is opening the door to both of them. And they find it cool and fun. So I think that is a change."

The two thousand brides and grooms who become members of TheKnot each day clearly agree. One million a month visit the site. Even mothers of the bride are seeing the light — 4 to 5 percent of the audience for TheKnot.com is moms on-line.

TheKnot is a vivid example of how attitude and technology

have converged to alter social customs of hundreds of years' standing. "It has completely changed the process of planning a wedding," says Roney. "There are things now that are a part of planning a wedding which have actually been invented by this Internet concept. It picked up on a trend which was happening anyway, that couples were now involved in planning a wedding together. That was already shifting, although the traditional media ignored it. They were just too steeped in tradition. But the Internet in particular really pushed that agenda forward, in that guys are often the ones who find TheKnot for their couple.

"Then there's the whole idea of having a Web site for your wedding. You send people to interact with your wedding long before the actual process. E-mail has changed a lot of things about weddings too. People can post questions or write e-mails. Take the whole concept of bridesmaid dresses, a previously painful process for everyone involved. Now a bride can go and find a bridesmaid dress, she sends off the file to her maid of honor and the bridesmaids, and so on. The whole concept of being able to manage the community of people through e-mail has been very interesting. People weigh in their opinion by logging onto the site, or by looking at different things. You have your own little community for the event, and people interact within it on the Web site."

"When you just think about the communication that goes on between the bride and groom and their bridal party," Liu says, "most people don't even live in the same city as their wedding anymore. Statistics show that 45 percent are living in a city where they are not getting married. So imagine trying to find a florist or a caterer or a limo driver from a different city. It is nearly impossible.

"Also, one of the changes that is happening in weddings today is that people want their wedding to be different and personal. The 1980s and '90s were all about the cookie-cutter, perfect wedding. Now people want their wedding to be unique and memorable, and I think the Internet has helped make that possible. What if you are planning a honeymoon in Bali? Or you want to honor your fiancé's heritage with food at the reception? Or you want to research ancient Greek traditions or some cool thing that people do on the other side of the earth? How do you find out about this? The Internet brings all that information together, it makes it a lot more efficient."

Imagining I was a bride, I checked the site and discovered that TheKnot covers a wide variety of weddings, including "Real Weddings," "Cultural Celebrations," and "Intimate Weddings." Interested in how somebody else pulled it off? You can find what TheKnot refers to as "The Oscar rundown of a wedding," the who, what, when, where, the invitations, the menu highlights, how he proposed, whatever. I was a bride with exotic tastes, in search of something that might not be too readily accessible through traditional means, and chose Egypt as a thematic for my wedding. No problem on TheKnot. Sure enough, there was a couple who had an Egyptian-influenced wedding, and every detail was on the site, up close and personal for me to study. Here's a smidgen of what I learned: The couple had a fascination with ancient Egypt, so Terrence, the groom, had proposed at the Washington Monument because it is in the shape of an obelisk, an ancient Egyptian symbol of fertility. The engagement ring had four ankhs, another Egyptian symbol. The cake was a confection in the shape of a three tiered step pyramid. The bride wore a traditional gown, but Terrence broke tradition by wearing a pharaoh's outfit. The food at the reception included some Egyptian delicacies. By the time I had finished reading about the wedding, I felt like I had been a guest myself. I had to wonder: Where else would I have found another couple who had taken the Egyptian path before me, for better or worse, and in a matter of seconds?

"It has really opened a whole other world," says Roney, "in the way that people talk to each other about weddings. It has expanded people's community. You might have a problem and in the past, you could ask your mother, your aunt, or your friends at work, but now you go into a chat room and you ask people from all over the world what they are doing for their favors, or how they are dealing with their crazy sister who is jealous that she is not getting married first, or all those different things. Weddings are such a community thing anyway, and expanding that concept worldwide, I think, is going to have a fundamental change on what people do with their weddings."

Roney and Liu acknowledge the importance of the role of tradition in weddings, but note that some traditions had almost crippled the process for modern couples. "Take registering for gifts," says Liu. "You call a store, say, Bloomingdale's in New York, and you say you want to register. The registry consultant will tell you, 'Well, on average it takes about six hours and we recommend that you space it over the course of three days.' Who has time to spend six hours doing this? I mean, that is insane!" TheKnot, on the other hand, allows you to register with a click, is open 24/7, and, if you can't find what you want among the 10,000 gifts—everything from blenders to whitewater rafting trips—there's always American Express Gift Checks. The goal is to end one tradition that nobody is anxious to keep alive—the seven-toaster wedding.

"Then there's finding the gown," Liu continues. "Basically, before the Net arrived, you had to buy these wedding magazines that weighed about five pounds each, flip through thousands of pages of ads, and then you see this beautiful gown, and it doesn't even give you the price or the style number. You may get a list of retailers, but when you walk into that retailer, you may realize, 'Oh my God, this whole thing has been a bait and switch,' because now this retailer may say, 'Oh, that is a $12,000 gown.

Here, let me show you the things in your price range.' And you realize then that you, the consumer, have been insulated from the information you really require. Ultimately, all this is a waste of time."

Online at TheKnot, a bride can choose from 20,000 images of gowns ranging from $800 to $5,000, including gowns by almost all of the major bridal designers. She can narrow the field and shop by price, neckline, waistline, style, or a wide choice of criteria.

"I think you could probably save at least 50 to 60 percent of the time that was traditionally spent on planning a wedding by using TheKnot.com," says Liu. "We can also empower people to make decisions so you can enjoy your engagement, enjoy the process, as opposed to get stressed over it because you feel like you are running out of time. One of the things TheKnot does is handle your lists and through its weekly countdown feed you the information you need when you need it, and give you reminders of things you may not have thought of. So you can rest at ease that someone has thought about this and someone is helping you through the process. And even though we are probably the best that is out there, there is so much more we can still do.

"The reality is that things have changed a lot in the past twenty years. When you think about the different influences that occur at a wedding, I would venture to say that, of the twenty weddings I have been to in the last two years, divorce had some play in it, some are interracial, interdenominational, perhaps even a second wedding, and some people have a child already. Now these things have become more and more a part of everyday life. Brides and grooms can use our site, print out articles or write-ups of other people's weddings, and take them to their parents. They are using us as a sort of voice of authority, to show there are other ways of doing it. We wanted people to not feel alienated while they are planning something that is really ultimately important to them.

"I think the underlying theme of what TheKnot is really about is that we were not technologists. We were media people who said, 'Oh my gosh, this is an incredible application that can help us change an entire industry. And impact lifestyles in the process. In our wildest dreams or projections, we never thought our audience base would exceed an institution like *Bride's* magazine, which had been the standard of the industry for sixty years. And for us to eclipse it twofold in only a matter of four years is probably more of an indication of the power of the medium than even our execution."

The response has been surprisingly emotional, the antithesis of the notion that the virtual world leads to an emotionless environment, a product without soul. "We have really intense relationships with our users," says Liu. "For instance, once our VP of sales was getting on an airplane, and he was carrying TheKnot gift box under his arm, and someone stopped him on the plane and started gushing 'Oh my God, are you with TheKnot? I love TheKnot!' That phrase, 'I love TheKnot,' is one we hear a lot— our salespeople, the community, these people are engaged. Even business people will say, 'I just had to come to this meeting because I really love TheKnot.' And you realize, if I was walking around with a bridal magazine or a tote bag from Macy's bridal registry, nobody would respond that way. There isn't a relationship that has been built up, in spite of dozens and dozens of years in the business on their part. That is the difference between what we are trying to create and what is out there.

"The one thing we believe is that the process of a wedding is a great incubator. We can understand or learn how people go about informing themselves to make a decision, because they have this big budget, they have a tight deadline for spending it, and they need a lot of information. We think the model of creating a service vehicle out of the online medium is only going to be better defined. And that is what we are trying to do with TheKnot, and we think that will lead into everything, and hopefully we will be the agent of change for that."

Still, TheKnot, like the most successful forces for change, manages to honor what we love about what has been while evolving toward what is to be. After a bride (or groom) has been registered for a certain amount of time, TheKnot sends an impressive, free gift box. Inside, among other treats, is a CD on honeymoons, a booklet with a ring-sizer, a wedding planning notebook, and a gift registry workbook. Elegantly scripted on the cover of the workbook is a quote from the very eloquent and entirely analog Robert Browning: "Grow old along with me/The best is yet to be."

Closing the loop on rites of passage, the Internet has, no doubt inevitably, entered into the business of death and the bereavement process. It is not unexpected that funeral homes and mortuaries now offer descriptions of their services via Web sites. What may surprise you, however, is the creation of a new medium dedicated to the grieving process, the virtual memorial. This is a permanent, Internet-based "album" into which the mourner and family, friends and associates from around the world can pay their respects by posting tributes to the deceased. These memorials can take the form of a few sentences or a poem, or numerous pages of text, photographs, letters, music, artwork, scanned documents, or videos. It is possible to post the complete life story of the deceased and preserve it on the Internet for generations to come. All of this can be created in the privacy of the participants' homes, and the online medium provides a convenient way for friends and loved ones to pay their respects or grieve without the expense or travel to a specific cemetery. In addition, there can be a link to a charity of choice for donations in the name of the deceased. Like a gravesite, an online memorial can be purchased "preneed." Or it can be established at any time following the death of the loved one. Presumably, you could even set up and edit your own online memorial.

I visited a number of these online memorial sites and found the memorials were unexpectedly moving, much more so than the physical experience of walking through a graveyard and looking at headstones. The sites were all extremely personal; many showed images that connoted the deceased or pictures of the individuals. Written passages about the deceased by friends and relatives were in many cases lengthy, personal and emotional enough to move me to tears in a way that no obituary or gravestone for a stranger ever had.

One eMemorial featured a simple picture of a crystalline blue sky, shot from above fluffy white clouds, as if from the window of an airplane. Soft guitar music played, and there was not much copy, just the simple name of a girl, the dates of her birth and death, and two words: *forever fourteen.*

More telling about the impact of the Internet as a benchmark medium for a certain group of people were the young ages of those who either were memorialized or who had posted the memorials. Almost all of those posted memorialized individuals under the age of thirty-five or were posted by young parents of deceased children. It seemed as if those who grew up and lived on the Internet retained a comfort level there even in death.

"Most of them are younger people," says Andrea Gambill, editor of *Bereavement* magazine, which manages the eMemorial site. "The response has been amazing." Gambill, herself a bereaved parent, sees the Internet as filling a unique gap in the grieving process. "Society is impatient with people who are grieving," she says. "When old Uncle Henry dies, and he's ninety-seven, that's one kind of grief, but it's not what I am talking about."

To Gambill, this particular kind of grief is more applicable to the young. "Every time a person who has had that kind of experience has an opportunity to remember the person they loved, they want to do that. The biggest issue is 'Will somebody remember?' Sometimes society is impatient with that."

The Internet, in its association with speed and instant gratification and impersonality, provides a contrarian haven via those very attributes for those with highly emotional issues that may be beyond the reach or grasp of the family or community in which a person actually resides.

Gambill feels the Internet meshes with the needs of the bereaved in unexpected ways. "The far-reaching aspects of the Web are important," she says. "It doesn't sound logical, but people don't care who remembers, they just care that *someone* does. Even though the Web is anonymous, it's important that someone out there remembers."

She was not surprised that I was emotionally impacted by the online memorials. "As you read about these people, you become invested in that situation. Whether we know it or not, we are invested in each other. If we choose to look at the situation, we care."

The Internet offers the opportunity, the accessibility, to care. "That's why we have online memorials," says Gambill. "Because people need it. It matters to people, it's important. At any given moment in the U.S., thirty million people are walking around with a grief situation that can impact their everyday life—by confusing, disorienting, distressing, or distracting them. There is a silent but powerful message from the people around them, however, to hide their natural feelings, so they put on what I call their 'fine mask.' People ask how they are, and they answer, 'I'm fine!' But they're not.

"The Internet gives these people a chance for intimacy and anonymity. They can be anonymous with their intimacy. They can disclose as much as they choose and at the same time be private. They can get the exposure of their feelings without criticism or judgment. The Internet offers that, and it is tailor-made for people who are grieving. They can maintain anonymity, yet open up to a vast audience of people who can connect with their experience.

"We also have bulletin boards where there is an opportunity for people to write in their questions and comments on a variety of topics—widowed, suicide, homicide, bereaved parents—and people can connect with each other."

As can the parents and pre-parents on the BabyCenter.com bulletin boards, or the brides and grooms on TheKnot.com. All of these unrelated individuals, mostly under the age of thirty-five, but all at a different stage of the life process, have reached a flashpoint of emotion and need that has compelled them to reach out—not just to buy a piece of merchandise related to their situation but to connect with others in similar situations. To join a very accessible yet intensely personal community of others in similar circumstances who, they hope, will understand, give direction or, at least, understanding and acceptance. To find a place where the answer to a timeless question can be posted and an individualized answer received.

This is more than kids hot mailing and e-mailing. According to the GenY2K Study™, 45 percent of those age thirty-five to forty used the Internet as a primary means of connecting with others, and of those who were heavily into technology, not surprisingly, the number reached 70 percent. These connections are much deeper and farther-reaching than are superficially apparent, possibly because their strength is in how they provide private solutions for the most personal situations. This impact, which may be below the radar screen, becomes apparent beneath the surface of the Web, where bulletin boards and connecting features on sites like BabyCenter.com, TheKnot.com, and eMemorial are becoming magnets for issues, questions, and emotions.

A woman who finds herself spotting at six weeks and shares her experience online at two o'clock in the morning with other women she does not know who have had a similar situation is unlikely to broadcast this experience to the world, as is the parent of a recently deceased child, or the sister of a twenty-two-year-old man who has died. Even a joyous situation like a wedding requires many private decisions and consultations with oneself and one's family, which, in this new virtual community, may take another form. Still, the impact is unmistakable. In the future, it is clear that the keyboard will become as critical as the telephone as an avenue of human connection.

For some who are comfortable there, the virtual world has already provided a particular sense of community, a safe harbor in a blizzard of anonymous "hits," that the real world cannot. Or, at least, a place where, at any hour of the day or night, someone, somewhere, is there.

13 REINVENTING THE FUTURE

The future isn't what it used to be. What was once written in stone is, increasingly, sketched in disappearing ink. Straight lines have splintered and dotted. The future used to be a chart, a course that one could follow — one that was pretty much predetermined in a step plan of short-and long-term increments. Any missing step, personal or professional, was a black hole and a cause for panic. Parents, educators, guidance counselors, and employers remonstrated the hapless goalless in a chorus of guilt and made them feel like a substandard species of shiftless wastrels. No clue what you'd be doing in five years? Gasp! No Big Brother corporation looking out for your well-being and putting together your benefits package and retirement plan? You might as well climb Everest without oxygen.

Today the Change Agents have taken an eraser to the mapped future. They are not only prepared to forge into uncharted territory, but many find it the only desirable course. Still, this does not mean a dead end for long-term goals, but a reinvention. The fact is, the generation that has the least problem leaving the future undefined is paradoxically the most likely of all to say it sets long-term goals. According to the GenY2K Study™, 65 percent of twenty- to-twenty-four-year-olds say they set long-term goals, which is actually 17 percent more than those over age thirty-five. There is also a strong indication that this is not a traditional career vision. Forty-seven percent of twenty- to-twenty-four-year-olds said they expected to work from home at some point in their career, as did 54 percent of twenty-five- to thirty-four-year-olds. Across the board, one-third of all respondents said they would leave work early if there was something else they wanted to do.

Here the definition of "important" is relevant. When my son was born twelve years ago, I remember feeling guilty when I went into labor at the office and had to leave at three. (Actually, I didn't realize I was going into labor since it was my first baby— but I did know I was eight and a half months' pregnant and felt strange. I had a debate with myself: If this is labor, then it's OK to leave work, but what if it's not?) Maybe this was because I had a boss who had extolled the virtues of my predecessor, who had stuck it out at her desk, at his insistence, until the pains came so close they had to call an ambulance and carry her out on a stretcher. Young women, and men, reading this today will think that this kind of mind-set was ludicrous—and they are right—but, the truth is, it used to be that life and death were about the only legitimate reasons for the career committed to leave work early, even, or especially, in one's own head.

Today the worm has not only turned, but it is spinning into a death spiral. One woman I interviewed, a forty-something senior executive in a traditional firm, was shocked when one of the young vice presidents who reported to her said she could not stay late to work on a proposal and walked out. The reason? "She had tickets to a rock concert. I mean, I could not believe it! If I had been in her shoes, I would have given away the tickets and stayed. I would not have even mentioned the tickets to my boss, even if I had to throw them out!" The senior executive had to admit that the young vice president ultimately did get the proposal done—it was her attitude toward commitment to the job that amazed her.

Fast Company's George Anders has similar stories. "I can think of friends who are in software design who will say, 'I go hike in Nepal every year. And you just will not see me in the month of October because that's the best month to go hiking there. And make sure you assign me projects that can be done by September 10, because come hell or high water, I'm gone for a month. And if you don't want to keep me as a full-time employee, that's fine, but hiking is every bit as important to me as what I do in my work.' The attitude to that kind of thing used to be, 'Take a hike.'" But we're now in an environment where people can do that, stresses Anders. "They feel they can get re-hired come November 15, when they're back. It's very disorienting for traditional managers, who used to be able to pull people into their office for that stern talk and send the guy out quaking. Now they try it and they literally get laughed at."

As long as job requirements are satisfied, this mind-set is defined by employee needs. The natural progression, attitudinally, is the free-lance mentality. And it has never been more accessible.

Where working independently was traditionally limited to a network of immediate contacts, the Internet provides a global platform. Web sites such as HotJobs, Career Mosaic, and Guru.com are already serving this marketplace, offering branded capability of connecting free-lancers with opportunities. The Internet is playing a role in making lifestyle free-lancing a strong option for a wide network of participants. There are the basic technical capabilities, of course, that allow corporate employees to be virtual participants at the office on many levels. But you do not have to be a member of a corporate structure to reap the benefits. More than enabling the work flow and process, the Internet is providing a new platform for putting people together with work.

Anders notes, "I would reinforce the argument that we're moving to a world where a lot more work is done on an outsource basis by people who are highly skilled, making good money. I think the Internet greatly enables people to do more of that. I was talking with a guy who runs a company that puts up for work serious computer engineering projects. And the guy said there are people in the Ukraine, there are people in rural Idaho, there are people in India who will bid for work on these three-or four-week projects. They can live wherever they want to, they can get paid, and there's no longer the feeling that you have to come into the office and have an employee badge to be getting a chance to be working for a big-chip company."

Jon Slavet, CEO of Guru.com, works with a base of some 300,000 free-lancers and consultants and has said that within ten years, "This trend will be in full bloom and will be an accepted part of the way that business happens and the way the world works. This definitely could not have happened ten years ago. The seeds of powerful technology are freeing people from corporate jobs."

The category is already starting to mushroom. Guru.com's newsletter began with 1,000 readers and within two years grew to 200,000. The roster of registered companies that are looking for freelance talent is about 50,000. Companies will outsource 20 million projects this year, more than double that in the next two years. And that is expected to grow to $80 billion in a few years.

Slavet sees the free-lance trend as going beyond the borders, with people utilizing Guru.com's services in 150 countries. "This is a very international trend," he says. "Technology is completely democratized as to how, when, and where people can work. You can take your laptop, you can have DSL at home, you can go to a teleconferencing center—all with no corporate infrastructure." People who have made the decision to be independent, he says, are looking for freedom, control, and "the capability to work with the people I want, on the projects I want, from where I want. So there is a values shift."

It is not surprising that almost 80 percent of those age sixteen to twenty-four surveyed in the GenY2K Study™—men and women alike—felt it was acceptable to take time out from a career for responsibilities at home. The commitment focus is shifting from the professional to the personal. But that does not eliminate the possibility of a peaceful coexistence between the two.

Could it be that, when the dust settles, we'll see a new category in the workforce, one that is based on neither the New Economy nor the old economy, but the next economy? This may be a world populated by lifestyle free-lancers, fluidity specialists who segue from one opportunity to another, depending on the opportunities and personal goals of the moment, taking out time when they feel like or can afford it, patchworking together a life. It is an opportunistic rather than long-term vision. But it is a vision, and the result is a patchwork rather than a smooth linear progression. Today, some 30 million Americans, or one in six adults, work outside of companies. By 2020 it is projected that 40 percent of the white-collar sector will be working in a free-lance or independent capacity. Futurists refer to this scenario as the coming free-agent nation.

The fact is, the number of Americans who are working for themselves has dropped in recent years, according to the Bureau of Labor Statistics. Between 1994 to 1999, the supposed entrepreneurial breakout period, self-employment actually fell for the first time since the 1960s. Is there a way to reconcile this with the soaring *motivation* to be not necessarily self-employed, but in control of one's career destiny? Yes, and that is the third alternative, fluidity. It is actually the only option that makes sense in the face of the facts. Here is the recipe: Work for one company for as long as you want or it wants, on reinvented terms that *feel* more like working for yourself. Then move on — work for someone else, or for yourself. Take off. Return to next situation. Repeat.

Perhaps this pattern will be merely a bridge to a truly free-agent nation in the future, but in the meantime, it provides both employees and employers with the best of both worlds. For the employee, there's organizational support and a measure of predictable security, enriched by whatever benefits and personal satisfactions can be gleaned; for the employer, there's lower long-term overhead and better capability to access and deploy the right resources for a changing environment. On both sides, there's less commitment, which, as in a relationship, is good when that's what both sides want. And, when it's over, as we've seen with today's ex–dot commers, there's not the postdivorce bitterness of being the one left behind. Rather, there is a feeling of something more gained than lost.

14 E-CARUS

According to urban legend, in the spring of the year 2000, after a particularly soaring season, E-carus flew too close to the sun. His virtual wings melted with his stock valuation, and he tumbled to Earth.

Or did he?

More to the point would be that the landing may have been hard, but E-carus has hopped a cloud. Although a very few of the Change Agents interviewed for this book showed a glimmer of concern, almost none expressed major worries for their future in a shaky market that had already materialized. This included those whose companies had evaporated from beneath their feet — some, more than once.

Typical was Aaron, in his mid-twenties. "I don't want to worry about ten years from now," he said. "I have a strong support group of friends and family around me to fall back on, so I am not really worried. I would love to retire young. That would be great, if I could retire at thirty. But I really don't have a plan. I have never even thought about it. My only goal is to enjoy life. I don't want to be one of those people that works twenty-four hours a day. I enjoy traveling, I enjoy spending time with my friends, my family, doing my music. And when I am ninety years old and looking back on my life, I definitely want to be able to say I enjoyed my life. There is always more to life than just work. Although, the thing is, I get up every morning and I look forward to going to work. The job I am doing now, I love to death. The only thing that would be better is to actually be a famous musician."

A Rolling Stone, perhaps?

"Exactly."

Since the judgment week of April 10, 2000, when the NAS-DAQ index fell nearly 1,000 points, puncturing the prospects of many dot com companies, a large percentage of which were existing on the furthest fringes of profitability, and following the roller-coaster dives of the markets, the Greek chorus has been raising its voice: *Hear ye, hear ye, the reign of technology is over.* Some old economy holdouts suppressed a sigh of relief, as if this whole thing had been some kind of virtual Brigadoon. The geeks were going to go back where they came from and things would go back to normal.

Well, normal isn't ever going to be what it used to be. Those brash and noisy young neighbors are going to be permanent fixtures on your block, and it doesn't matter where you live. Because, in retrospect, although there is no doubt that some segments of the original dot coms were built on platforms of less than long-term, self-sustaining, profit-generating capability, the underlying needs they met and the values they shaped are not only still standing but entrenched.

"There's uncertainty when you see negative news," says Chris Whittman of TechSpace. "But everyone still likes what they're doing and are working hard. There are a lot of companies out there that are still working, and it's going to make them stronger, better companies. That's the way it is for us. The fact is, most start-ups are high risk to begin with. We don't see so much of a hypergrowth mentality anymore, but we see it as a challenge. We've seen some companies move out (of the incubator environment) and then more recently move back in. Things are more fluid now. There are a lot of companies still out there that are changing the business models." Overall, Whittmann observes, "We are going forward."

"It used to be that as long as you had a pulse you could get funded," John Mecklenburg, an editor at *Red Herring*, the key tech industry magazine, was quoted as saying, echoing the business plan on a napkin analogy that I had heard in an Internet hangout. After the market faltered, however, funders were not so unequivocal and companies were not so casual. Venture capitalists who provided the funding tightened their requirements in the face of investments that would no longer be able to sustain returns of 100 percent and more. Yet the wherewithal is still there, as are the profits, a fact that often has been overlooked.

Venture capital investments for the first half of 2000 rounded out at $35 billion invested in 2,138 companies, according to Venture One. Compared to total 1999 figures of $37 billion invested in 3,153 companies, a boom market, the picture does not seem as dark as it has been painted. In fact, the thrust has simply shifted to different segments of the Internet market and to different kinds of requirements and expectations. There is no question that there has been and will continue to be a consolidation and winnowing out. Just as the dot coms with shaky foundations collapsed, so did venture capital that could no longer meet the demands of *its* investors—the wealthy individuals, pension funds, and institutional investors who were much freer with a checkbook when the bloom was on the rose. But this is not a dying breed. Three years ago, there were 507 VC firms in America. In 2000, there were 725. What is emerging is a more selective perspective. Investors are taking a cold, hard, and critical look at properties and plans presented to them. Incubator organizations are cutting back on both sides of the Atlantic. In England, where there were some 50 publicly traded incubators, their valuations have shrunk, forcing these organizations to reconfigure to survive. In America at the close of 2000, the bumper crop of 350 new incubators are braced for a shakeout.

"I think a lot of the dot coms will just go away," said Menlo Park consultant Valerie Frederickson, "but at the same time, a lot of people are still going to get money, they're still going to hire, and the venture capital funds have their money locked up five years down the road, so they're all still going to have to give out money. So VC money isn't going to simply drop off."

But the process is being impacted, which will in turn impact the people. Frank Quattrone, managing director of the Credit Suisse First Boston Technology Group in Palo Alto, California, has a unique vantage point in the new economy sector. In 2000 his group handled $7.4 billion worth of technology IPOs, and it continues to be the leading technology group in the investment banking industry. "I think that the get-rich-quick aspect of the gold rush is definitely over, in the sense that I don't think you'll see any venture capitalists or institutional investors put big money down on the come, and expect the public markets to risk capital in hopes that some of these companies might end up being the next Cisco or Microsoft," says Quattrone. "I think those days really are over, but I think that many of the category-defining companies in the sector, whether it's eBay or Amazon. com or Yahoo, will end up making major contributions to the economy.

"A leading indicator in our business is the venture capital that gets raised and invested in start-up companies, so in the past, typically in most cycles, it takes anywhere from two to five years from when a company first gets funded to when they either go public or get sold, creating transactions for investment banks. If you go back and take a look at what's happened to the amount of venture capital that's been raised and invested, it's just skyrocketed in the last couple of years. Maybe there was $10 billion a year raised between 1996 and '98, and '99, there was $45 billion raised. And in 2000, there was $100 billion raised, so that's a tremendous amount of capital raised, coming into the system, funding new companies. One thing that happened with the Internet which accelerated every possible time frame was it also accelerated the time frame from when companies could get funding to going public, so that instead of two to five years, it had shrunk to, in some cases, less than a year. The question is how much of the $45 billion that got invested in companies last year has already seen returns on investment, in the way of liquidity events (or IPO's, or company sales), and how many of those opportunities were invested in based on a set of assumptions that no longer exist. So one of the key questions is, will some of the venture funds be able to show the same degree of return, or will a bigger percentage of their portfolio never see the light of day? The good news is that a lot of money has been raised and not as yet invested, so they'll have the opportunity to invest in valuations and with economic conditions more reflective of normal times, and the accordion is expanding back out to companies taking two to five years to get sold rather than less than a year. So when you wrap all of that up in a bow, I'd say that while there are crosscurrents, the trend clearly points toward more start-up activity and more transactional opportunity for investment banks downstream of the venture capitalists."

Quattrone forsees a shift of emphasis, a reformatting of the business. "Maybe the mix of business at investment banks will shift from taking companies public and merger and acquisition activity to raising more money for companies while they're private through private placements and helping them with strategic partnerships," he says, "rather than taking them public so quickly."

As the economy and its vehicles reformat, the Change Agents may face an attitude adjustment. "People are going to be forced to adjust," Quattrone believes. "Things got so bad in 1999 and early 2000, there was an attitude that was outrageous and very frustrating to deal with — the entitlement attitude, 'I just graduated from business school, I should be worth $10 million in my first two weeks on the job, and if you can't give it to me, I'll go someplace else and get it there, because there's a lot of free money, and I don't have to work all that hard, and why shouldn't I get my stake?' The level of whirling around and spinning around to make sure that you were getting yours was just at an absolute peak right before the market crashed, and it was a very, very difficult time. I think when it first started weakening, the reality distortion field was still very much intact, where people said, 'This is a correction, but we'll get back to the normal level for these companies.' But after nine straight months of continual hammering and beating, and many of the stocks trading at anywhere between 1 percent and 10 percent of the value that they were trading at the peak, and companies going out of business, and layoffs, and venture guys pulling the plug on companies — you need to have extended periods of pain before it sinks in, and I think now it has definitely sunk in.

"I think the level of motion, the level of disloyalty, the level of job hopping has clearly slowed down," says Quattrone, "and I think these people are genuinely concerned for the first time in their working lives that the economy and the stock market might not always be up, and that maybe they should be worried about job security instead of going from X million of net worth to Y million of net worth."

The future, Quattrone thinks, will depend on the environment at the time, although "The young generation always has something to prove to the old, and they certainly have had their share of icons, whether it's Bill Gates or Larry Ellison. So for all the failures, there are still the visible successes, and there still are always going to be geniuses that might not necessarily have a very well-rounded portfolio of characteristics who are going to be passionate about changing the world and fight against all odds and succeed. But there are going to be a lot more that fail over the next three years than over the last three, when it seemed like anybody with a business plan, or without, could get venture capital funding and get their company public and create the sense of paper wealth. So there's always going to be exceptions, but there's not going to be 100 percent exceptions going forward.

"I think that people who like to start companies always have some mixture of wanting to change the world out of opportunity and frustration and desire for wealth-building, and those are the ones who have the unique passion and insight to change the world as the thing that really drives the behavior and drives the energy level. We were always very skeptical about people whose main objective was to build wealth and look for a means to get there. We were looking for people who were passionate about their ideas and clever about having thought through the details and willing to take advice and surround themselves with high-quality teams."

Moving ahead in turbulent times, those same talented, passionate, entrepreneurial individuals, on the crest and cusp of their careers and lives, with attitudes and affinities acquired before they could drive cars or vote, will be completely capable of sustaining and reinventing themselves as necessary. The next economy is in its infancy, and the need for those to serve it will, for the foreseeable future, far outstrip the level of talent supply.

Dot com orphans will seek and find new homes. And they will do it without sentimentality, as often as they have to, and fearlessly, because they have never had anything to fear.

Valerie Frederickson has experienced this firsthand in her recruiting business. "Even with the demise of some of the dot coms, young people still aren't worried about getting jobs, because if they've got good skills, people will hire them. They've got more confidence than anybody's ever seen."

Back to Aaron, who is philosophical regarding those of his contemporaries who have suddenly found themselves falling from the top of the dot com heap: "A lot of people don't deserve to be where they are." He shrugs. "Reality at times can be very harsh. But then, I say, they can get over it. These people, at the same time, have had an experience that not a lot of people have had in running a company." He also focuses on the upside of the situation. "Not many people can say that at such a young age, and if it was somewhat successful, then that will always be able to help them. And if they can turn the negative situation into a positive, then they will be just fine."

Cal Cooper (not his real name), twenty-eight, had just experienced the literally overnight shutdown of a seemingly prosperous dot com where he had had a top job. There was no warning to the staff. One day the company occupied two bustling floors of prime space in mid-Manhattan, with scaffolding and logo signs in place for expansion. The next, it was over. Three weeks later, "There's nobody there. They filed Chapter 11." To prove his point, or maybe to confirm yet again that it was really true, Cal pulled out his cell phone and dialed his former phone extension at the office. A massage parlor answered, and he laughed as he hung up. "If anybody calls me, they're going to think I went into a new line of work!" Then he sighed. "I guess that means it's officially over."

Cal did not blame his former management for the company's

abrupt demise; in fact, he praised them, claiming that sudden death was better than slowly twisting in the wind, cutting half the people to slow the burn rate and leaving everybody looking over their shoulder to see if they would be next, with no guarantee that in the end that would have worked. He preferred decisiveness, and he was not bitter. His immediate plans included a two-week trip with his wife to Thailand and China. "We're a zero-income household now," he said. If he didn't seem unduly fazed, perhaps it was because he'd been in four start-ups in six years. Still, looking around, he had to admit, for the first time in his life, "I'm worried."

Cal met me at his chosen hangout, a linoleum-lined booth at the Union Square Coffee Shop, a retro-hip place he called Central Alley, the one-time dot com epicenter where the New York tech types congregated. His routine had been to drop into the coffee shop in the morning on his way to work between eight and ten. There were always a few meetings going on, a buzz to pick up and be part of.

He picked a paper napkin off the table and held it up: "This is all you need to do business in the Alley."

This was intended as a joke, a reference to the good old days of, literally, yesterday. In spite of their inbred confidence, people like Cal are finding themselves having to make a few adjustments. Historically, they've never had to do this before. Cal spent his entire career in the Internet space, although he found his calling somewhat haphazardly. "I was a slacker in high school, and I had no idea of what to do after college," he said. "I liked to play this computer game and hang out online. I didn't know what that meant, but I had an affinity for it. It was cool to plug your computer to a phone line and go to a place where a million others were. I picked up a copy of *Wired* magazine one day, read it, and thought, 'Maybe there is an industry there.' Then I moved to New York. I took the first job out of school where I could wear jeans and a T-shirt to work and get there at eleven and work till eleven and make a lot of money. So I have no knowledge of the corporate world. The only industry I've ever known is the online industry, and the only economy I've ever known is this bustling, booming economy. I graduated in 1994, and the summer of '94 was when it hit. I was in the first e-commerce company." Cal describes himself as a veteran of a time and place "where if you could pick up a pen, you could start a business."

For Cal, and, he says, his friends, the hardest part of being out of work has been adjusting to the pace. The speed of twitch turns on you when your company vanishes before you can change your phone number, and, in an instant, speedup is replaced with an entirely unfamiliar phenomenon: slowdown. Meanwhile, you're left with an itch and nothing to scratch it with.

"When you're used to working twelve to fifteen-hour days, and all of a sudden you wake up and there's nowhere to be — it's not only difficult to find something to do with yourself," Cal says, "but suddenly you're not so important, maybe you're not the king of the world. Now you're not making big decisions anymore, but the world still goes on."

Cal's fledgling concern about his future is not deep enough at this point to change his approach. Instead of diving headfirst back into the job market, he is leaving for vacation. Leaving town is a typical approach to handling the crash of your dot com. Perhaps this is evading the issue, or maybe it is just a physical way of wiping the slate clean with a return to something physical rather than virtual.

Pam Lloyd, the former vice president of marketing at the now-bankrupt Urban Box Office, was going to the Yucatán. "The guys that worked near me are already en route to South America for a month. There was another person I know who had come down to New York from Minnesota for the job. By 2:00 P.M. the last day, he was back in his car, heading north."

Four months after we first talked, Lloyd's high-energy dot com had folded suddenly. "It was very surreal," she said. "Two days before, the CEO had a company-wide meeting, at which he said either we'll get the check promised from the investors for our fourth round of funding—or we won't. There were signed papers from these investors, legal commitments, but still, we knew the deal: The company hadn't made a profit. There were two schools of thought. One was complete devastation, feeling it personally. The first thing you feel is like the whole world is collapsing, especially since that week there were an enormous amount of companies that went under as well; even the companies that seemed relatively healthier, with strong brand names, were laying off. The other dynamic was a bonding, a feeling of us against the man—that something as banal as a little old check had ruined the whole vision.

"Two days later, the entire company lined up for the last paycheck, all together. Everybody was holding their laptops and their cell phones and beepers, the company-issued hardware. There was a heap of IBM Thinkpads in a corner of a conference room, with their cords dangling, all stacked in rows. People were taking pictures. Wednesday, it was a thriving company of three hundred people racing around; Friday, it was a ghost town, and you just saw plugs in the wall. It was like the set of a show that they took off the air."

Lloyd feels that she has had the benefit of having worked in other environments, and that gives her flexibility in this situation. "I've never worked in a very corporate environment and never will—but it would be challenging to find something in between. In ten years, I've worked at five places and I've never gotten any negative feedback, so it's all made sense to me. It's gotten to the point where nothing fazes me anymore. Nothing is surprising. But there were a number of people in the company age twenty-four or twenty-six, who had nice titles, like managers, and nice pay, like $85,000, and that spoils you. There were some people for whom this was either their first or second job, and for them it was utterly devastating." She wonders what those people will do. As far as transferrable skill sets are concerned, she shakes her head. "What's a skill set? This environment was much less disciplined than that. So many of the dot coms are. It's not like a world with templates and Power Point—it's so much faster."

Lloyd, like most of her peers, feels that even the downside of her experience in working in the Internet space—losing her job when the company crashed—was worthwhile. "The beauty of the whole thing is that people were able to take on enormous responsibilities. You had access to responsibility, access to the executive level, hiring and firing people, real decision-making capability—while in the traditional track, you would still be somewhere in lower-level management. There is a big difference from actually heading a marketing group where eight to twelve people reported to you. I had to lay off people, I had to hire people. Most people, at thirty years old, have never had to lay off anybody. Even if my former company was not run as well as General Electric or NBC, you can't get that kind of experience, even if you have to take some middle-management job. So if I go back to anything else, another dot com or something more traditional, even if I take something more mid-level again, you know you still have that experience. I am so glad I tasted that part of the frenzy. I am not scared off. What happened at my company was an awful experience, but it was a learning experience, and I think it definitely can be translated. The crash of my company wasn't personal—it wasn't like they laid off fifty people and I was one of them. I mean, literally the entire company went at once. I think it helps me. But I think my value has increased, and I'm definitely enriched."

People who have worked in the technology sector in the recent past expect their jobs to change—whether at their initiation or not. Their ability to view this serial existence as the status quo and put a positive spin on it enhances their survival skills in such a market. "You've seen the changes, you've rolled with the changes, it happens," said one Silicon Valley veteran, now facing his third layoff. "Because I've always been with leading-edge technology companies, I can't say that it hit me unexpected or unaware or unprepared. It's one of those things where if you live it for long enough, you understand it better. And it's not just about start-ups. I was with two start-ups, but I was also with Apple and got laid off from there, so you can throw that theory out the window. In fact, with start-ups, there's also more opportunity. OK, so there's risk. But there's risk with the restaurant industry. A new restaurant opens up every ten minutes, but how many of those are alive in five years? Established companies as well as fledgling companies suffer from a lot of the same things."

One reason why the tech-driven Change Agents don't feel as stressed as their predecessors did about job loss is not only because they feel secure in their value and their ability to get another job, but because the situation fits with their own program. Where the Baby Boomers saw their career as a linear progression, with as few breaks in the line as possible, this group is proactive about inserting those breaks. There is no end-of-the-rainbow retirement scenario at work here. The horizon has no horizon. Instead, personal interludes are an ongoing, integral element of the total lifestyle, and the goal is to keep it this way on a lifelong basis.

Frederickson explains it this way. "We work for a while until we get enough money and then we take off. The attitude is, I have to feel that if I wanted to, I could leave next week and go to Europe or wherever. I really don't care what the future brings, because I can always get a good job making a lot of money. No doubt."

Frederickson says she relates completely to her candidates' attitudes, because sees herself as a proponent of this philosophy. Flexibility is the key, and that attitude comes, in part, from the free-agent mentality. When you and your parents before you and most of the working people you know have been encapsulated in corporate jobs, family businesses, or traditional small businesses in an environment that stresses longevity, flexibility seems very hard to come by. But when you are a walking, single-entity value proposition with a free-standing, in-demand set of skills you can pack up and move on to the next situation, the situation seems totally within your rights and your control.

Frederickson stresses fluidity. "If for some reason all our clients quit, I could make a very good living doing career counseling. Or I could be a recruiter, or a VP of sales. I could teach French. I could clean houses. I'm completely not worried about it. I have my own company because I think I know better than anybody else and I think I am smarter than them." She admits, however, that she has never encountered a serious recession. "I've never lived through a bad economic time. When I was in high school, and then after college, any job I've ever applied for, I've gotten."

The fact is, both sides have already gone too far and have gained too much to go back. Mark Fragga of Wharton says, "It is like the dynamic of, will people ever go back to three-piece suits all the time as opposed to business casual? It's kind of hard to imagine us re-creating formality in the economic structure when informality has served us so well. And I think that is one of the things that will continue to change. That we will continue to believe that fresh, young people and fresh, young companies can make dramatic changes that all of us benefit from. And I think it is hard for anybody to deny that, even if they feel threatened by those changes. And so I think the window will remain open, even though how much gust there is to the winds pushing people through that window will change."

As those winds gust, the Change Agents will be the among the best prepared to weather the storm, whatever it takes. First, they have the more aggressive attitude. Seventy-six percent of Gen Y Change Agents who are technology involved say they play to win, versus 58 percent of those age thirty-five to fifty. This is the same group who are already frustrated and who have suppressed violent tendencies, 61 percent saying they would use a gun if they had to and 49 percent saying there are people they'd like to get even with, according to the Gen Y2K™ Study.

The indications are that the younger sector has neither patience nor the inclination to stand in queues. If the job market is squeezed, they may float on the surface because of their unique combination of skills, flexibility, and attitude. But in the case of a recessionary environment, a face-off may be on the horizon between the ambitious, entitled-feeling Gen Y Change Agents and the Baby Boomers, who are less confrontational yet have their history at stake, feeling they played the entire game and, just before the buzzer, somebody changed the rules.

Indicators are already abundant, even in day-to-day behavior. "Gen Yers will send e-mails that all say 'ASAP' in them," notes Valerie Frederickson. "It really sets off the Baby Boomers. If I take a Gen Xer or a Baby Boomer out to lunch, they'll thank me. A Gen Yer won't. And Gen Yers will say to me, 'I need a VP title.'

"I'll say, 'What do you mean? You're two years out of college.'

"They'll say, 'I should be the VP. Put a VP over me and I'll quit.' And then they do quit. Once we have negotiated the financial package for Gen Xers, they leave me alone. The Gen

Yers, on the other hand, bring up money approximately every ten days. They try to hold me hostage again to pay them more. I have worked with people like the individual who was offered a director title and wanted a VP title, quit, and is now making an ungodly $2 million a year—but no job is good enough. There is a high level of arrogance. They don't take no for an answer."

The corporate response has been a combination of placation and helplessness. "They try to go through the channels, and then they feel sorry to lose them. Half the time, you want to say fine, quit. And the other half the time, you can't sleep at night because you are worried about losing them," says Frederickson.

When there is no hierarchy, there is still usually somebody controlling the purse strings. As new economy start-ups evolved, a phenomenon developed called "founder friction." This has often boiled down to generational warfare. In this scenario, the original founders of the organization clashed with the expanded organization as its goals moved forward. "The board will bring in a seasoned vet to protect the investment," said one insider. "The former CEO will either take umbrage and leave or will kow-tow."

"I saw two thirty-year-olds who were trying to do a start-up," says Frederickson. "They both quit their day jobs, and they thought they had an idea that was better than any software company in the world, that they knew more. I gave them a number of Baby Boomers who were willing to be on the board and be mentors and help them out. And the thirty-year-olds quickly got into a fight with the Baby Boomers because they didn't listen to them or trust their ideas. The Baby Boomers kept saying 'You've got to listen to me, I've been doing this for twenty years.' It just exploded."

There is a third option, however, which is based on flexibility on both sides. "Some companies will look at what fuels the passion of the founder and put him in that area, a place where he is not running the company or focused on the boring, mundane stuff that a CEO has to do," says Sankalp Saxena, senior director of product marketing and strategy of Rightworks, located in Silicon Valley. "This can be positive. Say the former CEO likes technology; he will then become chief technology officer. Or he may become the chief evangelist, or spokesperson for the company."

On the day-to-day level, however, outright hostility can break out as Gen Yers attempt to apply muscle on the job to get their point across. "Last week, one of our Gen Yers ended up screaming at one of the Gen Xers," said Frederickson. "What was this about? It was about how to best input something into our database. I had to talk to both of them. The Gen Yer actually had a point, and we ended up applying the suggestion, but it took a couple of days to get there."

This aggressiveness, even hostility, has seeped into more traditional environments—indeed, any environment in which Change Agents and Baby Boomers find themselves interacting.

One reason why the Gen Yers are more liable to confront than back down or even negotiate is because they don't have the same sense of accountability to authority that their predecessors in the workplace had. Richard Kirshenbaum of Kirshenbaum Bond & Partners points out, "This is one of the first times in history when children actually are smarter in some critical ways than their parents. How many times have we seen this scenario: The kids are on the computer, the parents standing by helplessly. And the kids say, 'Oh, Dad, what do you know?' or 'Let me show you how to do this.' And the parents are just standing there with this sheepish grin on their face, trying to assume a parental role, when the kids have this new focus. That has found its way into the workplace as well. These people have no sense of authority, because parents don't have the same authority as they used to.

They aren't this omniscient source of information anymore. Now that's transferred to the children. And that's a dangerous situation to be in."

Moving into the workforce, workers who have had no mentors feel no "parent-child" relationship on the job. They aren't trying to please anybody but themselves. They don't miss mentoring, nor do they even want it when offered. "This group is really lousy at even accepting mentoring," agrees Valerie Frederickson. "For instance, they don't even like to be coached. If you make a suggestion, they'll make a rude, hostile comment."

Change Agents, accustomed since youth to making independent connections and finding things out for themselves on the Internet, frequently clash with traditional, hierarchical training techniques imposed by Baby Boomers. The result is that young people, even when new to the workplace, expect office cultures to adapt to them, rather than vice versa, resulting in conflict, if not outright hostility.

In Chicago, Sandy Anderson (not her real name), a market researcher who runs her own firm, learned this when she hired Violet, a bright young woman with a fresh degree from the University of Chicago—but no work experience. "Violet completely resisted training," Sandy states. "She came in for an entry-level position in my office. She had never worked in market research before—or in any office, for that matter. What happened was, I would try to show her how things had been done, or how our office did things, or how our clients were used to seeing it, or how we had some systems that were time-savers that would help her. We even brought back the person she replaced to show her the systems, but she totally resisted all of that. The woman she was replacing and I went all out. We made copies of studies and reports for Violet to review. I even took Violet to breakfast a couple of weeks before she started so she could look at them.

"But her first day on the job, when I asked Violet what she

thought of the material we had given her, she laughed and said, 'Oh, that was just too much for me to read!' This was a University of Chicago graduate, so I knew she could read! The point was, she had no interest at all in reading about the kinds of things that had been done for our clients in the past. That was my first clue that there was going to be an issue. Also, we have a lot of office systems that have evolved over time. Violet's predecessor had written an entire office manual, which was very thorough — but Violet refused to even look at it. She said she didn't want to follow what anyone else had done before her. She said she wanted, in her words, to 'make a fresh path' and do it herself and figure it out for herself. Learning from someone else's experience was not something she was willing to do, on any level.

"Whenever I gave her input or suggestions, Violet would get this horrible expression on her face, hunch her shoulders, kind of tune out, and she often wouldn't even do what we had already set up. She would just do something different. What she told me was that she wanted to find out for herself how to do it, learn it herself, rather than do it the way we showed her. My response was 'Well, you could teach yourself Italian too, but why bother, when someone is here to show you these things and save you a lot of time?' She was so negative that her attitude was actually infecting others. I had a meeting with her, and I said, 'Look, you have to learn market research, and I'm here to teach you. Market research is not something you can figure out for yourself.' However, her response was that I was, in her words, 'explaining overmuch,' and it was insulting for her to have someone explain things to her. She said she really wanted to be more independent and creative and left on her own."

The friction mounted. "Violet refused to listen to how to do even the most very basic things, for instance, how to send out a broadcast fax to a number of clients at once. This is a task that is frequently done in my office, where the same faxes sometimes are sent to dozens or even a hundred people. But she wouldn't even read the directions to figure out how to do it. When I saw her standing by the fax machine sending one fax at a time, wasting so much time, I couldn't believe it. I went over and suggested, 'Why don't you read the office manual and see how to do a broadcast fax?' When I said that, Violet's response was to get an incredibly nasty expression on her face. She rolled her eyes to the other people sitting close by, as if to say 'Here she goes again.' She acted like I had killed her mother or something! I wasn't trying to push her, just run an efficient office, and after all, it is my business, and my name is on the door. We reached a total impasse. She wouldn't let anyone tell her what to do, on any level. Even though she had no idea what she was doing, she insisted on figuring it out for herself."

Eventually things broke down completely, and Sandy fired Violet. "I gave her three weeks' salary and terminated her. The next day, which was a Saturday, Violet came in and cleared out her desk. She brought her boyfriend with her. As she was cleaning out her desk, the boyfriend was pacing back and forth in front of my office, scowling at me. He was right outside my office door, and he had an umbrella in his hand. It was not raining out. But he had this umbrella, and he was ramming the umbrella as hard as could into his hand—just Slam! Slam! Slam! As he paced back and forth, back and forth. He was very threatening to me—I guess that's why he was there. It was really uncalled for. But I just laughed—it was ridiculous, what with the umbrella and bright, sunny skies. I invited him into my office to sit down and relax, but, no, he preferred to walk back and forth in the hall and scowl at me and bang the umbrella. Violet just cleaned out her desk and glared at me while this was going on. Then they left."

A key reason for younger workers' lack of the traditional respect for, or even acknowledgment of, authority, in Valerie Frederickson's opinion, is the way they were raised. While Baby Boomers were growing up, their mothers were usually at home and provided an omniscient authority figure. Gen X and Gen Y, on the other hand, were raised by two working parents, frequently divorced parents (the divorce rate doubled after the advent of the working woman in the 1980s), often were in day care or situations where they didn't identify with an authority figure. "Their parents were so busy," says Frederickson, "either working, or finding themselves, going through multiple marriages, going off to ashrams or whatever on weekends, they tended to neglect their kids in lots of ways. So you end up with generations that can be emotionally hollow. To counterbalance that, the parents gave them lots of goodies. Gen X and Gen Y are the first generations where the parents had a tremendous amount of disposable income and there was a lot of stuff to buy. Baby Boomers didn't grow up with their own pager, their own cell phone, their own TV. They were lucky if they got a bike. Gen X and Y grew up spoiled, so they expect all the stuff they got, and they expect it immediately. They don't feel they have to meet an authority figure's approval in order to earn it, they are just used to getting all the goodies and money they want. They are not intimidated."

In the absence of traditional authority figures, Gen X and Y have turned to the Internet for answers and information. For Gen Y, in particular, their community is moving from the actual neighborhood, school, and family to the virtual world. Advice can be had in a chat room from anonymous sources that can have as much — or more — credibility as a parent or teacher. The authority of the Web is limitless, but, unlike other authority platforms, there is no accountability involved. And, if you don't like or agree with one point of view, you can click on to another.

The messenger has morphed. The new voice of authority is a street chorus, a phenomenon we have come to accept because the dynamics of the new economy paved the way. The presidential election in 2000 is a perfect example of the impact of this bottom-up dynamic, where no single person or group displayed more authority than the next. Without leadership from one acknowledged point of authority, with consensus focused behind this point of authority, the election process disintegrated. Even the courts could not decide among themselves whose voice carried more weight. The result became a political war zone. If this is the result at the highest levels of the land, imagine what can happen in your local workplace. The future is likely to bring a proliferation of such clashes, particularly between the Baby Boomers and the Gen Yers. In the case of this scenario, the Baby Boomers are often the less equipped and less aggressive. If the job market tightens, their frustration, pitted against the aggression of the younger generation, could well turn to resentment and backlash as they struggle to maintain a slipping status quo. But, unless both sides can adapt, both will lose.

Over the past five years, I have been in countless focus groups with hundreds of Baby Boomers, both male and female, who, when given an array of pictures and asked to choose which appears most like them, invariably choose pictures of people ten to even twenty years younger. Clearly, those who once epitomized youth and trusted nobody over thirty still have a hard time seeing themselves as even middle aged. Most cannot see themselves retiring, at least not in the conventional sense of the word. And they're not. For decades, historically, the percentage of people working at age sixty-five or over fell steadily. In the mid-1980s the trend halted and then reversed. Government data reveal that in 2000, the percentage of people over sixty-five who still work was the highest than at any time since 1979. Many simply cannot afford to retire; others just don't want to.

Yet the ambition levels of older people in the workforce clearly lag behind those of Gen X and Gen Y. According to the Gen Y2K Study™, 35 percent of those thirty-five to fifty feel they have ambitious goals, versus 64 percent of those sixteen to nineteen and 66 percent of those age twenty to twenty-four. With their ambition on the wane, will the Baby Boomers muster the motivation to hold their ground, particularly in tightening job markets?

"I'd love to see a comeuppance or crash," says Valerie Frederickson, referring to the empowered attitude of the younger segment she works with, "but I don't think so. It is boiling down to a polarizing thing: people who use technology and people who don't. People who can adapt to the way things are being done and those who can't. For instance, I have a constant fight with Baby Boomers because we only take online résumés to submit to our clients. The Baby Boomers argue about it, they continue to fax their résumés in spite of our very clear requirements — it's ridiculous."

This generational divide is becoming a scab that is picked at continually within departmental structures, reaching far beyond the technology world. Its fissures reach deep into all levels of the spectrum of organizations. The commonality is in the situation, not the industry.

Carole Castiglione, a midcareer administrative assistant to a top executive at Federated Merchandising Group, has seen it in her world. "I don't think these younger people understand the reality and the interaction and where the ladder goes and the whole interpersonal part," she says. "You have to assimilate what's going on and, as an underling, make the higher-ups sound like a beautiful symphony. As an executive assistant, you're there to help your bosses, and if you can take a little bit off their back, there's nothing wrong with that. That's what your job is, to make their job easier. The reward is, you know you are active in making everything happen. I don't say you have to be a slave, but these new people refuse to get a cup of coffee. You know, you can get the coffee, and there's nothing wrong with it. But they tell me it's beneath them. They come in wanting to be Michael Jordan, but they're unproven entities, without even a year under their belt."

Castiglione started her career in the 1950s. "I went to work where I had worked after school. I loved working so much, I didn't even realize everyone left after five. One day the CEO came out and asked, 'Do you take steno?' He gave me a project and I threw myself into it. All of a sudden, I heard the fire alarm, but I kept working. I was a nervous wreck, but I knew this project had to be done. The CEO came back, and he saw me working and he ran up and said, 'What are you doing here?' I had worked straight through the fire drill. Luckily, it was just a drill!"

Castiglione told another, more recent story in which the caretaker of her boss's country house called the office to report that the heat was not working and subzero temperatures were forecast. What should he do? Castiglione knew the boss was traveling and unreachable, so she swung into action herself. From several hundred miles away, she directed the caretaker to investigate further. He determined that the heater was not broken but out of oil. However, he had no idea what company supplied the oil. Castiglione rounded up the names of all the oil companies that supplied oil locally and called each one until she found the one that had her boss's account listed. It turned out that the bill had not been paid. The boss traveled constantly, and something had slipped through the cracks. Castiglione arranged for an instant charge to cover the oil bill and arranged the immediate delivery of the fuel. Crisis averted. When the boss returned, she told him what she had done.

His comment was "That's what you're here for."

She agrees.

"Today I hear about these younger people who go out partying late, and, the next day, they call in sick and don't come in." Castiglione bristles. "I can't imagine that. What happens now is, people come in to the job aspiring to be something else. Rather than aspire to do the best at what they are, every one of them seems to say 'I want to be in marketing,' or whatever. For instance, one young man came in as a production artist. This is a job in which they do comps and layouts, actually an entry-level type of position. He was about twenty-three or twenty-four years old and as a person, he was the nicest, sweetest guy. All of sudden, though, he thought he was going to be an art director. We have people who work here for years to get to that level. But this young man refused to go through the protocol. He always just insisted he had to go straight to the top person, not through the chain of command. It was unbelievable how he made the jump in his head from what he actually was to what he thought he should be. Finally they fired him, but he didn't leave; he just sat there and looked at people. I had to take his employee pass away."

Caroline Ott (not her real name), a senior administrative assistant with eighteen years of experience at a suburban-based Fortune 500 manufacturing company, is dedicated to her career and is a conservative sort of individual, always immaculately dressed in a tailored business style. She is interested in the people around her and their circumstances. She has a history of performing her job well and takes pride in it and in her company. But she too has noticed that things are not as they once were.

"Within the last five years, I've seen a change," Ott says, disillusionment tingeing her voice. "I've noticed the lack of loyalty, people wanting to get ahead—well, everybody wants that—but now they don't care how they do it. They don't care who they step over or step on." This became uncomfortably clear when a new administrative assistant in her thirties joined Ott's group. "It came down to the fact that she found out I was making more money than she was. I work for a department head and I've been there eighteen years! Then she had to take a course, which was required, and she got very belligerent. After that, she decided that when she was asked to do something by one of us, the other administrative assistants, she would flat-out refuse unless she got more money. I would never, never do that! Having worked in human resources, I knew there were sometimes new people coming in who made more money than I did. All of us did. It bothered all of us, but did we say something? No. We knew that was the way it was. Not this woman. She did not come in to learn the basics; she came in, in her mind, to run the department right away. When this didn't happen, she reacted by blowing up. She gave everybody a very hard time. For instance, we all share printers, and she refused to share a printer. When I asked her a question, something very simple about who to go to for something, she resented it. Then she called me at home and said, 'The situation is beginning to affect my attitude toward you. I loathe you.'

"I was in shock! I told her I had supported her and helped her, that I'm not here to hurt her, I'm here to help her. She said not to take it personally. However, this is a person who, when they told her she couldn't take a flex day after being out for two weeks 'sick'—having just started with the company—thought they were out to get her."

Ott reported the phone call to her home to the corporate human resources department. "They told me, if she gets violent, let them know!" she said incredulously. "I have worked full time for thirty years." Her eyes widened but her voice remained steady. "I started when I was nineteen. But the workplace has really changed. I really think people in our generation need to stand up to these people and say no. I think they have to be put in their place. If we don't stop this, the workplace is going to go crazy. What's going to happen?"

Sankalp Saxena also sees generational resentment bubbling

beneath the surface—in his world, spurred on by what he calls "those caught on the flip side of the Internet rock star syndrome."

Saxena says, "I think there are those who are going to look back at this time, versus the forty years they've spent in the workforce and taken to get to this point, and they'll look out the door and see a young kid driving a Ferrari without a care in the world, and they're just going to look up and say, 'Isn't this all screwed up?' Because they've worked their entire life to get to a certain point, and they'll always see many more of those exceptions who just came out of school and happened to pick the right place. And they'll have that more as a memorable instance than all the other ones that failed. They'll see that as being something that's very inequitable for them. I think it's a personal frustration, that they look at the irrationality of the world, and how it's changed from the time they entered the workforce to the time they exit. And I don't think they'll be able to answer that well enough. So they'll fall back on platitudes, saying 'This is just a trend. It is something in vogue at one point. It will crash. It has to crash.' They will be the Doomsday prophets. It gives them peace of mind to believe that it will all get corrected, and people will come back to reality. But maybe it won't crash. Maybe it will just morph."

In the morphing process, who is going to be the most vulnerable—is it going to be the people in traditional corporate jobs or those used to working on an independent, low-resource, or outsource basis? Those whose paychecks depend on the system, or those whose livelihoods depend on their own value propositions and ingenuity? As I write this book and review the recent past, the markets have continued to fall. In addition to the dot coms that were squeezed off at their funding sources, many traditional companies have been trimming the fat—however lean it was to begin with—in the traditional ways: letting attrition take its toll; cutting budgets and jobs; and outsourcing to keep head-count down and save the costly benefits packages.

In such an environment, which is the stronger position, being in the traditional company or floating in the outsource environment? "You may be better off being part of the oursource pool," says *Fast Company*'s George Anders. "Because the work still needs to get done and companies would rather have it be done by people who take care of their own health club memberships. Also, it gives the ability to expand and collapse the workforce. Because that's been the hard thing for a lot of companies — either they're understaffed or overstaffed. But outsourcing creates the ability to have a pool of people who come and go almost the way subcontractors do on a construction project — now we need an electrician. OK, we've got one. Months from now, we no longer need an electrician. And then we don't still have to be paying the guy and saying 'I'm sorry, I have no work for you.' "

Historically, recessionary environments have not favored those who were not full-time employees. In the 1981–82 recession, for instance, overall employment fell by 3 percent, while temporary employment dropped 12 percent, and recessionary environments in 1974–75 and 1990–91 showed a similar pattern. This pattern has led to some negative forecasting for the future of the independent worker should a recession occur. However, this analogy is flawed. At the time of these previous recessions, technology had not hit with its massive force, nor had an attendant workforce evolved to service that sector. The impact and requirements of technology are not going to disappear, no matter what the economic climate, and there will still be a massive workforce required to implement and evolve it. To not acknowledge this is not unlike ignoring the need for gasoline after the invention and widespread adoption of the automobile.

"You can argue that in a recession, the first to go may be the outsiders," Anders says. "But really, I think their opportunities are better. The thinking is: 'If one area starts to slow down, I have a lot more agility to figure out that people don't want, for instance, programmers in HTML, they want programmers in XML. I am then going to bone up my XML skills and go look for those kinds of jobs, as opposed to being stuck at a company that's programming in last year's language. They are not making the transition there, and my skills would be getting rustier all the time.' "

Also, the business dynamics have changed. "More and more, you look at all kinds of organizations where having a flexible workforce just makes more sense relative to the business mission," says Anders. "A lot of companies are changing strategies faster than ever. And, if you've got an entrenched workforce, it's very hard to do that. People three and four levels down the organization don't want to be told their mission is now different, their job is different, that all the skills they've built for the last eight years aren't really the skills the company wants these days. Whereas if you've got more fluidity, you can say 'Here's what we're paying the most for, and here's where we're giving the most projects. Come be part of our team for the next—whatever.'

"So I would reinforce the argument that we're moving to a world where a lot more work is done on an outsource basis by people who are highly skilled, making good money. I think the Internet really enables people to do more of that."

Even full-time job requirements are becoming shorter in term. "It used to be that recruiting firms did a job search and knew that person was going to either be in that job or at least in that company in that field for five to ten years. Now a lot of placements really are eighteen-month placements: 'We need someone to help this particular area for a year or two while we build it up, and after that, we're going to want something different.' So you need a workforce that's comfortable with that, the feeling that you don't have a lifelong career at one place, that you have a series of interesting, fun, and rewarding projects, but that they will not all come from the same place."

The inflated financial rewards of the technology sector have allowed a different career mind-set to evolve. "There is no degree of continuity," says Sankalp Saxena. "No such thing as a long-term plan. I think the finality for a lot of people is getting in the two-comma club—you know, hitting a million or more, and then being able to sit back and assess your options, or take six months off and then come back and dive into it again, recharged and renewed and refreshed. People are banking so heavily on that type of financial and social independence. When the company they're working for hits, it's almost this binary all-or-nothing effect. And, if you lose, you get up again and pump yourself up to believe that it can happen again with somebody else. It's ironic, because the goal of wealth creation is independence, but you keep postponing independence in anticipation of hitting it. It's like winning a big lottery."

The younger Change Agents are particularly comfortable with the concept of the serial career, with slight generational differences. "Gen Y feels they will have a series of jobs, but they are not signing up for a career," says Valerie Frederickson. "They seem to feel they will never climb a traditional corporate ladder. And there is absolutely zero loyalty to whom they are working for. Gen X is a bit more willing to climb the ladder, but they assume they will get the good jobs and screw their employer if the employer isn't going to cooperate—they will just go someplace else and do it. These people just have no interest in doing it. They have seen how previous groups have worked and they see how quickly life and technology are changing, and they just don't see any reason to invest in it."

The concept of the long term has also evolved as a result of the serial mind-set. As one Internet executive said, "You make a long-term plan, but do it in chunks. You have a goal in life and ten years to do it—you set milestones along the way. If my goal was to be the CEO of a huge company in ten years, then in two years, you'd want to hit one milestone, in another two years another milestone, and so on. If you were with a single company, it might be easier to figure out what those milestones are. But in this kind of environment, it's more figuring out what skill sets are needed, what are the titles needed, the kinds of experiences you want to have, what kinds of technologies you want to be involved with—a lot of the same questions, but on a little bit of a broader canvas. And that often gives you a chance to kind of branch out a little bit more. So not only have I advanced my career in terms of position—going from a senior manager to a director to a senior director, to a VP and so on—but I've also been able to dance around a little bit, being in different-focused businesses, from a B2B, to a B2C, to a B2B2C, to something that was entertainment focused, to something that was business focused, and so forth. I got to play with a number of different options that I wouldn't have had at a single company."

A key reason why the Change Agents are comfortable with serial careers is that the reward at the end of the rainbow is, for them, more personal. "I work to travel," said a woman who was recently put out of work when her dot com crashed. "And I know people who work six weeks, get paid nicely, then take off. There are people I know who take off the entire summer. It is a job. You're being paid to supply your skills, and that is all you should give them. You're going to the office—it's not a place where you're developing your soul."

In spite of the frantic schedules and hours worked by the Change Agents in the new economy, they seek a spiritual kind of element. There is a palpable yearning to reconnect with self, nature, and belief. The aspirational goal might be a rock-climbing trip, as opposed to a more material benefit that their predecessors might have chosen. Becoming the CEO is not the pot of gold at the end of these people's rainbows. "More and more people are focusing on the quality of life and lifestyle, on enjoying things," says Pam Lloyd, who claims she has learned a valuable lesson from both the life and death of her dot com. "Balance comes down to finding something you care about, but you don't want to get sucked into it." The job that Lloyd is considering accepting now, she says, would allow her to travel and to work from home.

"I feel more selfish now," says another ex–dot commer. "It's about me. I'm happy to give them what they want, but I will never work on a weekend again. Companies are going to have to be more flexible, or people will start designing a more free-wheeling company. So, whether someone's officially a W-2 pay-roll employee or whether they're a 1099 employee, you're going to get the same outcome, which is to have greater return on your workforce, and that's going to give you flexibility and fluidity, and people will be comfortable with that: 'OK, I did everything that I wanted to at this company or that, and now I'm going to work for this other company, or start my own business.' The one thing that fades away is the 'My dad worked at U.S. Steel for thirty years' kind of ethos."

The Internet makes working for yourself immeasurably more feasible in many ways. Ten years ago, working for myself in-volved renting an office, hiring a secretary and research assistant, signing on with answering and messenger services, buying a fax machine, and huge monthly bills for printing, Fed Ex, and travel. Three years ago, the Internet and other technologies had replaced or offered alternatives for many of those functions, and I was able to run my business with far less overhead and almost no outside help. People who are more technology-savvy than I can run one-person organizations that can produce deliverables that once required entire departments. As a result, freelancing is much more of an economical option from both the contractor and provider point of view.

Today's hirees for any kind of job carry with them the portfolio of skills that give them independence in the workplace, whoever they work for. Unless you are self-sufficient on a Tibetan mountaintop, your personal intellectual capital is no longer enough to launch a single-handed career. Everyone in business has a story about the brilliant seven-figure executive who can't open his or her own e-mail. (I knew of one who required secretarial assistance to figure out Velcro.) These individuals acquired the loft to sustain their current careers prior to the advent of the new economy, but their breed is becoming an endangered species. If they were starting out today on their own, without a cadre of support to buttress and implement their ideas—and a peer group who were on their equivalent dependency level—would these people be able to compete? Today, in most fields, and driven by the technology sector, the ability to execute is a given part of the equation. As a result, like animals bred for survival in the wild, workers at every level of the continuum are being born into the next economy on their feet. Have you returned a rental car recently? A few years ago, the person in the parking lot took your keys. Today he or she is wireless and fully capable of executing your computerized transaction on the spot, using a handheld device that links to the company system. There is an equivalent scenario in every field.

Valerie Frederickson says, "People who I work with may earn high in the six figures, but they also have all the ground-level skills. They have technology independence. They have superb computer and online research skills. They know every relevant program. They have to have superb Power Point skills, superb Excel skills, superb Intel skills, advanced Internet skills. They know how to be highly flexible, adaptable to change, feel comfortable listening to and respecting people even if those people are younger than their kids."

This kind of individual is not going to be stymied, or slowed down, by the lack or loss of a hierarchical support system, secretary, mentor, and mail room. The entire company could evaporate, but this is a person who would not—and does not—feel like a turtle beached on its back. If the economy dictates that some of the workforce will be cut loose, the squadron of virtual paladins are armed and ready, and, in turn, will inspire others.

We are all among those "others."

Think of it as a mothership. The technology industry, which began in relatively defined geographic locales, has bred a community with a unique sensibility that nurtured and supported its own particular needs. That set of skills and sensibilities, both economic and cultural, rippled outward in the whirlpool, creating a larger community, which, in turn, continues to grow. A correction of the market, even a recession or, most extreme, depression, may cause a hard landing of the mothership, but the community, and its mind-set, will survive, impacting all those with whom it connects. In leaving the mothership and infiltrating the greater community, the Change Agents will permanently alter our DNA. They've already done it. Just as we are now literally different creatures from what we were thousands of years ago, just as each generation brings its own mutations and evolution, they have triggered our metamorphosis as a culture.

Right now we are experiencing a massive process of opening up and fresh ideas. A revolution of any sort is a time when thinking that has not been considered has a chance to be if not necessarily embraced, then at least evaluated or reevaluated. There is an opportunity to consider options in ways different from what were previously thought possible. Which, in turn, creates both chaos and vitality. Meanwhile, we must cope with the friction of both the positive payoff and the churn factor that is involved in considering and evaluating a myriad of new options, scenarios that are playing out in every aspect of our lives that is touched by the Internet and attendant new technologies. Every segment of the current economy needs to learn from the other, to work better and more productively as a cohesive whole. The first step is to realize that everyone out there does not do things your way and does not have to. The next step is to learn from the other guys, until each segment has evolved and merged values to the point where there are no other guys.

As the continuum moves forward, the momentum is definitely becoming two-sided. "In a way, we're going full circle," says an Internet executive. "In the beginning, Internet start-ups felt that they were magic, they were golden, that none of the old rules apply. And nowadays companies are looking for more seasoned skill sets and looking for more traditional marketing focuses and processes. So whereas you used to see a lot of twenty-five-year-old VPs out there, now you're seeing more with gray hair." Whether this leads to friction or not depends on the company involved and the culture involved. "I've seen instances where it works quite well, and I've seen instances where it comes to loggerheads."

Clearly, positive coexistence and joint momentum are possible, but only if understanding, acceptance, and flexibility are incorporated on all sides. Ultimately both the new and old economies will have to give way to a fusion of the two. The Change Agents of today will, inevitably, become tomorrow's status quo. We are hurling, together, from dot com to dot bomb to dot beyond. Actually, the lines began blurring as soon as they were drawn, and a clash of cultures can result in only one finale: not a win for either side, but a melding of both into one.

It's how we handle that process that is up to us.

AFTERWORD

Two key proprietary research studies formed the foundation for many of the themes in this book.

The Gen Y2K Study™ is an online survey conducted by Nickles & Ashcraft in partnership with Greenfield Online. A nationally representative sample of 4,000 respondents was interviewed from the Greenfield Online panel. Since demographics of panel members are known, a nationally representative sample was invited to a custom Web site to complete the questionnaire. Of the 4,000:

- 1,982 were age sixteen to twenty-four

- 2,018 were age twenty-five to sixty

- The respondents were both male and female: 1,601 male; 2,399 female. When the data were tabulated, responses were weighted demographically to ensure national projectability. Interviewing for this study was conducted in May 1999, with further interviewing conducted by Nickles & Ashcraft in December 2000.

The Update: Women™ study consists of three nationally representative mail surveys designed by Nickles & Ashcraft and fielded among the Consumer Mail Panel of Market Facts, Inc. This panel is balanced demographically within census regions to be representative of the U.S. population. Respondents were female heads of household age twenty to fifty. Response rates ranged from 65 percent to 80 percent. Over 5,000 American women have participated in Update: Women™ surveys between 1980 and 1998. Information areas include career/home attitudes; attitudes toward motherhood and parenting; brand attitudes; relationship dynamics; self-image; stress; critical motivation triggers; role models; computer orientation; demographic differences; financial attitudes; psychographic subgroups.

In addition, Nickles & Ashcraft conducted hundreds of one-on-one interviews and focus groups with both women and members of Gen Y and Gen X across the United States. I also conducted fifty one-on-one interviews specifically for this book.

I would like to express my deep gratitude and appreciation for the use of this proprietary source information, much of which has never been previously published, to my research partner Laurie Ashcraft and to Greenfield Online. For further information on the Gen Y2K Study™ or the Update: Women™ Study, please contact Nickles & Ashcraft via www.nicklesandashcraft.com geny2krpt@aol.com, or see the Web site at www.nicklesandashcraft.com.

APPENDIX

TEN THOUGHTS FOR BABY BOOMERS

1. Conduct an honest self-assessment. Where do you want to be in five years? Ten? Two? If working at a traditional job is the answer, imagine you were fired tomorrow and construct a plan to keep yourself current and in demand. Do not assume that you are coasting toward your great reward. Divide the long-term into achievable and rewarding short-term goals. Go for them. Then, when you look back, you will have assured yourself of success.

2. Reconnect with your industry. It may have been some time since you attended industry functions, assuming that you had no need to network or learn. Drop that assumption and get out there. See who's who and what's what—before somebody else has to fill you in.

3. Learn your technologies. Your secretary's fielding and printing out your e-mail? Learn to do it yourself. Now. Most companies cover or contribute to the the cost of basic e-training.

---

4. Subscribe to a technology-oriented publication, and read that section of the newspaper. Nothing stays the same.

5. Brush up your résumé and put it in e-mail format. Have a knowledgeable associate help you edit ruthlessly.

6. Make a buddy. Get to know a young person in your industry and have lunch regularly. See what he or she is thinking. Listen and learn.

7. Give some rope. If you have a younger person working for you, don't assume things have to be done one way—your way. Things may happen a little more slowly, but you may learn something new and even improve on the status quo. At a minimum, you will improve relationships and cut down on friction in the office.

8. Get on a committee, in the office or outside, with younger people. Find a forum for sharing ideas, learn how another generation thinks. They'll learn from you too.

9. Watch MTV and VH-1 for a couple of hours a month. See who and what's being promoted, seen, admired. What goes in, comes out—eventually.

10. You are an expert. Allow yourself to believe it, because it's true. The traineeship is over (although learning never is).

TEN THOUGHTS FOR BABY MOGULS

1. Read the manual.

2. If you think you have a better way to get something done, discuss it with those who may have a different idea. Everybody learns.

3. Set up weekly status meetings. Progress speaks volumes. If you're getting it done, you're going to get the go-ahead. And the rewards.

4. Making enemies makes no sense, and, worse, they resurface elsewhere. Avoid.

5. Do not put anything in an e-mail at work that you do not want the world to know.

6. Explain. Time-consuming, but worth the results.

7. Learn from your boss. If you look hard enough, there is something from which you can benefit. If not, get out.

8. Join a committee with senior people. As above.

9. If someone tries to be your mentor, accept graciously. Mentor is not the same as mother. You can mentor them too and become a mutual-mentor society. Everybody wins.

10. Play this game: Imagine one major thing in your life changed. What would you do differently regarding your career? Figure it out. Pick something significant—you get married; have a child; are forced to move cross-country; get a long-term illness; win the lottery; whatever. This is a trick that will force you into longer-term thinking and planning. Just in case.

SOURCES

PRIMARY RESEARCH

Update: Women℠ Study © 2001, Nickles & Ashcraft
Gen Y2K Study℠ © 2001, Nickles & Ashcraft and Greenfield Online

SECONDARY RESEARCH

Articles

Ames, Sam, "Tech CEO's Add Hefty Salaries to Options Packages," CNET News.Com, March 24, 2000.

Anders, George, "Power Partners," *Fast Company*, September 2000, p. 146.

Andreessen, Marc, "An Archtyped Entrepreneur Says Mere Profits Are Not Enough," Interview, *The New York Times*, December 11, 2000, Sec. C, p. 5.

Atanasoo, Maria, "Merry Christmas E-Tailers," online article (smart-businessmag.com, December 2000).

Bale, Lewis, "Now It's Blair's Bewitching Hour: Low Budget Flick Set To Scare Up Big Box-Office Bucks," *The New York Daily News, New York Now*, July 1999, p. 46.

Barnes, Katrina, "Fast Factoids," online article (www.fastcompany.com/online/341/flash4.html.)

Beaupre, Becky, "Will Online Degrees Hold Up on Paper?" *Chicago Sun Times*, July 30, 2000, p. 34.

Belkin, Lisa, "An Office Tour for Mom and Dad," *The New York Times*, December 6, 2000, Sec. G, p. 1.

Chabrow, Laura, "Companies Are Willing to Pay for Performance," online article: informationweek.com/792/jobhop.html, September 27, 1999.

Edmonds, Patricia, "Now the Word Is Balance," *USA Weekend*, October 23/25, 1998, pp. 4–6.

Egan, Jennifer, "Lonely Gay Teen Seeking Same," *The New York Times Magazine*, December 10, 2000, Sec. G, p. 110.

Eisenberg, Anne, "The World through PC-Powered Glasses," *The New York Times*, December 14, 2000, Sec. G, p. 1.

Ellen, Abby, "Genies for Hire Cash in on Worker's Stress," *The New York Times*, December 14, 2000, Sec. G, p. 1.

Flavelle, Dana, "Casual Dress Choking Necktie Sales," *The Toronto Star*, Business Section, October 29, 1999.

Flusser, Alan, "History of Neckwear," online article (http://www.ties.net/history.html.)

Fridman, Sherman, "Report: Young Online Shoppers Out-Perform Adults," News Byties Special To Me, E-Commerce Times February 23, 2000.

Gentry, Mae, "Toddlers to Log On, Get Rescue Wherever May Go," *The Atlanta Constitution*, March 17, 1999, p. 8C.

Glater, Jonathan, "A High-Tech Domino Effect," *The New York Times*, December 16, 2000, Sec. C, p. 1.

Greenwald, John, "Instantly Growing Up," *Time*, November 6, 2000, p. 99.

Greeven, Amely, "Will Fashion and the Internet Click?" *Harper's Bazaar*, April 2000, p. 198.

Gross, Michael, "War Of The Worlds," *Talk*, December 2000–January 2001, p. 76.

Guernsey, Lisa, "Hard Hat, Lunch Bucket, Keyboard," *The New York Times*, December 14, 2000, Sec. G, p. 1.

Guernsey, Lisa, "MIT Media Lab at 15 Big Ideas, Big Money," *The New York Times*, November 9, 2000, Sec. G, p. 1.

Hamilton, Walter, "More Teens Making Trades—On the Stock Market," *The Los Angeles Times*, October 31, 2000.

Harmon, Amy, "When That Corner Office Is Also a Dorm Room," *The New York Times*, October 22, 2000, Sec. C, p. 1.

Hoffman, Havi, "Web School," *Chicago Sun Times*, Financial Section, July 20, 1999, p. 32.

Judge, Elizabeth, "Why Females Differ from e-Males," *The Times*, London, June 25, 2001, p. 3.

Kerwin, Jessica, "Electronic Empire," *W Cyberchic*, Supplement to W, Fall 2000, p. 8.

Kreahring, Lorraine, "The Company She Keeps," *C. Elle*, Winter 2000.

Lee, Jennifer, "Last Call for Silicon Alley's Famous Wingdings," *The New York Times*, April 1, 2001, Sec. 9, p. 6.

Lehmann-Haupt, Rachel, "Plug In, Start Up, Drop In," *Business 2.0*, November 14, 2000.

Leland, John, "To Loaf or Not to Loaf," *The New York Times Magazine*, December 17, 2000, p. 25.

Lewis, Michael, "Jonathan Lebed's Extracurricular Activities," *The New York Times Magazine*, February 25, 2001, p. 26.

Macfarquan, Neil, "Named a Market Swindler at 16," *The New York Times*, September 21, 2000, Sec. B, p. 1.

Marin, Rick, "The Uncrimped Lifestyles of the Rich and Feckless," *The New York Times*, April 1, 2001, Sec. C, p. 1.

McGeehan, Patrick, "At a Wall Street Firm, Juniors Voices Roar," *The New York Times*, April 4, 2000, Sec. C, p. 1.

Miles, Stephanie, "Urban Box Office Lays Off 330, but Gets Funding," *Wall Street Journal*, Dow Jones News, November 15, 2000.

Mui, Nelson, "Here Come The Kids, Gen Y Invade the Workplace," *The New York Times*, December 1, 2000, Sec. C, p. 1.

O'Havol, Robert, "Teenage Stock Phenom Agrees to Return Gains," *The New York Times*, September 21, 2000, Sec. A, p. 1.

Orr, Andrea, "Tech Start-Up Scene Undaunted by Market Setbacks," online article, Reuters News Service, May 14, 2000.

Schactman, Noah, "IT Pro Find Job-Hopping Pays," online article. (informationweek.com/792/jobhop.html, June 26, 2000).

Slatalla, Michelle, "Wedding Wishes Fulfilled Over the Web," *The New York Times*, November 9, 2000, Sec. G, p. 4.

Stein, Tom, "A Shakeout Finds a Return to Venture Capital Investment Basics," *Redherring*, December 4, 2000, p. 115.

Steinberg, Jacques, "Goal of $100 Million Gift Is Free Online University," *The New York Times*, March 16, 2000, Sec. A, p. 18.

Taylor, William C, "Those Were the Com Days," *Fast Company*, December 2000, p. 44.

Tierney, John, "Can Power Transcend Knotted Silk?" *The New York Times*, December 1, 2000, Sec. B, p. 1.

Tolela-Myers, Michelle, "Cyber U: What's Missing?" *The Washington Post*, March 21, 2000, Sec. A, p. 25.

Travis, James, "The Campus Is Being Simulated," *The New York Times Magazine*, November 19, 2000, p. 88.

Uchitelle, Louis, "Can the New Economy Navigate Rougher Waters?" *The New York Times*, December 18, 2000, Sec. C, p. 1.

Wallace, David, "The Dorm Room Economy," *Business 2.0*, November 14, 2000, p. 196.

Wallace, David, "Class Act," *Business 2.0*, November 14, 2000, p. 197.

Walsh, Mary Williams, "Reversing Decades Long Trend, Americans Retiring Later in Life," *The New York Times*, February 26, 2001, Sec. A, p. 1.

Welz Prafder, Erika, "From Little Acorns: Colleges Offer Courses in Entrepreneurship," *The New York Times*, December 19, 2000, p. 31.

Wolff, Michael, "Just the FAQ's, Maam," *New York*, June 2000, p. 34.

Yankey, John, "Computers to Wear," *The Journal News*, November 14, 2000, Sec. K, p. 1.

Yee, Roger, "Connecting the Dots," *Interiors*, October 2000, p. 52.

"Dot Dot Dot: What's Next in the Victims of Recent Dot-Com Layoffs?" *The New York Times Magazine*, November 19, 2000, p. 44.

"Interview with Jon Slavet of Guru.com," *House Of Business*, November 12, 2000, p. 44.

"Lunch Loses Out to the Desktop Dinner," *London Daily Mail*, September 27, 2000, p. 41.

"Net Ed: Growing Pains," *Los Angeles Times*, November 20, 1999, Sec. B, p. 9.

"New Parade Survey Finds Internet Shopping Has Reached Mainstream America," PR News Wire, Financial News, Source: *Parade Magazine*, May 31, 2000.

"On the Brink: A Poll," *The New York Times Magazine*, August 22, 1999, p. 13.

"Online Mortgages Slow to Take Off," online article, *USA Today*, November 24, 1999, Sec. B, p. 1.

"Sizing Up the Web," Jupiter Media Matrix, *The New York Times*, December 11, 2000, Sec. C, p. 5.

"Upfront People," *House Of Business*, November 12, 2000, p. 44.

"Warm and Wired," *Talk*, March 1, 2000, p. 66.

"Why CEO's Fail," *Fortune*, June 21, 1999.

"2nd Annual Hot List—9 Millionaires Under 30," *Entrepreneur's Business Start-Ups*, April 2000, p. 38.

"2 Net Concerns To Form Online University," Reuters, *The New York Times*, August 15, 2000.

Studies, Surveys, and Reports
A *Five-Year Review of Venture Capital Investments in the Internet*, Price Waterhouse Coopers LLP, 2000.

CEO Study conducted by Hanis and Associates, 2001.

"Employment Characteristics of Families in 1998," Bureau of Labor Statistics.

The Kepner-Tregoe Survey on Speed and Decision Making, www.kepner-tregoe.com, June 2000.

Marital Status and Living Arrangements, U.S. Bureau of Census, Annual data from current population survey for 1947–1998.

Newsweek/Kaplan Poll of Parents with Children K-8, Newsweek, Inc./ Kaplan, Inc., © 2000.

Number of Jobs Held, Labor Market Activity, and Earnings Grown over Two Decades: Results from a Longitudinal Survey Summary, <http:// stats.bls.gov/news.release/hlsoy.nro.htm>, April 25, 2000.

Women Pass Men in Internet Use, Media Matrix and Jupiter Communications, 2000.

1998 Census Bureau Report on U.S. Divorce Rate, <http://www. census.gov/population/www/socdemo/ms-la.hunl>

Books
Mandel, Michael J., *The Coming Internet Depression*, New York: Basic Books, 2000.

Nickles, Liz, with Laura Ashcraft, *The Coming Matriarchy: How Women Will Gain The Balance of Power*, Seaview Books, 1981.

Robinson, John P., and Geoffrey Godbey. *Time For Life: The Surprising Ways Americans Use Their Time*, The Pennsylvania State University Press, 1991.

Oxford English Dictionary Additions Series, Volume 1, Clarendon Press, Oxford, 1993.

PERSONAL INTERVIEWS

The following industry experts were interviewed for this book:
Tod Abrams, Alternative Marketing
George Anders, *Fast Company*
Laurie Ashcraft, Nickles & Ashcraft
Donny Deutsch, Deutsch, Inc.
Esther Drill, gURL.com
James Finkelstein, Luxuryfinder.com
Mark Fragga, (formerly) Wharton Center for Entrepreneurial Programs
Valerie Frederickson, Valerie Frederickson & Company
Amy Frome, Rate Yourself.com
Andrea Gambill, *Bereavement* Magazine
Dr. Chet Gardner, University of Illinois
Ray Gaulke, Public Relations Society of America
Renny Gleeson, iTurf
Abbi Gosling, Agile Enterprises
Jeffrey Gut, CollegiateMall.com
Doug Hall, Richard Saunders & Associates
Richard Kirshenbaum, Kirshenbaum Bond & Partners
Steve Klein, iballs.com
Marilyn Levey, Levey Marketing
Cindy Lewis, *Harper's Bazaar*
Ron Lieber, *Fast Company*
David Liu, TheKnot.com
Pamela Lloyd, Urban Box Office
Ronald C. Long, United States Securities Exchange Commission, Philadelphia, PA.
John Maienza, Maienza Design
Jim Marks, Credit Suisse First Boston
Caryn Marooney, Out Cast Communications
Robert Proctor, The Internet Exchange
Frank Quattrone, Credit Suisse First Boston
Carley Roney, TheKnot.com
Jack Sansolo, Eddie Bauer
Mark Selcow, BabyCenter.com
Lisa Sharples, Garden.com
Diane Silberstein, *Yahoo! Internet Life* Magazine

Elizabeth Talerman, Agile Enterprises
Mark Taylor, Global Education Network
David Waxman, Firefly; PeoplePC
Chris Wittmann, Tech Space

INDEX